Van Haren
PUBLISHING

ABC of ICT
An Introduction

Paul Wilkinson and Jan Schilt

B C
A
OF ICT

Attitude, Behavior
and Culture of ICT

VHP

GamingWorks

Other publications by Van Haren Publishing

Van Haren Publishing (VHP) specializes in titles on Best Practices, methods and standards within IT management. Architecture (Enterprise and IT, business management and project management.

These publications are grouped in the series, eg: *ITSM Library* (on behalf of ITSMF International), *Best Practice* and *IT Management Topics*. VHP is also publisher on behalf of leading companies and institutions, eg The Open Group, IPMA-NL, CA, Getronics, Pink Elephant). At the time of going to press the following books are available:

IT (Service) Management / IT Governance

ITSM, ITIL® V3 and ITIL® V2
Foundations of IT Service Management – based on ITIL® V3
 (English, Dutch, German; French, Japanese and Spanish
 editions: Spring 2008)
Introduction to IT Service Management (ITIL V3, English)
IT Service Management based on ITIL V3 – A Pocket Guide
 (English, Dutch, German, Italian; French, Japanese and
 Spanish editions: Spring 2008)
Foundations of IT Service Management based on ITIL® (ITIL V2),
 (English, Dutch, French, German, Spanish, Japanese, Chinese,
 Danish, Italian, Korean, Russian, Arabic; also available as a
 CD-ROM)
Implementing Service and Support Management Processes (English)
*Release and Control for IT Service Management, based on ITIL® - A
 Practitioner Guide* (English)

ISO/IEC 20000
ISO/IEC 20000 – An Introduction
 (English, German: Spring 2008)
Implementing ISO/IEC 20000 Certification (English: Spring 2008)
ISO/IEC 20000 - A Pocket Guide (English, Italian, German,
 Spanish, Portuguese)

ISO 27001 and ISO 17799
*Information Security based on ISO 27001 and ISO 17799 -
 A Management Guide* (English)
*Implementing Information Security based on ISO 27001 and ISO
 17799 - A Management Guide* (English)

CobiT
IT Governance based on CobiT4.1® - A Management Guide
 (English, German)

IT Service CMM
IT Service CMM - A Pocket Guide (English)

ASL and BiSL
ASL - A Framework for Application Management
 (English, German)
ASL - Application Services Library - A Management Guide
 (English, Dutch)
BiSL - A Framework for Business Information Management
 (Dutch, English)
BiSL - Business information Services Library - A Management Guide
 (Dutch; English)

ISPL
IT Services Procurement op basis van ISPL (Dutch)
IT Services Procurement based on ISPL – A Pocket Guide (English)

Other IT Management titles:
De RfP voor IT-outsourcing
 (Dutch; English version due Spring 2008)
Decision- en Controlfactoren voor IT-Sourcing (Dutch)
Defining IT Success through the Service Catalogue (English)
Frameworks for IT Management - An introduction (English,
 Japanese; German)
Frameworks for IT Management – A Pocket Guide
 (English, German, Dutch)
Implementing IT Governance (English)
Implementing leading standards for IT management
 (English, Dutch)
IT Service Management global best practices, volume (English)
IT Service Management Best Practices, volumes 1, 2, 3 and 4
 (Dutch)

ITSM from hell! / ITSM from hell based on Not ITIL (English)
ITSMP - The IT Strategy Management Process (English)
Metrics for IT Service Management (English, Russian)
Service Management Process Maps (English)
Six Sigma for IT Management (English)
Six Sigma for IT Management – A Pocket Guide (English)

MOF/MSF
MOF - Microsoft Operations Framework, A Pocket Guide
 (Dutch, English, French, German, Japanese)
MSF - Microsoft Solutions Framework, A Pocket Guide
 (English, German)

Architecture (Enterprise and IT)
*TOGAF, The Open Group Architecture Framework – A
 Management Guide* (English)
The Open Group Architecture Framework – 2007 Edition
 (English, official publication of TOG)
TOGAF™ Version 8 Enterprise Edition – Study Guide
 (English, official publication of TOG)
TOGAF™ Version 8.1.1 Enterprise Edition –A Pocket Guide
 (English, official publication of TOG)

Business Management
ISO 9000
ISO 9001:2000 - The Quality Management Process (English)

EFQM
*The EFQM excellence model for Assessing Organizational
 Performance – A Management Guide* (English)

SqEME®
Process management based on SqEME® (English)
SqEME® – A Pocket Guide (English, Dutch, mid 2008)

Project/Programme/Risk Management
ICB/NCB
NCB Versie 3– Nederlandse Competence Baseline
 (Dutch, on behalf of IPMA-NL)
Projectmanagement op basis van NCB V3 - IPMA-C en IPMA-D
 (Dutch)

PRINCE2™
Project Management based on PRINCE2™- Edition 2005
 (English, Dutch, German)
PRINCE2™ - A No Nonsense Management Guide (English)
PRINCE2™ voor opdrachtgevers – Management Guide (Dutch)

MINCE®
MINCE® – A Framework for Organizational Maturity (English)

MSP
Programme Management based on MSP (English, Dutch)
Programme Management based on MSP - A Management Guide
 (English)

M_o_R
Risk Management based on M_o_R - A Management Guide
 (English)

Other publications on project management:
Wegwijzer voor methoden bij Projectvolwassenheid
 (Dutch: fall 2008)
Het Project Management Office – Management Guide (Dutch)

For the latest information on VHP publications, visit our website:
www.vanharen.net

ABC of ICT
An Introduction

Paul Wilkinson and Jan Schilt

Version 1.0

Van Haren
PUBLISHING

Colophon

Title:	ABC of ICT An Introduction
Authors:	Paul Wilkinson and Jan Schilt
Editor:	Steve Newton
Publisher:	Van Haren Publishing, Zaltbommel, www.vanharen.net
ISBN:	9789087531409
Print:	First edition, first impression, october 2008
Layout and design:	CO2 Premedia bv, Amersfoort -- NL
Cover Design:	O2 Creative, Norwich
Copyright:	© 2008 GamingWorks

For any further enquiries about Van Haren Publishing, please send an e-mail to: info@vanharen.net

Contents

Foreword

IT is becoming increasingly important to just about every company on the planet. Most of us in the developed world use computers to find information or order and purchase products. IT must work. As such, IT must be managed as a strategic asset. Because if it doesn´t work the consequences can be extremely costly, highly embarrassing and even disastrous. Frameworks such as ITIL are becoming increasingly popular and increasingly important, but why is this the case? These are seen as a solution, as a way of bringing IT under control. However we still have problems adopting frameworks such as ITIL and making them work. Why do we keep failing? And what must we do to finally ensure that ITSM becomes a strategic capability? This book hopes to address these questions. Why are we writing this book now? The time is ripe; failure is no longer an option. We can no longer afford to do with ITIL V3 what we did with ITIL V2.

In the last 10 years we, the authors, have been travelling the world extensively. We have been giving 'worst practice' speeches at international IT service management conferences. This has given us the chance to talk with hundreds of IT professionals that recognize and agree with our 'worst practice' observations and findings. We have also had the opportunity to deliver hundreds of ITSM simulation workshops which have brought us into contact with literally thousands of customers implementing, or struggling to implement, ITSM practices. During these workshops we have been able to discuss key issues that people recognize in relation to ITSM success and fail factors. We have discussed these issues with IT operational employees, team managers, line managers, process managers, project managers, even CIOs and, occasionally, business people from the boards of directors, as well as end users. We have also had a chance to discuss our findings with those of our 100 or so international GamingWorks partners who help and advise their customers to adopt and deploy ITSM best practices. So, all in all, we feel we are able to say what we have found represents truly global 'worst practices'…..but, more importantly, what we have found represents truly global 'best practice' approaches to dealing with the issues that just about every organization adopting ITIL is faced with.

Fortunately many people recognize and understand that the ITSM frameworks and procedures are just an instrumental part of the solution. To be brutally direct, any idiot can design an ITIL process flow and a book of procedures. Participating in our presentations and our workshops, people recognize and agree that the single most critical success factor, or fail factor, is the way in which the frameworks are applied. The way in which the 'Attitude', the 'Behavior' and the 'Culture' within the world of ICT and all of its stakeholders, are taken into account and consciously addressed. In other words 'The ABC of ICT'. It is addressing this ABC of ICT that will ensure a real, lasting, sustainable success when adopting and applying ITSM best practices; by success we mean ensuring that ITSM delivers, and continues to deliver, recognized and demonstrable value to both the business and the IT organizations.

What we have also discovered is that, although managers, consultants, trainers and those responsible for deploying ITSM recognize these issues, they do not know, and have not been taught how to tackle them, and existing ITIL best practice literature or ITIL training and certification schemes currently do not help them. This is a very worrying situation and indeed a symptom of why, in the last 10 years, too little success has been realized using ITSM frameworks,

We have also noticed with concern that in the numerous conferences we have attended less than 5% of the sessions and presentations address these ABC issues, whilst more than 90% of the attendees recognize and agree with the issues and the need to resolve them.

The worst practice presentations we give at the conferences often receive the highest scores, the cartoons and examples we use are instantly recognizable. People laugh at the cartoons but afterwards they say 'how true'. How true are the examples of Attitude, Behavior and Culture that need changing.

What is equally worrying is not the fact that ITIL training and certification fails to currently address the ABC issues adequately, but the fact that some experts say that ABC has got nothing to do with ITSM and, as such, it shouldn't even be given special attention! ABC is something relevant to ALL organizations and all branches and is, therefore, something that managers should already be doing. Therefore, we should already know how to address these issues! Therefore, if we ignore them they will go away by themselves....just like they have in the last 10 years? We are afraid that ignoring it and hoping it will go away, and assuming that these are management capabilities that all companies should have is simply not helpful. People need help and guidance in solving these issues, and the people and organizations that should be helping solve them haven't done a good job so far. We include ourselves in this as ex-ITIL consultants and ex-ITIL authors.

Furthermore, with the increasing importance of IT we can no longer afford not to bring IT under control. ITIL and ITSM frameworks and best practices must work. In the words of Gene Kranz, Flight Director of Apollo 13, "Failure is not an Option...". IT organizations that fail to successfully adopt and deploy ITSM practices place businesses at risk.

These were reasons enough for us to write this book.

This book will challenge and confront you, and hopefully make you think. We strongly advise you to think carefully about the cases presented and seriously reflect upon these in relation to your own organization. Simply assuming that this doesn't apply to you or your organization is an attitude we see all too often. Helping you change your attitude, to look at things differently, may be the first and most important learning point from this book.

This book is also a handbook to help you to become the most important instrument of change within your organization. After reading this book and attempting the exercises using the ABC of ICT cards you will be better able to recognize and hopefully tackle the ABC issues most relevant to your organization.

Whether you are a manager, consultant, trainer or process manager, this book is equally applicable and will give you an insight into how you can, from within your role, become an agent of change.

In the 'worst practice' presentations we give, we usually finish with three simple best practice tips. The first one is this: we ask "What is the most important instrument for making ITIL work?". People call out "Tools", "Assessments", "Maturity framework". We then say "YOU". You are the single most important instrument for change. You, the people listening to these presentations, or in this case reading this book.

One thing is fairly certain, you will probably be one of the few people in your company reading this book. The line managers, the operators, system managers, application people, the CIO… none of these will be reading this book. None of these will have been confronted with the ABC issues, none of these will see the need to change. As such, none of them will change by themselves. You are the only one who has been confronted, you are the only one that can make a difference. You must change your attitude and behavior if the cultural issues, and the attitude and behavior issues of others, are to change. If you don't do anything then we can guarantee that we will be back in 10 years giving the same worst case presentations and having people nodding their heads in recognition at the conferences. The choice is yours.

We would like to share our vision and our solutions, together with those of our colleagues who have contributed, and we hope that their insights and practical tips may help you in your ITSM journey. Who are these people we have invited to contribute? They are individuals who have demonstrated a track record in helping organizations improve through the use of ITIL and other best practice frameworks. They are also representatives of some of the leading delivery companies, who we are giving a chance to express their views and experiences. They are also people responsible for deploying ITIL, and customers who have used ITIL and have tried addressing the ABC issues. We tried to involve people from different countries and a cross section of the industry. If a leading player or individual is not here it is not because we found them unworthy, more because we do not know everybody and some didn't have the time to contribute. If you are looking for a guru, an expert, somebody who can help you ensure your ITSM initiatives do succeed and will address the ABC issues, then our advice is to ask them for the credentials, ask them for their demonstrable ability to realize effective change. After all, it is experience, not just credentials and qualifications that count.

We thought it would also be a good idea to allow some of those who are currently responsible for the new ITIL and the deployment of ITSM best practices to express their views on ABC in this short introduction. The first is that of **Richard Pharro** from the APMG: "My personal view is that ABC is essential. Success with ITIL or any other similar framework is all about people. People need to have the right attitude, skills and knowledge channelled towards the right behavior, otherwise you will achieve nothing. In this book you call it the ABC, we call it professionalism. ITIL will give you the knowledge. But knowledge alone is not a guarantee for success."

Also **Sharon Taylor**, the chief architect for ITIL V3 and now chief examiner. In response to the question about the relevance of ABC, Sharon responded "…Likely more important than any system, tool, framework or method. The best practices in the world don't work if people are not committed to them and do not espouse the ABCs that are needed to bring frameworks, tools and systems to life."

We also wish to add that the contributors to this book actually made their contributions without having read any part of the book, so it cannot be assumed that they agree with everything else in the book. One thing is for certain, what they have contributed represents their belief and view on the ABC of ICT.

Paul Wilkinson and Jan Schilt

Contributors

The following people contributed case studies to this book. None of the contributors saw the rest of the book, so it cannot be assumed that they agree with everything we wrote in the book. This list identifies the author, the company and the country to which the individual case study applies.

Martin Andenmatten, Glenfis - Switzerland
Mats Berger, Westergaard - Denmark
Jack Bischof, Accenture - United States
Aad Brinkman, Apreton - Netherlands
Gary Case, Pink Elephant - Canada
Alejandro Debenedet, Exin - Argentina
Arjen Droog, itSMF NL - Netherlands
Rob England, IT Skeptic - New Zealand
David Bathiely Ferdandez - Spain
Bartosz Górczynski, CT Partners - Poland
Jeremy Hart - United States
Brian Johnson - Global
Benny Kamin, itSMF Israel - Israel
Alexander Kist, Newskool & itSMF International
Erna van Kollenburg, EducaSimula - Netherlands
Aidan Lawes - United Kingdom
Paul Leenards, Getronics Consulting - Netherlands
Peter Lijnse, Service Management Art - Canada
Vernon Lloyd, Fox-IT - United Kingdom
Ivor Macfarlane, IBM - United Kingdom
Kirstie Magowan, Verso Solutions Ltd
Martin Ng, Deloitte - Kuala Lumpur
Paul van Nobelen, Suerte - Scandinavian
Don Page, Marval - United Kingdom
David Pereira, ITXL - Brazil
Harold Petersen, Lucid IT - Singapore
Richard Pharro, APMG group
Colin Rudd, ITEMS Ltd. - United Kingdom
Walter Servaes, CTG - Belgium
Mark Smalley, Getronics (Applications) - Netherlands
Clive Strawford, independent consultant - China
HP Suen, itSMF - Hong Kong
Robert Stroud, CA - United States
Sharon Taylor, ITIL Chief Examiner
Pablo Coutere de Troismont, Xelere - Argentina
Ken Turbitt, Service Management Consultancy (SMCG) Ltd. - United Kingdom
Stephane Vleeshouwer, CTG - Luxemburg

Richard Voorter, Ideas-to-interconnect - Netherlands
Ken Wendel, HP & itSMF international - United States
David Wheelden, HP - United Kingdom
Katsushi Yaginuma, ITPreneurs - Japan

Chapter 1
What is this book all about?

This book is about the Attitude, Behavior and the Culture in ICT organizations. We call it the 'ABC of ICT'. There is now a growing recognition in the ITSM community that the ABC factor is important in ensuring ITSM improvement initiatives work. However we have also noticed that ITSM professionals have difficulty addressing these issues. Why is this? Because it is inadequately addressed in the best practice books, there are currently, at the time of publication, no training courses available as part of ITSM certification, and little attention is given to it in IT conferences as a subject. Yet if we present these issues at conferences in our 'Worst practice' ABC presentations, we are surrounded by people saying 'how true', and 'we recognize this…you are so right'. So if we all recognize it and all know it needs changing, why haven't we done anything about it? Maybe we are hoping that if we ignore it, it will go away. Well it hasn't gone away in the last 10 years and we really don't think it will in the next 10 years unless something changes.

So what exactly is it we are talking about?

'Attitude'
This is what people think and feel. It is their demeanour and how they react to the world about them. How they react to a change initiative, a colleague, or a customer. An example of attitude is somebody thinking "The users are ALWAYS complaining….just ignore them, they will soon go away!"

'Behavior'
This is what people do. Behavior is influenced by attitude and by the culture of the organization. An example of behavior is 'saying you will follow the ITIL procedures but not doing so', Behavior can be 'not registering a resolution, or not transferring knowledge to a first line employee even though you know it would help, and even though you know you should be doing it'.

'Culture'
This can be described as the accepted ways of working within an organization, the values and standards that people find as normal. An example of culture is 'knowledge is power', or the 'hero culture'. In this type of culture people believe that sharing knowledge diminishes their own value, therefore they

want to be the only ones with the expertise and knowledge, they are the heroes. This type of culture can negatively influence attitudes and behavior.

In fact you could say that 'attitude' is individual and comes as a result of personal beliefs and experiences which influence 'behavior'. Culture is often difficult to grasp but could be described as the corporate attitude. Often employees in an organization are unaware of the culture and how this influences their personal attitude and behavior. This is why culture is one of the most difficult things to change. It is 'soft', you can't see it, you can't touch it, you know it's there, you can get bogged down in it and unable to move, it can stop a change program in its tracks. It is something to be taken seriously if you want your change program to succeed…..it would seem that the most common approach is to ignore it and hope that it will go away or change by itself.

"ABC is like an iceberg, much of it hidden beneath the surface and yet capable of inflicting enormous damage".

This book will help you develop the most important instrument for realizing a successful ITSM improvement initiative. That instrument is YOU. You are the most important instrument for changing the attitude, behavior and culture in your organization; however it may be that before you can become that effective instrument, you may need to change your own attitude and behavior.

This book will give you a theoretical background to the most important aspects that you will need to be aware of so that you can develop and become an effective 'instrument for change'. This theoretical background is important so that you can understand ABC and what influences it. But more importantly this book will help you to identify and develop your own 'interventions' to help change ABC.

This book also contains practical examples from your peer colleagues and other experts who have experienced the ABC issues and have successfully done something about them. Armed with the theoretical building blocks and practical examples we hope that the reader will be better placed to make conscious interventions in their own organization, interventions that may finally solve some of the ABC worst practices that have been preventing us from realizing real, lasting results using ITSM frameworks and best practices.

We will also go into detailed descriptions of some of the 'worst practice' examples of attitude, behavior and culture. Why? So that you can recognize them, so that you can identify whether they exist in your own organization. We will show you how these worst practices negatively impact the performance of the IT organization and, more importantly, the results that ITSM needs to realize for the business. ITIL V3 stresses something new, namely 'risk management'. We strongly suggest you add ABC to your list of risks, as being one of the most potentially serious. The advice in this book will help reduce the risk that ABC will damage your organization and enable you to ensure that ITSM capabilities really do become 'a strategic asset' as described in ITIL V3.

In order to help you, and others in your organization to be able to effectively recognize and deal with ABC issues we have developed a card game. These cards, and the 'worst practice' cartoons they contain, are based upon the most common worst practices people tell us about, and worst practices we see in our travels around the world of IT organizations. The cards can be used in your own team or department to make the ABC issues visible, to bring them into the open and discuss them. Discuss them and the consequences that they bring for your organization. Once they are recognized, agreed and the consequences known, you have a basis for the next step, agreeing how to tackle them. There are a number of exercises you can perform with various stakeholder groups, using these cards. They are, in effect, an awareness and assessment instrument.

In order to help you apply what you discover reading this book, we have added one or two practical exercise you can apply directly in your own working environment.

Chapter 2
Who is this book aimed at?

As we have already mentioned. Our worst practice presentations get a lot of people nodding their heads in recognition and agreement. Many people come up to us afterwards and ask us 'How can I address these issues?' 'What should I do?' This is what prompted us to write the book, and these are the people we are writing it for. This book should be valuable to the following people:

1. **ITSM professionals who agree that ABC is one of the most critical success or fail factors for ITSM improvement initiatives.**
   They will learn how to recognize and address the ABC 'worst practices' or potential fail factors. They will learn how to become one of the critical success factors, 'an effective instrument for change' and what type of interventions they can initiate to change ABC.

2. **ITSM professionals who think the ABC issues are nonsense, or something that managers should already know and do, and therefore there is no need to give them any 'special treatment'.**
   For this target group we hope that their eyes will be opened, that they will realize how misplaced their 'attitude' and 'belief' is. We gave our 'worst practice' presentations 10 years ago. 10 years later we gave almost exactly the same presentations. The presentations STILL received wide recognition and high scores. Since then we have had ITIL V2 and now ITIL V3. The problems persist and are becoming even more important to resolve as IT becomes increasingly important. We can no longer afford to ignore them and hope that they will go away. These people may see and read the worst practice examples in this book and, by using and discussing the cards, may learn how these ABC aspects are equally relevant in their own organization. Indeed they may see that these ABC aspects are preventing their own ITSM improvement initiatives from realizing real, lasting results. For this type of person we'd like to point you to the case example of using the ABC cards, described by the card the 'Queen of clubs'.

3. **For anybody interested in ABC aspects in ITSM or organizations in general.**
   This book is written for anybody and everybody who has anything to do with ITSM. We are adding this because it makes our publisher happy and increases his potential sales audience!

No, but really it is written for anybody that needs to play a role in making ITSM initiatives a success. CIO's, IT managers, process managers, service managers, operational managers, project managers, team leaders, human resource managers, trainers, advisors, consultants, suppliers…..and indeed even those who are often the victims of misguided, poorly applied ITSM initiatives, the people who have to use the books of procedures that are produced on their behalf. The operational level staff….of course let's not forget end users and customers of ITSM. Let them have a laugh and see what kind of strange world we live in and what kind of issues we are faced with. Also let's not forget that end-users, customers and business executives also have a role to play in making ITSM a success.

Hopefully everybody can find something in this book they recognize that is standing in their way, and recognize something that they themselves can do to change 'attitude' and 'behavior'. Many people, such as operational staff feel 'victims' of these ITSM initiatives, they feel dumped upon from a great height by everybody. They just want to do their work and get on with managing (or mismanaging) IT. This book should also give these people an insight into 'interventions' they can make. Take control of their own role in ITSM improvement initiatives. If you don't take ownership and initiatate some kind of action then quite frankly, sorry to put it this way, but you deserve to get dumped on.

Don't believe us? Thinking to yourself "That's easy for you to say…"? Well here is an example.

A small case:

We have chosen this case as a result of a recent poll we conducted on the itSMF website in the Netherlands. It was in response to the following worst practice card:

Specialist talking to Help Desk employee: "If I told you how to do that, then you'd know as much as ME….That will NEVER do" (knowledge is power).
The poll was 'We are not very good in IT at sharing knowledge' – 86% agreed. A significant number. How can you change this?

A Help Desk manager, and Help Desk staff were the butt of all internal IT jokes. Poor quality, lousy service, user complaints, complaints from support staff. Senior managers didn't see value in the Help Desk, little money was spent on improving it. ITIL was being adopted and the Help Desk manager was told to ITILIZE her domain. **Management commitment** was sadly lacking. In what way? The Help Desk manager needed a new Help Desk management system, she needed more authority to ensure she could get better, faster support from the specialists. The specialists generally put the Help Desk work that came their way at the bottom of the list of things to do……and let's not forget the poor, long suffering end-user that everybody seems to have forgotten about.

The Help Desk manager felt sorry for herself, the Help Desk staff felt demotivated, depressed, powerless and, to make matters worse, they were given a book of ITIL procedures that they now owned……written by some consultants that had never even seen a Help Desk, let alone an end-user. ("What is that?" asked the consultant.)

What did the Help Desk manager do to become empowered? To change things?
She asked us if we could help change the **attitude** of senior management towards the Help Desk, try to get managers to **change their behavior** toward the Help Desk.

We suggested some interventions:

1. Get the IT manager to visit an effective Help Desk and let the Help Desk manager explain how success was realized and describe the role played by IT management in making it happen.
2. Play a simulation with the IT management team to let them see, feel and experience the impact of a poor quality Help Desk, and see, feel and experience the success when the Help Desk works effectively.

Fortunately the IT managers wanted to organize a getaway, a brain storming event to help focus attention on process working. It was decided to play the Apollo 13 business simulation with the IT management team and the heads of all of the specialist departments. We put the IT manager on 'Capcom' (Capsule communications), which is the Help Desk. As the simulation progressed the IT manager was getting more and more stressed. His face went red, he started sweating as the Astronauts (users) demanded status updates, 'where is my incident?', 'when will you resolve this, it is important!?' He was receiving fragmented, incomplete and late information from the second and third level specialists in the simulation. 'It is just like reality!' was the general observation, and the general feeling.

We helped the team scope some improvements. A better registration and tracking capability, more authority placed with the Help Desk (Incident manager) for ensuring incidents were solved on time, increased responsibility by the second line for up-to-date information and knowledge transfer to the Help Desk staff, better registration and availability of common work-arounds. After the improvements were made we played the next game round. Suddenly everything went smoothly, the Astronauts (users) were happy. Availability improved, costs went down, resolution times increased. The IT manager was relaxed and smiling and feeling proud to be on 'CapCom'. We then reflected on what the success factors were and, more importantly, what were the impact of the changes made during the game to real life.

The IT manager sat at the back of the class, deep in thought and nodding to himself. Finally he declared there would be more funding to adequately 'tool' the Help Desk, there would be more authority and, even more importantly, the second line managers were given the 'task' to ensure their staff spent time doing 'knowledge transfer'. The Help Desk manager sat with her mouth open as she heard the IT manager **commit** to the changes that she had been proposing for a long time. Why this sudden turn around? We asked the IT manager and his response was: "In the simulation you are confronted with the impact of poor behavior on end-users. You are confronted with the pain and frustration of end-users not being able to do what they NEED to do….you are also confronted with the dependency of end-users on the Help Desk and how the Help Desk NEEDS to be a calling card for IT quality and service….I realized we NEEDED to make our Help Desk equally as effective as the simulation. Then it was a no-brainer!".

The Help Desk manager said that, ironically, the IT manager had recently read an article from CIO.com in which the following key success factors for the Help Desk were mentioned:

"Make sure your online knowledge base is simple and easy to use by focusing on the 10% of problems that account for 40% of the calls..."

"Put together a sample group of affected users, Help Desk technicians and project team members to brainstorm a sizable list of FAQs, and post the results on the Help Desk website..."

"Make sure you've got very clear metrics around average handle time and average speed-to-answer, and train your team to use these metrics effectively"

However, it wasn't until he was confronted with the actual situation that he changed his behavior.

Chapter 3
An analysis

Where are we now?

For the last 20 years or so we have been busy trying to adopt and deploy, no, sorry adopt and 'implement' ITIL. We use the words 'trying to' deliberately because the majority have not succeeded in realizing the 'hoped for' gains and benefits promised by ITIL. Often ITIL gets the blame for being too bureaucratic. In response we have produced ITIL V2 and now ITIL V3 to fix things and make ITIL work. However ITIL is not the problem. Indeed we can go on and make ITIL V4 or ITIL V5 but until we address the real reasons why ITIL 'implementations' fail, we will continue to disappoint ourselves and, more importantly, the business.

We have decided to include a small extract of the 'worst practice' article Paul wrote for the itSMF best practice year book to describe 'where we are now'.

When I began my career in computing 25 years ago as a system manager, otherwise known as 'technoid', I was informed in the computer publications of the time that IT'ers would need a new focus if they were to survive:

- **I** would need to communicate in terms the business could understand, and deliver services to customers and users as IT was becoming more and more important …..10 years later I was a manager of a team of system and network managers, a herd of 'technoids', the industry was preaching to us ITIL and how we techies would need a new focus if we were to survive;
- **We** would need to communicate in terms the business could understand, and deliver services to customers and users as IT was becoming more important.

In 1996 we first produced our worst practice book. We included an extract of an article written by Lew Young, editor in chief of the Business Week publication, in which the state of IT was clearly described from a business manager's point of view. "*Probably the most important management fundamental that is being ignored today is staying close to the customer to satisfy his (or her) needs. In too many companies the customer has become a bloody nuisance*

whose unpredictable behavior damages carefully made strategic plans, whose activities mess up computer operations, and who stubbornly insists that purchased products should work."
We certainly agreed that the customer was a bloody nuisance.

Now we are in 2008 and, of course, things have obviously changed. Because, after all, we have had all that best practice to help us. In which case can somebody please explain to me why the latest survey of the itSMF in the Netherlands shows the number one strategic priority of IT organizations is 'to improve the quality of services and products'. This reminds me of that film 'Groundhog Day' every day you wake up and relive the same day.

A technoid is somebody who grunts in technobabble and doesn't know what a customer or user is, apart from some annoying creature that interrupts his (or her, not to be sexist) work and breaks the IT.

This cartoon is accurate in one respect. 'People' are indeed the worst practice that is standing in the way of realizing the benefits of IT, people that can turn a best practice into your worst nightmare. The technology itself is no longer an issue. It is the way that it is used (abused) and managed (mismanaged).

SO WHY HAS SO LITTLE CHANGED?

Darwin proposed a theory of 'survival of the fittest'. A species would evolve from generation to generation, adapting to the demands of its environment in order to survive. Based upon his premise you would logically conclude that from generation to generation the technoids would evolve and adapt to changing business demands... apparently not. It would appear the theory doesn't apply to technoids. Or perhaps the technoids are like the great white shark, perfectly adapted to their environment, they haven't changed in millions of years. **Perhaps the technoid is a perfectly evolved and adapted species? Grunting in technobabble and annoying the business is what it was designed to do.**

However, a species can succumb to some sudden external influence that can make it extinct within no time, look at the dinosaurs. For the technoid (the modern day equivalent of the dinosaur), this sudden external factor is 'sourcing' (out and offshore), threatening the survival of the in-house IT'ers unless they adapt…. and fast. 'Survival of the most adaptable?' A somewhat more topical and controversial solution is at hand and offers another new perspective. Gene manipulation.
Perhaps the only solution is to genetically modify the technoids. Research has already shown that lazy monkeys who only work when rewarded can be made to work hard at all times when they have undergone simple gene manipulation. If you see copies of 'New Scientist' on the desk of your P&O manager then it's time to start worrying….. But of course, this doesn't concern you.

So that explains where we are now. We still needed to change. If you want to assess where you stand now, then you can use our ABC cards to perform an assessment, or review Chapter 5 which describes the cards, the symptoms and some example cases.

Importance of IT for business growth
So after all these years, and having thrown ITIL V2 (and now V3) into the equation, we are still poor at improving the quality of IT service to the business. Why do we need to? Let's just carry on doing it the way we do. It keeps us busy, keeps the consultants in business, everybody happy, the cycle of life goes on. Only, let us take a look at IT today. IT is becoming more and more mission-critical. IT is a way of life. The cyber-consumer forces the adoption and deployment of IT in just about every industry. IT organizations face the need to demonstrate control and compliance. Bring IT under control and prevent risks and protect business continuity. On the other hand they face the need to demonstrate performance and added value. Demonstrate how IT contributes to business success and value. These are the driving demands in fact for IT governance, and indeed what ITIL V3 stresses in its Service Strategies book.

This drive for governance is one of the reasons why many CIOs are adopting ITIL. ITIL is exploding. A survey of 197 CIO's in March 2006 by the CIO magazine revealed that 95% of CIOs will adopt ITIL to address business goals. The success of ITIL is no longer a 'nice-to-have' but a 'need-to-have'. Failing to get it right THIS time could mean the red card for many IT organizations. So the status quo is no longer acceptable. We must change. The sense of urgency is clear to many. But is the sense of urgency felt by all.

This has prompted the authors of ITIL V3 to declare ITSM capabilities as a strategic asset. The need to use ITIL to achieve a strategic alignment between business and IT. Or, as many of those involved in the creation of ITIL V3 have declared, it will finally enable business and IT integration! This is one of the reasons I have written this article. The alarm bells are ringing. WE may have CONvinced ourselves we are a strategic asset, but go and tell that to a business manager and when he stops laughing and wipes the tears away from his (or her) eyes you can ask. "Why are you laughing?" This article tries to explain why.

Another reason for writing this article is that we do not see anything in the ITIL V3 certification schemes at present to address the ABC issues.

As a result we will send tens of thousands of people through ITIL V3 certification training, arming them with 22 points. We will then let them loose as 'strategic assets' to reap havoc with ITIL process flows and books of procedures within their own organizations.

It has been promised that things will change. But until such time.....

"...I have 22 points. Therefore I am fully certified in ITIL, therefore I am right...therefore you must be satisfied..."

ITIL certification means I know what I am doing

So basically governance is one of the biggest drivers demanding the need to bring IT under control. Minimise risk, demonstrate value. If we look at a definition of *Weil and Ross* ('IT Governance', Harvard Press) describing governance we will see where our first worst practice stems from:

'Specifying the decision rights and accountability frameworks to encourage the desirable behavior in the use of IT'.

Why have I used this definition from Weill and Ross? Because their book is based upon proven best practice taken from numerous case examples. Why have I split the definition above into three lines like this? Because one of our primary worst practices is that we focus so much on the first line (adopting the frameworks such as ITIL that will define some responsibility and accountabilities) that we forget and do not adequately address the second part **'encourage the desirable behavior in the use of IT'**. Which is what IT governance is all about - 'doing the right thing to responsibly manage the IT assets in an organization such that it poses no risk to business continuity, and such that the investments we make deliver value'. One example of this worst practice is the books of process flows and procedures we produce and 'hand over' to the organization assuming they will then follow them. Believe me this is still a reality.

We in IT adopt our own 'process' framework to bring IT under control.
Process working is adopted and organizations realize they don't always deliver the expected and needed results. Process managers are created and installed into organizational structures. Books of process flows are enthusiastically produced, often with the help of expensive, 'expert' consulting companies. But the results are often sadly lacking.

Simply handing over a set of new ITIL procedures and hoping this will suddenly change peoples attitude (to become more customer focused) and behavior (Following the procedures) is like expecting all of the countries in the world to suddenly stop CO_2 emissions because of Al Gore's film.

Why is this the case?

(1) Line managers are often not prepared to change their role and accept process managers, whilst process managers often have little authority as far as claiming resources goes and are continually battling, and losing, against line management.

(2) Employees don't accept the role of process managers, especially when they see how line managers behave.

(3) Senior managers do not assume responsibility for enforcing new ways of behaving, and also fail to walk-the-talk. If they say process-based working is important and must be done, then they should be the first to show how serious it is.

(4) There is often no relationship between the strategic goals of the business or IT and the key performance targets to be realized by processes; processes are often not monitored or actively steered.

(5) Process working implies crossing organizational boundaries; too often SILOs and SILO thinking remain in place and the end-to-end process chain breaks down. A chain is only as strong as the weakest link.

This focus on 'frameworks' is also a worst practice that I still see evident at just about every ITSM conference I attend. What do I mean by that? Take a look yourself. The next conference you attend, look at the program and the titles of the sessions. 95% will focus on some framework or method or approach or specific process, very few will focus on addressing attitude, behavior and culture, telling you how to embed the solution in the organization, what sort of resistance you will encounter and how you overcome this. This leaves many organizations, new to adopting frameworks, with the naïve belief that they can simply be 'implemented'.

This is the first of our worst practices – we rush to adopt and deploy the formal frameworks and process models, and fail to address the bit about 'desirable behavior'.

ITSM as a strategic asset

Once again I have decided to use an extract of my worst practice article to highlight one of the reasons this book is needed, and one of the reasons this book has been developed.

"The achievement of strategic goals or objectives requires the use of strategic assets. This guidance shows how to transform service management into a strategic asset." (ITIL V3)

This is brilliant, and is my favourite bit of ITIL V3. It is something that sums up our culture and our attitude. I'll explain what I mean. Strategic assets are:

Resources	Capabilities		
Financial capital	Management		
Infrastructure	Organization		Processes
Application	Process	Embedded in	Systems
Information	Knowledge		Technology
People	**People**		**People**

When I saw this, I asked myself, "Am I the only one to see this?" Because obviously the ITIL refresh authors, boards, reviewers and QA didn't, otherwise surely they would have said something about it? ……about what? PEOPLE. What is revealed here? PEOPLE are resources, capabilities and one of the elements of PPT. So PEOPLE are a crucial strategic asset??? Oh no!!!

If people are such a strategic asset then why isn't enough energy and attention given to the ABC in ITIL V3 to explain how to transform the 'technoid' into this strategic asset? Also, if people are such a strategic asset, how come the new ITIL certification scheme doesn't address this? Ensuring they have the necessary skills and competencies to become strategic assets? Ensuring that they have the necessary skills and competencies to change ABC? And if people are so important, why do we not see this reflected in all the itSMF conferences, presentations and workshops to help address this? I thought perhaps it is just me and my view and doesn't reflect Industry expertise. I looked on the internet and found these two items:

- **Bita Planet article**: Survey shows continuing adoption of ITIL but persistent challenges. 'Number 2 on the list of challenges strikes a chord, in its recommendation of the need to ingrain process into the culture…'

- **Tech Republic**. 10 things you should know about being a great IT manager.
  #1 Spend time (and money) developing your PEOPLE.

So, here's another reason why the time was right to produce some practical guidance on addressing the ABC of ICT to enable us to become a strategic asset.

Failure is no longer an option – ITSM improvement initiatives must work
We have seen that failure is no longer an option. This time our efforts to deploy ITSM must work. If we want the business to truly see us as a strategic asset we must demonstrate we can bring IT under control. So what are some of the key reasons for all these failures in applying ITSM successfully? The following list is by no means complete but sums up the essential elements:

1. Inadequate link to the business value or performance outcomes to be achieved using ITSM.
2. Too much focus on ITIL as a goal in itself, and not on the desired behavior that ITIL is trying to achieve and the results that ITIL must realize.
3. Not enough alignment and dialogue with the users and customers to ensure they are involved and committed to the initiatives, the expected results, and their role in making it a success.
4. Not enough ownership or commitment from senior management to ensure that the desired behavior change is embedded at all levels and within all departments in the organization.
5. Not enough buy-in and commitment at operational level to the need for adopting ITIL, or the results to be achieved.
6. Getting an ITIL certificate is more important than proving you can do something with ITIL. The certification and training does not focus enough on developing capabilities, it focuses more on getting a certificate.
7. An unrealistic planning and approach to deploying ITIL. Thinking that ITIL is something that can be 'implemented'.
8. Inability to measure and demonstrate the impact of ITIL on results. What has it actually done for us?
9. Lack of involvement from operational staff in designing and developing THEIR own new ways of working. Books of procedures are produced and thrown over the wall.
10. A TOOL will solve all problems. Thinking an expensive ITIL tool is the answer to the problem. 'A fool with a tool is still a fool'.
11. Failing to embed the results into the line organization and ensure 'continual improvement' is part of the culture.

Where do we need to be?

Apart from the obvious fact that where we need to be is where we should have been 20 years ago, let's just quickly summarize for those of you that may have skipped the last chapter. 'We need to ensure that ITSM initiatives deliver the value we promised the business that ITSM would deliver, if the business agreed to let us invest in ITSM.'

• We really do need ITSM to be a strategic asset. An asset that reduces business risk, guarantees business continuity and delivers added value for the IT investments made.
• We must ENSURE that ITSM initiatives work. Failure is not an option.

- 'Failure is not an option' must be an attitude that is accepted by all involved.
- ITSM improvement initiatives must be managed as a strategic project. ITIL V3 will help describe the approaches. ITSM improvement initiatives must also be seen as a 'management of change' initiative. The ABC issues (Attitude, Behavior and Culture) must be consciously addressed.
- We need to ensure that we create and embed 'desirable behavior' in the organization, at ALL levels, as a result of our ITSM initiatives.
- We need to ensure that 'continual improvement' is embedded in the culture, that everybody's attitude is they are personally responsible and accountable for ensuring ITSM delivers value and they behave accordingly. This is a tough challenge and requires all managers to behave in a way that ensures and enables this.
- We need to engage and collaborate with the business to ensure both the business and IT accepts each other's role, and both start displaying 'desirable behavior'. Once again this is a tough challenge and meas that IT management must play a leading role in breaking down the 'victim' role that many IT organizations adopt.
- Pigs really will one day fly.
- Making a wish in a wishing well really works.
- Father Christmas does exist.

See we can make a list of bullet points as well. These are easy throw away lines. Quickly read and equally as quickly forgotten. Where we need to be is this:

'**Make change happen**'.

How do we approach things now?

ITIL V2 and ITIL V3

We have an instrumental approach to applying ITSM best practices. We focus very much on the process frameworks and procedures, deployed as part of a project and program initiative. The results get thrown over the wall, the project is disbanded, things go fairly well for a while and then slowly things start to break down, people revert to old behavior and attitude, there is not enough authority or commitment to keep things on track. Because of the project approach to implementation, continual improvement is not embedded in the attitude or the behavior or the culture. Processes fail to align with new projects, and IT solutions or new IT projects fail to align with processes, whilst processes are out of date. Because we never really specified the value that was to be delivererd, we never set the correct measurement indicators to demonstrate success. And because we are unable to demonstrate success and everybody had different expectations, very few, if any, stakeholders declarc ITIL to be a success. Those who were skeptical at the start, now voice their dissent, and more and more people believe processes don't work. We blame process managers, we blame line managers, we blame senior management, we blame the operational staff, we blame ITIL….see we told you it was no good. Then we look around and see that ITIL V3 has come and everybody who felt they were being blamed suddenly shouts, there see! A new ITIL, it wasn't our fault. So we all go towards the new instrumental approach. Buy a new framework, a new tool and try to 'install' or 'implement' the new one.

The good thing about a new way of adopting and deploying ITIL is that a lot of people now 'recognize' and 'understand' the need for a holistic approach. We like using holistic because it is used by everybody in ITIL V3. It is this decade's 'buzzword'; the 1990's buzzword was 'leverage', so if we 'leverage' a 'holistic' approach then it must be a double whammy and our bullshit bingo card is probably filled up. Unfortunately we recognized the need for a holistic approach (People, Process and Product) in ITIL V2, but now ITIL V3 has enhanced this with the fourth 'P' – Partner. However the effort allocated to each 'P' is unbalanced and is usually related to the maturity of the organization adopting ITIL.

What do we mean by that? An organization with high technical expertise and the 'hero' culture towards the IT and the IT experts looks for the 'Product' focus. A tool solves all problems….. a fool with a tool is still a fool. They look to purchase an expensive all singing, all dancing ITIL compliant tool; thinking that 80% of ITIL can be solved with a tool. The tool suppliers, who predominantly still struggle with the concept of processes are eager to oblige and sell their tools, many come with ready made process models. We have literally heard this statement "…but the process flow in your tool doesn't meet our organization's!",….."That is because your organization is all wrong" declared the smiling, confident tool consultant.

Process way of working

Another level of maturity, equally dangerous is the 'Process' focused level. The organization has seen the light and has been converted to the need for ITIL. Not necessarily 'process based working' but more ITIL. ITIL is the silver bullet. In this type of organization the books are followed to the letter, processes may not deviate from the 'word' as recorded in ITIL, a slightly less mature version of this is the 'me too' level of maturity, everybody else is doing ITIL so we should as well. "What are they all doing?" asks an IT director…"They're all implementing ITIL processes" is the answer, so the focus is on process.

Both of the organizations above recognize that they need to have some people trained up on this 'ITIL stuff'. So they send some managers and process owners on ITIL training. The idea seems to be that once you have had ITIL training and you have passed an ITIL certificate then you are ready and able to 'implement' or 'install ITIL'.

Very often the people charged with installing ITIL do not have access to customers, users or the senior managers who knew why ITIL had been chosen and what it was they were all 'HOPING' that ITIL would deliver. As such, ITIL processes are designed and implemented without ensuring they are designed to realize specific outcomes (we believe ITIL V3 calls this value?). So the general approach is ITIL for the sake of ITIL.

If you don't believe us, then go into your organization and ask any process manager: "When is your process a success? When is it delivering VALUE to the business? Has that value been agreed with the business?". Let us ask it another way …if we went to the business and asked them "When is this process adding value to your business?", what would they say? We would love to know the answers to these questions. However we don't think we will be surprised. Why not? Once again we will use the example of our simulation, Apollo 13. Why this example all the time? Because we have played it with thousands of IT specialists from all levels in the organization, in most countries in the world and it gives us an incredible insight into common behavior models. And we want to share these common behavior models to help prevent you from falling into the same trap.

The teams in Apollo 13, including CIO's and senior IT managers, all make the same mistakes. They all design their processes without any direct relationship to the targets given to them by the business. When we confront them during the improvement round and ask them: "So you are spending 250.000 dollars in fact to improve your ITSM workflow tool, to improve your processes, to embed process ownership in the organization….what will I, as a business manager, see differently?". In more than 85% of the cases the answer is "Eh?". When we reflect on their own real life situations, the answer is usually the same. Little link between the processes as designed and executed, and the desired, agreed value that needed to be realized.

The 5th P of Performance
ITIL V3 has added a great new model - the design principles of the 4 P's: People, Process, Product, Partner. However they missed a P. It was there in V2 but seemed to have disappeared. The whole of the Service Strategy book talks about nothing but, so it ought to be the 5th P. What is that? Value or PERFORMANCE.

However the People side in the 4 P's approach is not given enough emphasis. Indeed in most ITIL implementations the people side is focused on technology and process training. The focus is on certification not on demonstrable capabilities to apply ITIL. Not enough attention is paid to how to create buy-in, how to motivate people, how to get people to own ITIL, how to get people to improve their own work, how to ensure desirable behavior. There are a lot of generalistic comments about how important it is, and then the books quickly skip onto the next set of bullet points. In a study we did with more than 1000 students the most important key learning point and success factor in Apollo is 'People'.

We buy a tool, we write procedures and we HOPE that people will use them and follow them and do the right thing. There is a very large gap between hoping and realizing.

A skeptical view...
A book that takes a slanted look at the world of IT would not be complete without some kind of statement, comment or observation from Rob England, the IT Skeptic.

We asked Rob if he would care to add his insights and vision on the ABC.

"Ten years ago, the ITIL community spoke of 'people, process, technology' as an important mantra Some ITIL sources add a fourth dimension: partners (An Introductory Overview of ITIL, Colin Rudd, itSMF 2004). An even more complex model includes 'vision and strategy, steering, processes, people, technology and culture' (Planning to Implement Service Management, Vernon Lloyd, The Stationary Office, 2002). Personally I like 'people, process, things', and I like to add "...in that order". But the people, process, technology model is the most commonly used form. Ten years later it is as commonly spoken of and as seldom applied. . .

As Paul and Jan say in this book, little has changed. IT organizations still charge into the fun stuff, technology, with lip service to process and a nod or nothing for the people who will live with it. So I commend this book to you for its focus on what should be our first priority, people. (Known as 'wetware' to the geeks.)

I like the idea of breaking down the people aspect into Attitude Behavior and Culture. Not only is ABC catchy (people like their frameworks nattily packaged and easily digestible), but it is a useful and accurate analysis of real cultural change. Good people and culture can cope with bad processes, and good processes can deal with bad technology, but it doesn't work the other way. Fix the people or your other efforts are doomed. Fix the ABC."

Rob England ('the IT Skeptic').

But, there is also good news!

The good news is that in ITIL V3 people are strategic assets. Not directly though. ITSM is a strategic asset which includes people, processes and technology, implying that people are therefore a strategic asset. The CIO or business manager reading the Strategy book will be confronted with the following description:

"The value of people assets is the capacity for creativity, analysis, perception, learning, judgement, leadership, communication, coordination, empathy and trust."

What about the bit about the risk side of people assets. They are busy with ad hoc firefighting, lack of customer focus, don't stick to agreements or follow procedures, account for 70% of IT outages through mistakes, communicate in technobabble, have no empathy with the business of business processes, demonstrate a lack of testing........your mission critical IT is in their hands. Do you trust these people with your critical strategic information technology? Where is the lifeboat?

The ITIL V3 Strategy book gives us some sound, solid, advice of course about culture:

"Culture is transmitted to staff through socialization, training programs, stories, ceremonies and language and example."

That is it. Well. That's really going to help me shape and change culture then!?
And then the Service Transition book, tells you not to worry because:

"The Service Transition Team will soon become familiar with the need to change attitudes and the operation of converting culture for them it is a routine task, holding no threat.!!!!"

If this is so, then please tell us which ITIL training and certification made this a routine task holding no threat? Another reason for producing this book to show people the THREATS of the ABC issues.

What is the effect of all this?

The effect of this superficial naming of culture, of implying that it is nothing of real concern and of paying lip-service to addressing it is this:

- Resistance to change, ack of belief, buy-in and commitment;
- Value not being realized, with people not understanding their role and contribution to delivering value;
- Wasted money;
- A bad name for ITIL - 'too bureaucratic', 'it's all about procedures';
- A belief that ITIL V3 will solve all our problems.

And now, what should we do?

We need to change the current way we approach ITSM adoption and deployment. The approaches we describe in this book are based upon our own experiences and the feedback from the thousand of participants in our simulations who describe their approaches that worked. Check your role below in order to see what YOU must do in the next few months or years.

IT management:

1. Must show 'leadership' as desirable behavior in ENSURING that ITSM initiatives do not fail, and that they realize demonstrable results.
2. Must reward desirable behavior and make an example of undesirable behavior.
3. Must 'walk-the-talk' if they expect others to change their attitide and behavior.
4. Must understand the 'value' that ITSM should realize for the business. If this is not known and not communicated to all, if this is not translated into process designs and flows, if this is not embedded in accountabilities and responsibilities, then the old saying will still apply: 'If you aim at nothing, nothing is what you will hit!'.
5. Must have patience and accept that changing attitude, behavior and culture takes time and effort.
6. Must engage with the business and gain credibility and trust.
7. Must ensure that 'continual improvement' is embedded in the organization.
8. Must apply suitable 'leadership styles' until true ownership and personal accountability is realized.
9. Must create an environment and commit time, energy and resources to ensure that change can and will happen.
10. Must 'empower' people to change by allocating resources, time, energy and by removing barriers and obstacles that stand in the way.
11. Must ensure that all IT staff are aware of how they contribute to business value and results.

Line manager:

1. Must visibly show commitment to processes and process management.
2. Must continually communicate the importance of process working in both words and deeds to their staff.
3. Must be prepared to reward desirable behavior and make examples of staff displaying undesirable behavior.
4. Must commit resources to process activities.
5. Must support their employees with prioritizing line work versus process work.
6. Must facilitate operational staff in realizing their change in ABC.

Process managers:

1. Must be able to assess their capability of being an 'agent for change'.
2. Must develop skills and competencies for addressing ABC issues.
3. Must ensure that all are aware of their tasks, roles, responsibilities and accountabilities in the process.
4. Must ensure that the process activities are embedded in behavior.
5. Must learn to focus and manage the end-to-end chain.
6. Must learn to engage with line managers and resolve resourcing conflicts.
7. Must learn to engage with the business users and customers and ensure the business is engaged in, and commited to, the processes and their outcomes.
8. Must help convince people to follow process working.
9. Must focus on embedding processes as the normal way of working.
10. Must continually analyze and improve processes.
11. Must learn to ensure process design and process delivery are aimed at realizing demonstrable results.
12. Must devote a large part of their time to motivating and winning over people.
13. Must facilitate operational staff in realizing their change in ABC.

Operational staff:

1. Must accept the need to change ways of working.
2. Must understand how their roles and activities contribute to overall success.
3. Must show personal ownership and accountability for process working.
4. Must accept responsibility for giving feedback and improvement suggestions in relation to processes.
5. Must learn to give feedback to colleagues when procedures are not being followed.
6. Must learn to find ways of quantifying and qualifying their concerns and making these known.
7. Must be shown how to work using new processes and procedures.
8. Need to change their attitude and behavior to become more customer focused. There is a difference between saying and thinking we are customer focused and acting customer focused.

Consultants:

- Must identify who the problem owner is and who is empowerd to say that an ITSM improvement initiative is successful.
- Must learn to help customers recognize and agree the problem to be resolved.
- Must learn to position ITIL in relation to the agreed problem that is to be resolved and not sell ITIL as a product or solution.
- Must learn to think in terms of Attitude, Behavior and Culture and learn to recognize the shift in ABC needed to get ITSM frameworks to work.
- Must be creative in designing inteventions required to make ABC issues visible and to openly discuss and address them.
- Must change their approach from developing processes and procedures to ensuring that the people using the processes and procedures are involved in and own the procedures.
- Must ensure adequate communication and training to gain buy-in and to understand and tackle resistance to new ways of working.
- Must help process and line managers to understand what 'process management' is.
- Must focus on embedding processes as the normal way of working.

Trainers:

1. Must ensure customers understand the ABC issues involved with adopting and deploying ITSM best practices.
2. Must relate the ITSM theory to the customer's situation and needs.
3. Must ensure that customers understand the holistic approach to deploying best practices.
4. Must help staff to identify ABC issues and discuss solution approaches to dealing with them.
5. Must help students transfer what they have learnt into their own daily situation.

Business managers:

1. Must have an attitude that reflects the statement that 'IT is a strategic asset within their organization'.
2. Must show 'desirable behavior' in managing IT as a strategic asset if this is the case.
3. Must ensure that the 'culture' within the business at all levels is focused on realizing the benefits of IT as a strategic asset and for ensuring that the risks associated with poor IT decision making and 'undesirable business behavior' are well managed.
4. Must take their role seriously in relation to defining requirements for new IT solutions and services.
5. Must be seriously involved during IT projects and for testing IT solutions.
6. Must ensure all business users are well aware of agreements relating to IT services and their role in interfacing to IT services.
7. Must ensure that end-users are well trained in the use of information systems.
8. Must responsibly manage the demand and prioritising of all requests for on-going and new IT in support of the business.

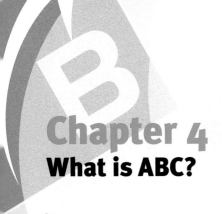

Chapter 4
What is ABC?

In this chapter we will discuss several aspects of the ABC elements. We will give some definitions, some descriptions of the words and we will try to make you aware of how to use these ABC aspects to increase the effectiveness of your ITSM initiatives.

Attitude

Embarking on a change program means changing people's attitudes. Getting buy-in for the change, identifying and addressing current attitudes that are counter productive to the needs that are driving the requirements for improvement initiatives.

What is 'Attitude'?

One of the definitions we found is: 'a feeling or opinion about something or someone'

Everybody has an attitude or opinion in relation to someone or something. Let's look at some examples:

- *"We expect a positive customer focused attitude towards our customers that you could read in a positions vacant advertisment."*
- *"The employees of the Help Desk must have a proactive attitude towards helping the users" declares a Service Center manager.*
- *"Your ' I couldn't care less' attitude towards these complaints is not what we want to see" declares a Help Desk manager towards an employee.*
- *"His attitude is WE have to follow the new procedures but if the customer calls him directly HE can ignore the process flow" say the disgruntled operational employees as a manager circimvents the change procedures.*
- *"The process manager has a positive attitude, she doesn't want to point the finger of blame, she wants to ensure it doesn't happen again."*

Some examples of attitude

There are various types of attitude. In this section we will look at some of the more common types and examples we see in IT organizations. We will also look at some possible approaches for dealing with them.

Cynicism and sarcasm

Cynicism: 'An attitude of scornful or jaded negativity, especially a general distrust of the integrity or professed motives of others.'

Cynicism, as we see, can arise as a result of distrust of professed motives. For example distrust in a 'best approach' proposed for an improvement program. Distrust of a manager's intentions or capabilities, Distrust that an improvement initiative will succeed, Distrust that a support person is smart enough to be able to solve a problem. Cynicism is often expressed as well grounded observations and comments made at the wrong or inappropriate moment.

Some examples of cynicism:

- *'A good workflow tool, have we got one of those?'*
- *'Consultants, that is just pouring money down the drain'*
- *'Procedures? That'll really make the difference then'*
- *'WE have to follow procedures and MANAGERS follow them just so long as they don't get in the way.'*

Sarcasm: 'A cutting, often ironic remark intended to wound', or 'a form of wit that is marked by the use of sarcastic language and is intended to make its victim the butt of contempt or ridicule'. Sarcasm is 'cutting' and may expressed, for example, as comments of praise that are the exact opposite of what is actually meant.

Some examples of sarcasm:

- *"So that is an example of a well managed change then!" "says an employee to a change manager whose change has just been backed out after bringing the network down.*
- *'We tried that before it didn't work then EITHER!'*
- *"So that is what management commitment looks like!" says an employee as the senior manager declares the importance of ITIL and then leaves the meeting for another appointment.*
- *"That is what the last bunch of consultants said too......before we kicked them out!" says an employee to a consultant explaining the need to adopt processes.*
- *"This is really going to create world peace and solve the hunger problem"" says an employee to a process manager explaining the importance of procedures.*
- *'I am sure the users will sleep safely and snugly in their beds at night knowing that we have a large book of ITIL procedures locked away in our cupboard.'*

Cynicism can have a productive effect. We can call this 'professional cynicism', which, when applied can keep people sharp and critical. Cynicism is often an indication that people's criticism has not been taken seriously and is ignored. Continued cynicism may however have an adverse effect and ensure that people are no longer asked, that they will be ignored and will be left alone to get on with their work….until they retire and pick up their pensions Perhaps continued cynicism is an attempt to avoid becoming involved.

However cynicism can impact the morale of other team members, team members who may have been more positive. They will be negatively influenced and, as a result, may also adopt a negative attitude causing projects to take longer and cost more, or result in projects and initiatives being stopped due to resistance. Well thought of, respected individuals displaying cynicism can have a serious impact on others who are not yet convinced. Imagine what the impact will be if, for example, a manager declares:

 "Process managers? What do they do again? Oh yes, now I know, they are the ones that write all those procedures that nobody reads"

or

 "…an improvement program? Remind me again which one is it now? I lost count?"

This can be the kiss of death to an improvement initiative.

The question is why does an organization become cynical?

Should we just give more attention to cynical people? People are cynical because they are not listened to and feel powerless. They place quotes and cartoons on notice boards, or make cynical comments intended to raise a reaction. Investigate why. What is the reason behind their attitude? It might be that these people have something to suggest that may be a solution, it may be that they want to change but are not involved, not engaged and not empowered to do so.

Cynicism can be caused by the loss of professional honor and by not recognizing group and individual achievements.

A distrust in the intentions and motives of managers can create cynicism, especially when managers do not walk-the-talk; they make statements and release memos but they are not backed up with deeds and example behavior. This can also be the result of managers using buzzwords and theories learnt from a book or a course they have just followed. You can see this as 'buzzword cynicism'. An example of this is 'bullshit bingo'.

Managers that say procedures are important but they are the first ones to bend the rules when necessary. This is the attitude 'don't do as I do, do as I SAY'. This type of management attitude and behavior causes employees to become cynical and they then start to resist and work against change.

People copy behavior. They will copy the behavior of a group or the behavior of people they look up to. Look at pop stars and footballers, their attitude and behavior is copied by many people. Well respected figures in an organization can also influence attitude and behavior by the way they conduct themselves. Making use of these people as 'champions of change' can help influence attitude and behavior where there is cynicism and lack of respect for management.

How to approach this:
- Look for and identify signals of cynicism.
- Why are employees frustrated and cynical and what has happened in the past to make them this way?
- Is there a sense of urgency for the change and do people understand the reason for, and the need to change?
- What is the feeling towards management and leadership within the organization?
- What is the history of change programs and the attitude towards change?
- Do people understand what the change will mean for them, particularly in terms of how the change might be positive for them?
- How is the change communicated? Are people involved? Is there dialogue? Is there a chance for people to give feedback and input? Is there a channel for people to state their concerns?
- What is done with feedback in an organization? Or criticism. How is this usually dealt with? Is it ignored?
- Ensure that the mission and vision are explained in normal language and avoid the buzzwords.
- Stimulate teamworking, as without the team effort we will not succeed.
- Organize events (meetings, workshops) to capture and structure feedback from people.
- Use the cartoons in the card game and see which ones cause the most reaction. Discuss examples of this attitude or behavior and agree what 'desirable behavior' should look like.
- Agree upon the type of attitude we should expect from each other.
- Try to convince leaders to show desirable behavior and reward desirable behavior. Show them the cartoons about leadership and behavior and ask them: "What do you think the employees would say if we showed them these cartoons?". Suggest using the cards in team workshops to capture how people really feel towards the change and how important they find leadership and management commitment.
- Managers should be present on the workfloor to gather feedback.
- There must be visible examples of action being taken as a result of the feedback to show that it is being taken seriously and management is committed to changing things as a result of workfloor input.

Passiveness

One of the definitions of passiveness we found was: 'Receiving or being subjected to an action without responding or initiating an action in return'.

Passiveness can manifest itself in numerous ways. Examples include:

In a meeting the service manager presents a proposal for a new way of working. The service manager has invited a number of people from the workfloor to gain feedback and create 'buy-in' for the new way of working. During the meeting the service manager tries to initiate a dialogue.

Service manager:	"What do you feel about the proposed way of working?"
Employee 1:	"Looks good" says one employee without looking up.
Employee 2:	"Not bad!"

Service manager	" Has anybody got any feedback or suggestions?"
Employee 1	" No, that looks fine, let's go for it," (while he is closing his notebook and packing it away in his bag).

The attitude and behavior of these employees is not helpful. Certainly when the non-verbal communication shows disinterest, and there is an urge to get out and do something else. This attitude can arise as a result of not wanting to be the first to show interest and involvement, or the fear of having to become involved and do something. Fear of having to accept extra work and help think about new ways of working. Perhaps fear of failing. Perhaps as a result of not seeing or recognizing any need to change. It could also be that they don't believe in the procedures but don't want to say as there is no feedback culture and they don't want to get into arguments. It could also be because they have heard it all before and know it will not work for whatever reason. It is important to identify what the motives are so that you can try to think of an appropriate intervention.

Another example is an agreement made between a process manager and some employees:

Process manager: "We will start using the procedures and, if there are any faults in the process or procedures, this will be reported to the process manager so that process improvements can be made."

A few weeks later in the team meeting:

Process manager: "OK. I have had no feedback or problems reported, so we can now go on to the next set of procedures."

Suddenly there is a wave of comments:

Employee 1:	"What do you mean ready? The procedures don't work!"
Employee 2:	"We stopped using that as it wasn't adding any value."
Employee 3:	"What procedure? Nobody told me we had to use new procedures?"
Employee 4:	"I wasn't asked for feedback, if you had come to me I would have told you…."

These reactions are hardly helpful for the progress of the change initiative, the trust in each other, or for the future of the team or department. Why didn't the employees give their feedback? Is this because what was agreed was unclear? Is it because they are hoping the initiave will fail? Is it because they want the process manager to fail? This 'passiveness' can have many reasons. It can be the result of the demanding workload in the organization. It can also be the result of distrust in management, or distrust caused by earlier change programs that failed.

Other examples of passiveness:

• Not offering ideas or feedback to emails or documents;
• Not offering ideas or input into work sessions;
• Not improving own work;

- Not following new procedures;
- Waiting to be told to use the new procedures.

How should you address this type of situation? Task focused leadership is one possible solution:

- Give employees a clearly defined task.
- Check to ensure they understand the task.
- Ask them to give and commit to planning for the task.
- Ask them if they have all the necessary resources and information to enable them to complete the task.
- Ask them what help they need to be able to complete the task.
- Coach the employee in the execution of the task, maintain contact about the progress, check to see if there are any new questions and that the task is still clear.
- Adress employees directly if they have failed to meet their agreed targets and have failed to report this is a timely way.
- If somebody is unable to complete the task for any reason, consider giving the task to someone else.
- Give tasks to employees that match their capabilities, or are likely to challenge them.
- Ensure that the managers of employees who have been allocated tasks give them the time and opportunity to work on the task.

Complacency

Complacency is a feeling of contentment or self-satisfaction with your own, or your team's, behavior. Types of statements here are 'Our Help Desk performs well' when in reality there are 20 complaints each month, or 'Availability management is really mature', whilst the users' biggest complaint is availability. 'There must be another reason the change went wrong, we did everything right'. 'We don't need to change the way we work, our procedures are good. It is the other departments', This final comment is something each department will tell you, so who has the right impression?

Complacency is one of the reasons that people do not seriously look for reasons for failure. We do not see ourselves or our behavior as part of the problem so we look elsewhere to improve things. This means we will not improve our own performance.

This type of attitude can be deeply embedded within the organization. If this is the case it can cause organizations to fail. What is particularly annoying in this type of situation is that others can see that things need to change. An example:

In an IT organization 'customer friendly' and 'customer focused' were keywords in the IT strategy documents, flyers on the wall and IT newsletters. Imagine you are consultant/coach or even a manager standing by the Help Desk department. A user comes along with a laptop that needs repairing.

User: "I have brought my laptop here for repair. When can I pick it up again?"

The support worker is on the phone (with another user), and signals with a wave of his hand that the user can put his laptop on the table next to the door and everything will be arranged. While the support worker is still on the phone the user tries to get an indication as to how late he can pick up his laptop. The Help Desk employee signals with his fingers between 2 and 5.

User: "Between 2 o'clock and 5 o'clock?"

The support worker sighs with frustration and irritation, lays his hand over the mouthpiece of the phone and says: "At the end of the day, I want to finish this call. OK!? Come back later this afternoon and ask if it is ready yet" and then carries on with the phone call.

The situation isn't exactly 'customer friendly'. Without making any judgement you ask them "What do you think of this situation?". The replies are:

"I don't see any problem, we said 5 o'clock!"

"The user should see we are on the telephone and can't do two things at once!"

"So, two satisfied customers in five minutes."

"He helped two customers at the same time. That's pretty good."

Organizations that say they are customer focused and believe they are customer focused often do not **know** what the customer sees as satisfiers and non-satisfiers. Often they think they know or they assume.

"We KNOW what the customer needs, we don't need to do a customer satisfaction survey. If we do a customer satisfaction survey we will set expectations."

These are typical examples of complacency. If you ask the customer what their perception and feelings are they will have a totally different answer to that of the IT organization. Later we will focus on how to address this.

This complacency is a barrier preventing the organization from improving. Complacency can occur at all levels within an organization:

- Managers who say staff need to go on ITIL training, I don't need to go, I don't need to change.
- Between departments, the help desk complains about support as being the problem, support complains that the Help desk is the problem, neither admit to being a part of the problem.
- IT managers continually accepting additional projects "Oh the techies can manage, they'll complain a bit but they can do it."

How to address this situation? One way is to create direct feedback loops:

- Let somebody who has factual evidence that something is failing talk directly with those responsible.
- Ensure that complaints go straight to the department responsible.
- Perform a customer satisfaction survey.
- Let the customers and users come and explain a situation that directly impacts upon their business.
- Try to use a non personal feedback mechanism. For example 'what I saw', 'what I felt', 'what the consequences were' rather than 'you really screwed up you idiot!'

Example:

We brought a user in to talk to our support staff. It was the first time many had seen a user, certainly the first time they had heard how the systems supported the user and what the consequences were when the system was down for a certain times. The user explained what he found valuable about the service and then went on to report dissatisfiers with factual evidence. We then brainstormed how we could address the dissatisfiers.

Saying yes and doing no

This is a common attitude we encounter in many IT departments. It appears as if people are willing to cooperate, but it is just that – an appearance. In reality they don't. It can be a symptom of thinking 'If I say yes they will leave me alone and go away and I can carry on doing what I always do', it can also be a symptom of not wanting to disappoint somebody by saying 'no'. Like many IT organizations we are so eager to please the users we say 'yes'to everything. We never say 'no'!

There is little you can say in the beginning when somebody says 'yes'. It is only later that you realize the 'yes' actually meant 'no'. It is important to realize that behind the 'yes' are a whole set of hidden assumptions, conditions, rules, time contraints and interpretations that belong to the person saying 'yes' and not to the person 'asking the question'. It important to be aware of what these potential constraints can be so that you can try to determine the possible risks.

Example:
A service manager asks a technical support person to ensure that a patch is installed on the server.

Support employee: "Yes, sure!"

At the end of the day the service manager asks again:

Service manager: "Is the patch installed, will it be available at the next reload?"

Support employee: "I was just about to do it, I'll do it next."

After two days it appears the patch wasn't applied and a failure occured. The service manager asks why it wasn't done.

Support employee: "Listen, I've been really busy this week, everybody keeps asking me to do things and everbody says it is important, so I didn't have time."

If you know that people are pressured by this type of situation and are really busy with conflicting priorities, and you ask them to do somethingthen you can make an agreement: "I appreciate you have many other tasks and priorities continually change, but let's make an agreement that you will do this and if, for any reason, you suddenly find you cannot, you will escalate to me immediately and I can discuss it with you and anybody else to determine the right priority".

Consciously saying 'yes', whilst doing 'no' is also a delaying tactic. The person giving the task is suddenly confronted with delays, the person giving the tasks becomes increasingly uncertain as to whether an action will be carried out and can no longer commit to planning. This type of attitude and behavior is not constructive.

Another form is saying 'yes' but actually thinking 'I'm doing it in my way'.

An example:

During a team meeting the problem manager discusses with the team the plans for structurally resolving a known error. It is decided to make use of a new printer type and everybody agrees. A few days later the problem manager discusses the list of open actions and sees that the printer has still not been replaced. The answer from the support worker is "Oh we could also fix that by installing a new driver, it is much quicker and cheaper".

You can imagine that the problem manager is a little angry, as this solution was originally accepted and agreed as the preferred solution and the employee never offered any alternative solutions.

This type of attitude makes it difficult to plan and predict the workload and the results. It becomes increasingly difficult to know what to believe and who to trust.

This type of attitude and behavior can be tackled with 'task focused steering' What does this mean?

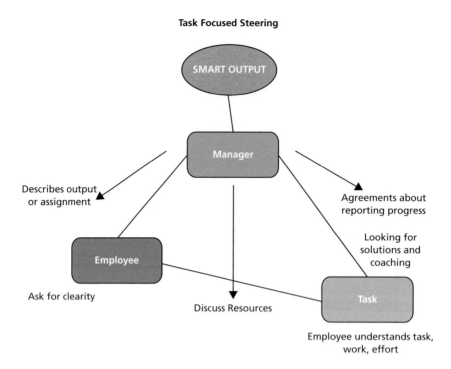

Task Focused Steering

A manager has an assignment for an employee. The manager needs to define this task very clearly in terms of SMART (Specific, Measurable, Achievable, Realistic, Time related) output. The employee needs to understand the task and will ask questions to clarify and check if he does so. The employee knows, from experience, which resources he will need in order to fulfil this task. His attitude is that he only needs to say 'yes' to this assignment if he can deliver the result as agreed. That is why he informs the manager that he needs some extra resources. For example: "I need to have at least three days because I need to do some research". Or "I can do it in two days, but then you must help me with the other task I have". It is important that the employees knows his job, he doesn't want to promise something he can cannot deliver and he wants to help his manager. Then both agree on the resources and the requested output. It is the responsibility of the employee to imform the manager about the progress. It is the responsibility of the manager to help the employee if there are any issues. It is also the manager who wants to have the solution.

This way of working has a few important aspects to think about:

1. The manager needs to define the output of this task in a SMART way.
2. The employee needs to know his job, knowledge and competencies in order to 'calculate' the impact of this request in terms of time, money, effort, risk etc.
3. The manager must be sure that the employee has the capabilities and can be relied upon to 'walk-the-talk'.
4. The manager must trust the employee's impact assessment.
5. The manager must help with the resources.
6. The manager must accept the impact and support the employee.

7. If there are issues, the employee must report this (ask for help) and the manager must give help.

This approach to managing people will increase the responsibility of employees. They must come back with a realistic answer in terms of time, effort and money. They must do it in such a serious way that if the manager agrees, there is no way back. Even if after a few days the employee cannot deliver the output, he cannot come back and say: "Sorry I cannot do it". In this approach the manager will ask the employees several times (depending on the time planned for the task) about the status. If there are some difficulties, the manager will offer help to the employee.

It is important that the manager recognizes how much 'hands-on' management he needs for any given task, for any given employee. A employee who lacks confidence and capabilities will obviously need more coaching and regular status checking, the same applies to employees who may be highly capable but are very busy and there is a risk they may let other tasks and priorities get in the way. There is a risk of 'saying 'yes'….but meaning 'no'.

This saying 'yes' but meaning 'no' can also be addressed by agreeing rules of accepted behavior within teams. Often these are made as part of some vision document or culture program and don't get further than slogans and lines in a report. The rules need discussing and agreeing at shop-floor level and managers need to agree how they will behave when employees continually flaunt the new rules, agreements and accepted ways of working. An accepted rule can be discussed at team level: "Our attitude must be 'an agreement is an agreement', if you are not going to meet an agreement you communicate this and agree the priority and any eventual escalation."

You are not allowed to do anything here! Why bother!

This attitude is common in organizations in which good ideas are ignored. People are often listened to and asked for feedback or input. The answers are always 'too expensive, we tried that before, let's do it differently, next year we'll do that….'

This attitude is strongly influenced by management. Either the manager doesn't believe in the idea but doesn't dare to say that, or he has no budget, or doesn't want to argue the case with his superior. Or it could be that it requires too much effort for the manager.

This is an example of a proud manager declaring: "we empower our employees to change their own work", "what do you do with all those requests?", "we pick out the ones we were going to do anyway and ignore the rest!".

If this attitude exists within a team or department there are various solutions:

For employees/teams:

- Discuss the problem within the team, let the person who suffers the most as a result explain the impact and consequences, involve the sponsor or budget holder who can sanction a solution.
- Investigate the willingness/urgency felt within the whole team to tackle the issue.
- Seek a solution that everybody agrees to.
- Work the solution out on paper in the following form:

- what is the problem?
- who has the most impact as a result of the problem?
- what are the effects in terms of wasted time, money, risks, delays and outages if we do not solve the problem?
- what is the proposed solution?
- why do we need this solution and not another solution?
- what are the costs?
- what is the impact in terms of time, effort, money, resources in solving the issue?
- Test the proposal with various stakeholders. Put yourself in the position of the person needing to make the final decision and read it critically. Assume that it is your company and your money. Would you invest?
- If it doesn't feel right think of alternative scenarios and solutions.
- Ensure that you and the team really endorse the solution and are ready, willing and able to implement the solution if the decision maker gives a 'go'.
- Present the plan.

For managers:

If employees come with ideas and proposals to improve things use the following guidelines:

- Prepare to listen to the request seriously.
- Ask questions to ensure you fully understand the request.
- Be business minded and critical from a business perspective.
- If you do not want to solve the issue then say so immediately and explain why. Take accountability and responsibility for the consequences if the solution is not implemented as proposed.
- If you agree that the problem needs resolving but do not agree with the solution, actively seek and help define a new solution. Explain why the initial proposal was not chosen.
- If you have budgetary problems with the solution then tell the team and explore alternatives.
- Search together with the team for an optimal solution.
- If you are unable to explain the solution to your direct manager, but you support the solution, then ask somebody with expertise in the matter to accompany you during the meeting with your manager.
- Be proud of this type of initiative and praise staff for their focus on cost effective business focused solutions.

For consultants and trainers:

As a consultant or a trainer you are often confronted with this type of situation. You would like the team to find a solution. Use the following guidelines to help:

- Coach the team to develop a small problem description, business case and action plan proposal.
- Motivate them if you see that the team agrees with the plan.
- Play devil's advocate and read their proposals from a manager's perspective.
- Ask the team questions that a manager would ask, if need be explain why you asked the question.

- Let the group practice presenting the proposal to each other before they present the proposal to their manager.
- If you have the opportunity, make the manager aware that the team will be coming to see him with a serious request and ask the manager to seriously consider the proposal.

Using container terminology

This attitude is characterized by using terms that actually don't say anything. Example: During a team meeting with the Help Desk and support staff, a Help Desk employee was asked "How is it going?". The employee replies "The communication lines between the back-office support and the Help Desk need improving", or "Not everybody understands the way it is supposed to work", "Management needs to be made aware that we have a problem." These words don't actually say much or help much.

There may be a variety of reasons why these container terms are used. It may be that this is part of the 'culture', nobody reacts to these words or feels they are being criticised. It avoids conflict and is a safe way of giving feedback.

The use can be conscious. It appears as if feedback is being given, it looks as if you are actively participating. It sounds as if something useful is being said, however the person saying it is being 'safe' and 'non confrontational' and the person listening to it doesn't feel personally confronted. Therefore there are no consequences for the people speaking.

The use of container terminology also gets in the way of making real improvements. It ensures we never get to the heart of the problem and that employees who need direct feedback are never confronted with a need to change. It is also a good way of burying or confusing issues. By using these words, nobody really knows what the issue is and it avoids risks of confrontation and arguments. If people talk to each other using container terms then there is actually no effective communication. Each of the parties involved interprets the words from their own perspective and paradigm.

A practical example:

Let's go back to the previous example in more detail. A Help Desk employee doesn't get adequate information from the second line. As a result the Help Desk employee cannot help the user and the user is irritated. The Help Desk employee is also angry and frustrated. During the team session the Help Desk employee is asked about the situation. The employee says: "The communication between second line and first line needs improving", The second line people in the meeting don't react. They don't feel personally responsible. An effective intervention could be that the team leader asks the Help Desk person to be more specific: "What information do you need and from who?". At this point the Help Desk employee becomes uncomfortable, he doesn't want to tell everything so he says: "I need more status updates about incidents from the network support guys, the information I get now is inadequate, I need to know what has already been done and when it will be solved". There now comes a direct reaction from Network Support: "We can't always give the information, we are busy trying to solve it and we don't always know how long it will take, besides which you guys need to document the information better and share it amongst yourselves. Often we give one of you status information and it isn't shared, so we get continually requested for status information again!". By avoiding container terms a healthy dialogue now occurs that can lead to a real identification of problem areas and some concrete improvement needs.

How should you deal with these types of 'container terms? Well, you should ensure that container terms are questioned. Ask questions such as:

- "What exactly do you mean by ….?"
- Who needs to do that precisely in your view?.."
- Be more specific, who and when?"
- "When you say management, who do you mean exactly?"
- "When you say communication is poor, can you give me a concrete example?"

Giving feedback:
Using container terminology can also be a symptom of the fact that we do not know how to give effective feedback. Often feedback is seen as personal. An attack on me personally, criticism that I am no good. It can become emotional and painful, both for the person giving and the person receiving feedback. We expect and prepare for confrontation to avoid this personal attack.

Feedback should be detached from the person but focused on the behavior. Behavior that can be changed. "This is the behavior I saw, this was the consequence, this is the impact, what I would prefer to see is…, how can we ensure that this behavior now occurs?"

Another rule is that positive feedback works and improves performance, whilst negative feedback demotivates. This is also known as the feedback sandwhich, where you begin first with positive news, then give the bad news feedback with constructive criticism to try to change behavior, then finish with a word of encouragement.

Example: "Incident 1 was really well handled. The customer was happy and it really helped us in terms of the information we got from the support team (support team does good work that adds value). Unfortunately the second incident caused us and the user a lot of pain, (support team failed to deliver). What can we do to ensure we can get the timely status information like we did with incident 1? That would be beneficial to our guys and the users. I am sure you guys can come up with some great ideas."Encouragement".

It sounds a lot like soft gooey, feely stuff that doesn't fit into the hard techy world of IT, but research reveals that giving positive feedback improves performance by more that 35%.

Feedback also needs to be specific (so avoid container terms), and it needs to be clear and precise (so avoid container terms).

How do you recognize the attitude of somebody towards something?
An attitude towards something is often difficult to recognize. Often the attitude is characterized in the form of non-verbal communication. Body language. People give away their attitude by the way they sit, the way they look or avert their eyes, the way they sit with arms crossed, the way they react to events or situations, the way they behave. If an employee sits slumped in a chair,

staring more out of the window or answering his SMSs, continually sighs and nods his head from side to side, then declares "I fully support the initiatve you can count on me 100%", you can almost guarantee that his attitude will not stimulate the desired behavior.

A research study by Professor Albert Mehrabian, a pioneer in understanding communication, into the non-verbal aspects of communication indicated that you can divide up interpersonal communication into the words we use, the tone of voice and gestures or body language. His conclusions showed that your words make up 7% of your communication, your tone of voice 38% and your body language and gestures make up 55% of your total communication.

Attitude is also evident in the things that are not said. If somebody is questioned about the current ways of working, and you know that people complain and are frustrated and the reply is "Yeah, it is OK I suppose", it signals an attitude of 'I'm not going to rock the boat', or 'if I say that it is OK I won't have to do anything about it'. This form of passiveness can be an attitude to avoid generating additional work or additional confrontation.

For example, a manager might ask his employees for feedback on a plan and there is stillness. People eye each other nervously of fidget in their chairs. This could signal an attitude of 'It doesn't matter what we say it'll happen anyway', or 'This'll never work but I'm not going to be the one to say', or 'I'm not going to say anything I might have to do something'. This form of passiveness could be a symptom of not wanting to accept responsibility, or of letting somebody else do all the work. If this type of attitude is not questioned, then the risk is failure, without knowing why, or being able to do anything to mitigate the risk.

It is also interesting to visit and observe the areas around coffee machines. Often there are notice boards where people hang up news clippings, quotes or cartoons. These often give a good indication of the attitudes of people. It is also here where people are more relaxed and more likely to verbalize their attitude to what they have seen or heard.

What does it say about attitude when there are numerous Dilbert cartoons about being blamed for everything that goes wrong, or articles about bad IT management?

It is worth looking at these and investigating why they are there and what the underlying cause was for putting them there; often this gives an insight into an ABC issue that the organization needs to resolve.

A very effective way of identifying people attitudes is by playing a business simulation. In a simulation people are taken out of their 'normal' working environment and are placed in unfamiliar, difficult situations. During the reflection moments in a simulation, the facilitator can ask questions to the team. This can often give an insight into underlying attitudes.

An example:

During a simulation the Help Desk became overloaded with work. The second line were not very busy. The staff sat with nothing to do and enjoyed the obvious suffering of their colleagues. They didn't make any attempt to support their colleagues and the Help Desk people didn't take the initiative to ask for help. The result of the simulation was poor. Not enough situations were resolved and resolution times were poor. During reflection the following was discovered about the underlying attitude in the organization:

- If you are struggling you don't ask for help, you solve it yourself, asking for help is losing face.
- If you see that somebody is struggling, you don't ask if they want help because you make them feel they cannot cope, and they will feel inferior.

During a business simulation these attitudes can be discussed in detail. If the organization wants this type of attitude and the corresponding behavior changing, then the team is stimulated in the next simulation round to ask for help or to offer help and support. At the end of the round the improvement in performance and the reduction of stress can be related to changes the team made.

Another way of discovering attitudes is to hold interviews with various stakeholders. The interviews with the different stakeholder groups often give a good insight into how people think and perceive things, and where the differences are in perceptions, opinions and attitudes.

Example:

During an interview with the customer of an IT organization, the customer said: "The IT organization needs to be more flexible. Standard services are OK for some services but we need flexibility to enable us to capitalize on business opportunities."

An attitude can also be influenced by putting information into context. What do we mean by that? For example saying "We need to improve the service delivery to reduce costs". The attitude of an employee hearing this can be: "What do I care about costs. It doesn't impact me…", in other words "Do I look like I care?". It leaves the employee feeling neither a sense of urgency, nor 'what is in it for me'. 'We need to improve the service delivery to prevent us being outsourced' has an entirely different impact on attitude.

If you can create a feeling of 'that is why I need to change' then this is the first step towards changing attitude.

It is important to think with the perception of the recipient in mind when communicating an improvement initiative or asking somebody to change the way they do things. Ask yourself the question: "If I was them and asked myself 'what is in it for me?', what would I want to hear?"

For example:

- Will it make my job easier?
- Will it give me more challenging work to do?
- Will it give me more value? Something to add to my CV?
- Will it help me develop and get a new position and more salary?

Think about this before communicating and try to explain it from the recipient's perspective if you want to increase the chance of buy-in. Remember also in times of change people may be thinking:

• Will this take interesting work away from me?
• Will this make me less valuable?
• Does this put my job at risk?
• Will I be capable of doing this?
• Why do we need to do this, it costs effort, time and may be frustrating?

We realize that to many people this may be simple common sense and we should be embarrassed writing something so obvious in a book. But it is suprising when we ask service managers giving a presentation: "Imagine I am an employee and I ask what is in it for me?", they say "I don't know, let me think about that", or "you'll be working in a more professional organization, we'll be more effective and efficient" – container terminology and a chance for me to play bullshit bingo.

What is the effect of a negative attitude?

The attitude that somebody has determines, to a large extent, the interaction that will occur between two or more employees. Examine situations from your own experience:

You have to give a presentation to a group of managers about the benefits of process working, knowing that you will be working with these managers to make it happen. You have prepared a number of slides and enter the room full of enthusiasm. After a few slides you are beginning to feel uncomfortable. People sitting in front of you are yawning openly and loudly, others are reading emails on their telephones. Somebody makes a comment about the colour scheme in one of your slides. Now answer the following questions:

• "What is the attitude of the people in front of you?"
• "How would you feel when this happens?"
• "Do you feel enthusiastic about working with this group?"
• "What would you do in this situation?"

The Help Desk employee who thinks that ITIL will soon blow over and all those procedures are a waste of time will, without consciously trying, communicate this attitude to the users calling the desk. The users will notice this attitude and interpret it as a non user friendly attitude.

Question: what will you observe in a Help Desk employee's manner that reveals an attitude of 'ITIL, what a waste, that will soon blow over'?

Some examples:

• "Help desk, what do you want?"
• "Sorry I have to ask you a lot of questions before I am allowed to help you?"
• "Yeah hi Frank, I know it's you but I have to ask you 'what is you name? what is your user name? what is your telephone number, what is your CI number?'….Frank? Frank? Are you still there….ha,ha what a joke eh!"
• "Sorry you'll have to wait, I have to type all this in my Help Desk system first."

Changing attitude is the best way to change behavior

In order to change attitude it is important to first make the attitude conscious, visible and open. People need to 'be made aware'. Next it is important to relate the relevance of attitude to behavior. To then get people to change their attitude in response to behavior, it is important that they feel the negative consequences and pain that arise out of not exhibiting the desired behavior.

Behavior

Let us now take a close look at the aspect of behavior. We will look at some examples of behavior, how it can be influenced by attitude and by culture, and how this behavior can impact, positively or negatively, upon your ITSM initiatives.

What is that 'Behavior'?

We found the following definitions: 'to act in a particular way'. 'Behavior refers to actions usually measured by commonly accepted standards.'

Behavior is influenced by attitude and culture.

To implement ITSM or to improve processes means behavior must change. As ITSM impacts all levels within an organization, from operational, to tactical and line management, to strategic managers, as well as the user and the business community, both IT and business behavior will need to change to some degree. This is a significant realization because, as we have said earlier, 'people do not like to change behavior', they will be likely to resist in one way or another until they have bought into the need and the benefits. Until they have bought into the need and the benefits, their attitude will be one of distrust as well as unrest at having to change the way they do things.

Behavior is what people do, it can be directly seen and experienced. The behavior can be supported by non verbal communication or body language. The non verbal communication can increase the effect and impact of the behavior.

Behavior stimulates a reaction to behavior. A support employee that doesn't take a user seriously will receive a behavior response in return of irritation and a failure to take the support worker seriously. The way in which two parties react to each other is also influenced by the attitude of both parties.

Example:

The user reports that the printer no longer works since he replaced the toner cartridge.

The Help Desk reacts as follows:
"You shouldn't play with the printer, then this sort of thing won't happen. Just leave them alone and let somebody who knows what they're doing fix things!"

User 1 may react as follows:
"OK I won't touch it anymore. Are you going to come sometime this year to help this stupid user……like you promised last time and didn't do!"

User 2 may react as follows:
"Sorry, remind me again whose printer this is, who pays for it and why you have a job? ….and now tell me Mr. guy, when you are going to come and fix it!,,,,if you can find your way here without a map!"

User 3 reacts as follows:
"Listen I am not really impressed with this 'user friendly' attitude. I'd appreciate a bit more respect and understanding toward your colleagues."

You see here totally different reactions. Behind every reaction (behavior) there is an attitude that influences the behavior.

User 1: Cynicism. Distrust
User 2: Sarcasm. This is unacceptable. I won't be put down like this. I will show you…
User 3: Respect. You treat people with respect, behave in a way that you want people to behave.

You can now imagine how a Help Desk employee would, in turn, react to these responses. The remainder of the exchange will be significantly impacted by the attitude of both parties.

The ideal situation is to know the desired behavior you want to see from each role involved in service delivery. Desired behavior that matches the goals and aims associated with adopting and deploying best practices.

It is a good exercise to define this behavior within your team. In this way people become consciously aware of the agreed and expected team behavior. You will then get a reaction from people about the desired behavior. What they think and feel about it. This will give some insight into their attitude (what they think) in terms of the desired behavior.

Behavior is often influenced by an attitude towards something. If a Help Desk employee has an attitude that the users are always complaining, then this will influence their behavior. In order to create desired behavior it is important to understand the attitude of people. It is important that people have a mirror held against them so that they become consciously aware of their attitude. In doing so, attitude can be related to current and desired behavior.

Some examples of behavior

Complaining about others
"If someone can not fulfil his task, he tries to switch the attention to somebody else."

"I could not install this package because the Help Desk asked me to wait!"

"How can I do my work if somebody else is holding the form to be filled in..."

Deliberately circumventing procedures
There are procedures in every organization, they all have a reason. But there are always people who see it as sport to circumvent them.

"Hey!, I know a way to change the setting of the router without registering a RFC!"

"If you tell the head of operations there is a error in his computer room, you do not need an access code to the computer room."

Avoiding responsibility
Sometimes you try allocating a task to somebody with the intention of improving working practices, for example:

Service manager: "Ok, so we all think this is the best idea ever? Tim, can you set up a first proposal of a procedure to make this idea successful?"

Tim: "Yes, I'd love to but I have to go and see my grand mother, she is 100 years old today!"

Passing blame
Passing blame is not good for team spirit. If someone makes a mistake, the cause is allocated to someone else.

Service manager: "John, you installed a new patch last night and this morning the system was out for three hours. What do you do wrong?"

John: "How was I to know that this patch was wrong. Peter tested it but he didn't obviously didn't test it properly!"

Refusing to accept or listen to others
This is one of the most irritating examples of behavior. This behavior is rather common in organizations where we have process managers, line managers and employees a;; working together. Let's look at the following example:

John is part of the release management process. He knows a lot about the financial applictions.

Process manager: "John, last week you prepared the release for that financial application. We did some testing and we found some missing files. A lot of customers are waiting to proceed with the test, can you quickly resolve this for us?"

John is very busy, but he also doesn't really know how to solve this. He could have said this, but he finds another way of saying 'NO'.

John:	"I know, but I am very busy. Can't you try someone else?"
Process manager:	"But we need the files now, everybody is waiting."
John:	"I told you, I'm currently very busy, try asking Tim!"

Process manager: "No John, you did the preparations, you need to do this."
John: "Listen, if you want me to do it, go and ask my boss, he can order me!"

Deliberately withholding information or miscommunicating

This is something that is very critical and is seen by some managers as a reason for firing a person. This behavior is often seen if people need to do things which they perceive as completely useless, wrong, stupid or impossible. As a reaction the people who need to support a manager or process manager, or even a collegue, will sabotage the situation. Here is an example from our own experiences as IT managers:

During a meeting a decision was made to select a new tool to register the workload on the routers. This router was not the best but the cheapest. It showed the best price/quality ratio of all alternatives. This tool however needed to be installed by one of the technical support staff and needed some customization work. Some settings needed to be changed.

The person who was responsible was asked to produce a plan for this. After a few days (and after being asked 10 times) he came up with a plan. This plan contained three actions. We asked the specialist (Rod) some questions for clarification:

Manager: "Rod, is this all we need to do?"
Rod: "I think this is all, well I hope it is!"
Manager: "What do you mean, 'I hope'?"
Rod: "I don't have any experience with this tool...I hope it will work!"

After a few days the tool was installed. Then the system broke down. We asked Rod if he could analyse what happend:

Manager: "Rod, what happend?"
Rod: "It is like I said, I hope..."
Manager: "Rod, I need to know what went wrong. I need to go to my boss to explain why this system is out!"
Rod: "Now you see what happens is you choose this kind of rubbish. I'll take a look."

After a few hours Rod came with an answer:

Rod: "Our machines are too slow and the buffer became full, we need to buy larger computers or the more expensive tool."

After consulting the supplier we found:

• Wrong installation;
• Computer is ok;
• Wrong settings and parameters;
• After two minutes, fast operations and uptime of 99.9 percent.

This example shows what can happen with people (Rod) if you (as a manager) choose a wrong solution (in the eyes of an employee). They will try to prove that you made a mistake.

Deliberately delaying activities

This last example is all about people who do not like or agree with the ideas of others. They will be (artificially) enthusiastic and they will accept actions but they will delay them ('let's just hope it will all go away').

Examples include:

- People need two weeks to read a document;
- People tell you after the deadline that they cannot make a decision because they miss information;
- They said they would do something and then a week later they say "let's wait until a colleague comes back from their holidays";
- Let's wait for the next version;
- If Tom is not here we cannot make a decision.

All these examples of behavior can cause problems in your organization. Let's look at a few:

- It costs an awful lot of energy from managers, project managers, process managers and employees;
- It can slowdown the project or program;
- It can even stop the program;
- It can even become a real threat for the IT service continuity element of business continuity;
- It can make really good people want to leave the company

So we need to so something about this.

Working on behavior

Resistance, how to address that?

'Resistance' is the one of the most common terms encountered in organizations attempting change. It is also one of the most difficult issues to address and, as such, it is something that is sometimes ignored or avoided.

What is resistance?

Resistance, like culture, is difficult to precisely define. The following is a theoretical description that may help to scope it:

1. An emotional or behavioral reaction to change.
2. A natural reaction to something that is enforced upon you.
3. A sign that there is energy and life.
4. A part of the pain (mourning) process of transitioning from the known to the unkown.

5. A timely intervention designed to create time to be able to think.
6. A label we give to people whio don't want to cooperate.

(source: COPP, University of Leuven)

Resistance can be an action of individuals or of groups. This group resistance is more prominent and powerful if the initial resistance comes from individuals who are seen as powerful, or well respected. This gives the group more certainty, power and confidence in how they act. Something even more dangerous to those attempting change is the fact that resistance can be organized and orchestrated by forming coalitions.

Resistance can arise from realistic motives and facts, but it can also arise from fear, or from a feeling that cannot be directly attributable to facts. The attitude and behavior can result from of a culture within a group. 'We don't want to adopt this new way of working. If they try to introduce that here then we will refuse to follow procedures'.

Resistance can have an active and visible character. Such as discussions, questions, complaints, or 'yes, but…', which may be a way of saying no. Sometimes this can be highly emotional or aggressive, such as strikes or protest actions. But resistance can also be passive and hidden. In this case it is often difficult to determine what the problem is. The signals are often subtle and are not immediately seen as 'resistance'. Often people give themselves away by body language. The way that somebody sits with arms crossed and a serious frown on their face. If you were asked to describe this you may say that it as an attitude of '…I disagree and am ready to argue' or somebody who continually looks away or avoids eye contact. Often we see these signals but they are not discussed or brought out into the open.

A form of passive resistance is also saying 'yes' but later doing 'no'. The resistance becomes visible later.

How do you identify negative resistance?

Resistance is often an indirect expression. For this reason it is difficult to immediately recognize it. We can all name examples of behavior that we perceive as negative resistance. For example:

• Negative reactions to a proposal for improvement;
• Complaints about 'management' or 'wrong choices' made in the organization;
• Saying 'yes' but doing 'no';
• Letting things fail and situations deliberately get out of hand;
• Passiveness, not saying anything or giving an impression of agreement;
• Delaying things by continually complaining and asking questions or demanding explicit detail;
• Cynicism;
• Sarcasm;
• Doing precisely what was asked and nothing more;
• Discussing something until it becomes so boring, tiresome and time consuming everybody gives up.

How do you recognize positive resistance?

The following types of behavior could be a result of positive resistance. This type of behavior can possibly be channelled towards supporting the improvement initiative:

- Emotionally defending what currently works and saying how the new approach needs improving.
- Asking questions that are focused on clarification and a desire to understand, not to undermine.
- 'That's not going to work unless……', where the 'unless' can be used to illicit suggestions.
- 'Yes, but….,', this can be an indication of buy-in for some things but not others. A management expert who advised large organizations said that 90% of good ideas are killed by 'yes but', sometimes without a desire to actually kill the whole idea.

What is the effect of negative behavior?

In general you can be sure that this negative behavior will cost a lot of energy, increase frustration, make the program considerably more difficult to succeed and will probably cost more time. Or, even worse, create a risk that the business or user may suffer as a result.

Delaying the program

Because this type of negative behavior requires more attention and reaction from the project leader, the process manager, or the manager, it will require time. Time taken to organize work sessions and discussions, and for individual sessions with employees. Time delays also occur as a result of employees not doing what should have been done, or not doing something correctly, or deliberately taking longer. This may require rework or extra work for other people.

Frustration for the process manager or team leader

Dealing with resistance costs a lot of energy. Not just for people in a management position but also for the employees. When the program doesn't go as hoped, or results are not achieved, or things need doing again, it can lead to frustration and even anger. It can result in positive, motivated employees becoming demotivated, and, in a worst case scenario, employees or managers looking for work somewhere else.

Frustration for employees

Working in situations with a lot of negative resistance can impact upon employee morale. It can create a spiral of negative energy. Motivated employees may become frustrated and disillusioned if management or leadership is not actively seeking to address the resistance. Ignoring resistance, or not taking it seriously, can increase frustration, cynicism and sarcasm and a general disbelief and distrust for the whole program. All employees can become less productive, less involved and less caring in what happens as a result of negative resistance. The working atmosphere can become unbearable for all.

Degradation of the service performance

The quality of the service delivery can be seriously impacted. Because employees perform sub-optimally they can make mistakes, they may ignore the consequences of their behavior, and not take things as seriously as they should and would normally do. Their general attitude and behavior can lead to dissatisfaction amongst customers.

Risk for business continuity

It is evident that resistance which leads to mistakes (conscious or unconscious) could have a serious impact upon business operations and business continuity. For example: A support employee wasrebuked for resolving something that he considered important and was told he could only solve things when instructed by the incident manager or problem manager. An evening job failed and the support employee was called by a user who was working late. "I need this report for tomorrow it needs to be presented to the minister in a government debate" pleaded the user.."Sorry" said the support employee. "I can only work on things when told to by the incident manager". Now this is a real life example. You can imagine the discussions the next day and the resulting complaints and apportionment of blame.

Failing projects and wasted investments

If projects need to be stopped before they have been completed, this can cost organizations a considerable amount of wasted money. Also projects that fail to deliver the expected and anticipated results can be a waste of money. The business loses value and faces increased risks.

Where does resistance come from?

If we could answer this question with certainty we would package it up and make a fortune in consulting engagements, and the ITSM community could organize and manage projects more effectively. However the fact of the matter is that resistance comes from all angles, all stakeholders and possibly at all times throughout the process. Quite simply, resisitance is a normal part of the process. It is something that must be gone through. The trick is to make it as short and as painless as possible.

Personal attitude towards change, preference for stability and continuity

Many employees want to maintain their own personal status quo. Enjoyable, easy work; pleasurable working environment. It is easy to forget that the reason for employment is actually to realize somebody else's goals and objectives, and that sometimes these goals and objectives require a new way of working for the employees. A need to reduce costs or to increase productivity, or a need to offer new products and services, or to meet regulatory demands. Often these changes require us to perform new or different work, often to acquire or relinquish responsibilities.

As we said earlier, people don't like to change and what may be seen by shareholders and managers as a necessary change to realize hard, impersonal goals affects people on a personal, emotional level. Very often managers have had time to think and discuss the change, time to consider its implications and make considered choices. These are then communicated to the organization. The employees are now confronted with a change, they feel they have no say, are powerless, and have too little time to understand and accept the change before it becomes a hard reality.

Fear of the unknown, fear of failure

If people are uncertain of what the new work will mean for them, and if they are unsure of their capabilities to perform the work, this can also cause resistance. They may see the change as necessary and even want the change. However they may fear failing. They may be driven by the need for, and the comfort of current successes. Successes they are used to and come to expect. The possibility of failure may cause a reaction that can be interpreted as resistance.

A feeling of not being involved or not being supported

When change initiatives, new procedures and ways of working are suddenly presented to people who have not been adequately informed or involved in the choices, the decisions and the designs may be seen as something dreamed up in secrecy by people who believe they know better. Try to reflect and remember if this has ever happened to you? And how you felt?. The same applies when you are suddenly confronted with change but nobody bothered to consider the impact this may have upon your knowledge, skills and competency. Too little consideration paid to your needs for training, education or coaching. Leaving you to sink or swim. This can come across as unfeeling and uncaring, and can cause anger and resistance.

Personal conflicts and rivalry

Resistance can also arise from the fact that employees may have personal problems and conflicts with a consultant, team leader, process manager, line manager or director. This situation can also result in ideas not being accepted, even if they were good ideas.

Resistance can also arise when an employee doesn't get a function, role or responsibility they expected. They may suddenly display a behavior that is confrontational. A behavior that is aimed at creating 'failure' in order to show that they could have prevented the failure if they had been given the opportunity.

Lack of tact or bad timing

The way in which a change is communicated can also have a significant impact on resistance. Indeed a survey a few years ago revealed that the biggest reason for changes failing, according to managers, was 'communication'. The same managers also knew this in advance, but for some reason they failed to spend enough time, energy or attention on communicating in the right way. The same managers declared that the reasons changes failed in their company was 'too little time or effort communicating'! This is like knowing that banging your head against a wall is going to hurt but you do it anyway.

Some managers deny any issues with communication. They have told people what will happen and why.....therefore it will be so. But communication is more than a one-sided monologue. If the message is too direct, too one-sided, fails to take account of personal feelings and fears, is without respect, is seen as arrogant or too authoritative, then this can quickly cause irritation, anger, frustration, fear and ultimately resistance. Think about messages you may have heard from politicians on the TV.

Successful communication in the context of organizational change initiatives is all about dialogue, giving people the chance to respond and vent their emotions and feelngs, giving people the chance to offer feedback, the chance to discuss and ask questions in order to clarify and help with understanding. Often what is missing from the message that is sent is the 'what is in it for me?', 'what does it mean for me?', that the recipient is looking for. If the recipient does not hear or understand what it means personally, then they will not have a feeling of buy-in and will not be fully committed.

The timing is also important. If a new change is communicated at the same time that a press release is announced relating to cost reduction initiatives, you can imagine the reaction to the message. It would have been received differently if it had been carefully communicated well in advance, explaining in detail the reasons why, as well as the various options that had been considered.

The purpose, the motive and the background are not understood

Effective change programs are focused on solving a problem. The better that the problem and the need to change are understood by all concerned, the better the chance of acceptance for the change. If the purpose, the background and the motive for the program are unknown, then they will be open to all sorts of negative interpretations and assumptions which could result in delays and resistance.

Distrust

There can also be distrust, or a lack of faith in the competencies of the leadership team to implement the change successfully. This could be the result of the failure of previous change programs. Or a distrust of the chosen approach to implement the change. For example, hiring in a large amount of expensive consultants to sit in a room and design books of procedures that will be thrown over the wall. This may meet a certain amount of resistance!

Employees only see the downside of the improvements

Change can lead to fear. Fear of the unknown, or losing position and status. Fear of failing. Fear of losing control. Fear of too much control. As we have said earlier, people do not 'like' to change. This is something that needs carefully managing to ensure that the downside is negated and, wherever possible, the up-side is promoted; the 'what's in it for me' is clear to employees. They are more likely to get on-board and buy-in to the change when their fears are removed.

Dealing with resistance

The behavior that arises as a result of resistance to change creates a counter push that can delay the change or cause it to fail. More energy and effort is needed to overcome the counter productive attitude and behavior. There is a tendency to 'attack' this type of behavior and see it only as negative and ill-intentioned. However the behavior can be a positive form of energy that we can use in our favor to help support the change. This type of resistance is a symptom of energy for the change. The trick is to channel this energy towards the right things.

Consider the complaints procedure at the Help Desk. We want customers to be able to submit their complaints. We make a note of these complaints and we allocate somebody to consider and address them. Often they may be negative or aggressive complaints. However we treat them seriously and use them to try to improve the level of service.

This example shows how we can treat feedback seriously and give them attention. This gives us a lot of valuable information to enable us to give better shape and direction to our improvements.

In many improvement programs a suggestion to undertake a customer satisfaction survey is met with the response: "Oh no! We don't want to do that, we'll get loads of complaints and the users will expect us to do something about them". Isn't that the idea of a service improvement program? To increase the level of service to the customers and users?

Some examples of how to deal with resistance

Give all resistance attention

Consider all forms of resistance as a gift. We know this sounds weird. Like going to the dentist, you know it is going to hurt, but ultimately it will make things better.

For example, an employee may have a problem with a change initiative but is unable to clearly articulate their concerns. Or an employee has negative resistance and displays deliberately unclear signals aimed at derailing the program. In both examples it is important to give attention to the signals. With positive resistance we can identify ways of improving the program, or gain an insight into the cause of the resistance, enabling us to remove it. In the second example we give attention to the attitude or behavior so that the person displaying it is confronted with the impact and forced to make choices. Either they must explicitly state that they are no longer willing to participate under any terms, or they must make concessions and learn to accept the change and come to terms with it.

It is important to show well intended interest in what the employees have to say. Try to understand the underlying cause of the resistance. Ask questions. "Can you explain what you mean by…", "I do not understand, please help me understand so that I can try and help or do something about it", or "If I understand you correctly what you mean is…".

Example:

At the start of an Apollo simulation we were told that this particular group was filled with 'resisters', 'these people will not accept it…', 'these people will work against you'.

We did an introductory round. "What do you expect from this day's training?". The response was: "I expect this will be a waste of time. I could be doing something more useful. I do not believe in this process stuff". When asked to clarify it came down to, we were told: "Too much unecessary registration and bureaucracy that nobody needs…"
"I don't have the time to explain or hand-over…."
"It will just give me MORE work and more people telling me what to do…"

It was clear that the resistance was due to time pressures, workload and not believing that processes could help in any way.

We played Apollo. The initial round was a disaster. There was stress, frustration, anger and a general belief of 'see we told you processes were a waste of time'. The sponsor for the workshop was getting worried. We had made the resistors even angrier and they had even more reason to believe they were right.

The interventions in the game, thought up by the resistors themselves, were to:

• Get rid of the annoying repeat work that was wasting their time.
• Agree a priority mechanism to help everybody decide what work needed doing first.

- Agree an escalation mechanism so that somebody else could make a call on priority when there was a conflict about what to do next.
- Agree to give each other the right information to enable people to do what they need to do.
- Agree to give each other feedback when things are not working as agreed.

We tested their new procedures, process design and agreements. The next round went much smoother. They achieved their goals and targets. We asked them "How does it feel?"

"Smoother, easier, less stress, more time to pick up the difficult projects, more ability to plan."

"How come?" we asked.

They concluded that it was because they had agreed their own procedures, they had all done what they had agreed and promised, they had handed over some of the workload to other people. They had, in fact, done all of the things they were being asked to do but now they were able to experience the difference on their own tasks.

We reflected back on what had happened and how we had listened to their underlying concerns and tried to show them how these could be solved by doing the very thing they were resisting.

When you show that you are listening and really looking to help find a solution to the underlying cause, the employee will get a feeling of really being listened to and taken seriously.

If an employee refuses to reveal the real causes, then each time you answer one concern another one will appear. It feels like you are continually banging your head against the wall. The fact is that not everybody will change. There is an 80/20 rule. It will cost 80% of the energy to get the last 20% to change. You may want to ask yourself is this worth the effort?

When you continually get this mushrooming resistance you can address this in a team setting. Like a business simulation. At the start of the day we had 90% resistance, as the day progressed 80% were buying-in and convincing the others of the need to change. It was suddenly 'peers' who were trying to convince the resistors. My role as a change agent was put aside, the employees themselves were becoming change agents and convincing people from their own team. However there are always some who will continue to resist. Even if they believe, they may have a hidden motive which they don't want to reveal, such as wanting it to fail so that a person they do not like also fails.

Two examples to illustrate this.

You have developed a plan, together with some employees, to improve the level of service from the Help Desk. Not all Help Desk employees were involved. Three people from the department took part. One of the new agreements was to record the amount of time spent by a support worker on an incident. This would enable the department to get a better idea as to which types of incidents were causing the most amount of effort and work. This way they could highlight the need for additional training or capacity. This would help the Help Desk to try and solve their own frustrations. The plan was presented to the IT department. There were also employees from second line and third line support.

One of the employees from second line called out "I don't see why that is important, That just wastes time and effort better spent solving things!"

"What do you mean by 'that'?"

Second line: "…well…that registration of the time you spend on a call, sometimes that is five minutes. I will spend more time writing that down than I spend actually fixing the problem!"

"How would you prefer to spend the five minutes then? Have you got an idea?"

Second line: "Yeah! Wait a minute, who thought of this?"

"The Help Desk improvement team. But let's get back to your point. You think that five minutes worth of administration is a waste of time, correct?"

Second line: "Yeah, you might as well not do it."

"So how could you capture these sort of activities without it costing so much time?"

Second line: "Maybe you can just close it with a code or something that shows it was closed in five minutes."

"Sounds like a good idea, we'll try that. Anybody got more reactions on this proposal?"

This example shows that you shouldn't go deep diving on the negative aspects. The reaction appears to come from a negative attitude of not wanting to administer and seeing it as a waste of time. Try to focus on the positive points. Discuss the orginal reaction and work through it point for point until you solve the underlying issue. Don't be detracted by switching the discussion from point to point and losing the initial focus and purpose. By switching the focus, the person could be deliberately trying to avoid diving in deeper on the motives, the cause and a solution. Ask also for ideas and suggestions, even if the initial reaction is negative, search for a possible solution focus.

Another way of looking at this is the 'yes but….', which kills an idea. For example:

The idea is presented: "…administration so that we can identify training needs and areas where extra capacity is required…"

Second line: "Yes but that wastes time…..we could be doing something else."

The 'yes but….' kills an idea, and negates every positive thing in the initial idea by association. What do I mean by that? You could react by saying: "Wait a minute, tell me two positive things in the suggestion that are worth keeping?". What you are looking for is an agreement that it is a good idea to identify areas for training or improvement to make life easier. "OK so how can we gather the information to support this?"

Sometimes you can't come to an immediate solution, but you do gather additional, relevant information that gives an insight into the deeper reasons for resistance. Below is a second example of a reaction to the same initial proposal:

Second line: "I couldn't be bothered with all that registration. You've obviously never been to our department."

"Please explain what you mean by that."

Second line: "Well if you want to know what we do all day, come and sit in our department and see how busy we are."

"Oh, do you mean you see this as a way of checking to see if you are busy or not?"

Second line: "Yeah, otherwise why would you want to register all that information? Who's going to use it?"

This short dialogue highlights the precise fear and suspicion of the employee. He doesn't understand the real reason, and interprets and assumes a totally different hidden motive; perhaps from experience or mistrust. You need to bring this back to yourself and the way the idea was presented. You need to spend more time describing how the problem was originally signalled by employees themselves, and how this was a suggestion from themselves about taking control and improving their own work pressure and demands.

By giving attention to this resistance you discover a lot about assumptions and fears that drive resistance. When you directly confront statements such as 'I've got better things to do than register all that stuff…', by insisting that they should do what has been asked, you will probably end up getting even more resistance.

Not fighting against resistance
Do not try to address the negative aspects of the statement, or try to convince somebody. If you do then you will probably not identify the real reasoning and argument as to why somebody is against 'registering'. By directly counter-arguing you put yourself in a defensive position where you may run out of arguments. You will then end up losing your position and your credibility. This can result in employees feeling sorry for you or pitying you. Not taking you seriously or not respecting you.

Do not try to talk employees out of their resistance by showing how good you are at arguing and presenting facts. If you simply counter with "what difference does five minutes make…", or "…don't worry nobody wants to control you", you may increase the resistance. You face the risk that other employees will also begin to call out and expand upon the negative issues: "Yeah but the five minutes happens about 20 times a day!..", or "…yeah, you say we don't need to worry that it will be used to control us but that is what management wants to do…". This only creates more negative feedback and energy and makes it even more difficult to address the resistance.

Don't ignore or deny
Some comments may, in your opinion, be worthless, unnecessary, cynical or totally negative.

An example:

Second line: "That registration. Does it have to be in exact minutes and seconds?"
Second line: "Can we write it on a post-it and give it in to you so that you can register it."

You also need to pay attention to these comments even it feels uncomfortable, makes you mad or you find them too stupid for words. Don't forget you are responsible for improving the quality of service delivery and that the initiative is important.

Example reactions to these points could be:

"Why are you asking that question?"

"Why are you looking for exact details in minutes and seconds?"

"Why give it to me first on a piece of paper?"

Try, by continually asking questions, to identify the reason underlying the resistance. It is the cause that you may be able to address, not the symptoms and the statements made.

If the answers are obviously not serious, or a deliberate attempt to belittle the subject and make it seem laughable, then stop the discussion and address the person afterwards in a one-to-one session.

You should also avoid simply denying. This can lead to 'yes, but.....no, but' situations. Denial can have the same effect as trying to fight against the resistance.
If you looking for a comparison between dealing with resistance and playing a sport, then it is more like judo than karate. In karate you attack, it is more thrust and counter thrust. Judo is more about using the energy of the other to maneuver them into a direction they didn't want to go.

One-to-one discussions with employees
It can often help to have serious one-to-one discussions with employees. You take the employee out of the comfort of the group, removing the reactions and behavior aimed at impressing the group, and you take them out of the comfort and safety of their environment. It may seem a strange analogy, but this is what police do when they take people in for interviewing. When they want to ask questions to get to the truth. What you want is to ask questions to get to the real reason for resistance. This sort of discussion can be highly effective, however you must handle the person with respect and it must be a dialogue aimed at getting to the heart of the situation, not a monologue or an emotionally charged session where you get angry and are trying to win an argument or bully somebody into submission.

Intervene in the case of destructive resistance
If the resistance leads to destructive situations such as a negative atmosphere, boycots, mistakes deliberately being made, arguments or personal attacks, then a management intervention needs to be made.

This could be, for example, a discussion with the employee, with a line manager being present, a formal discussion with an HR employee or, in the worst case, somebody being removed from their position. The last intervention may seem too drastic but there are times when it may be the only realistic solution.

We want to use another example from the Apollo simulation. We actually got to speak to James Lovell (Commander of Apollo 13) and Gene Kranz (Flight Director) about simulations. James Lovell said it was difficult, but people that failed to learn from the simulations or who failed to change their behavior to ensure mistakes were not made, were removed from Mission Control. They were allowed to make the same mistake only once in a simulation.

The argument being, these people are dealing with mission critical systems, and the consequences of failure are unacceptable. Now, in most cases, the consequences of IT procedure failure won't result in death. However business failure can occur as a result of badly managed IT. "So if you tell me" said James Lovell "that IT is mission critical and failure has unacceptable business consequences, then maybe the same should apply. If you can't or won't make the grade…."

You will often find notorious opponents within organizations, who, through their position of respect, influence, or power, are looked up to by other staff. People look to them for an example and listen to them. These types of people often have an unspoken 'permission' to sidestep the desired or agreed behavior and procedures. The impact can be dramatic.

Others will emulate this behavior. There are often bypasses thought up to avoid this person and leave them out of the change initiative. "Don't invite or ask that person, we know they will refuse to agree…", "…no need to invite them…I'll tell them myself later". It sometimes becomes a full time task for the process or project manager to remember how they should deal with various prima donnas. It should be evident that this type of situation is unworkable.

That is why it is also necessary in this type of situation to have a serious discussion with this type of person, in order to consider and agree a series of countermeasures to be taken when undesirable behavior occurs.

Giving attention to desirable behavior
Mostly we put our energy and attention towards those people displaying resistance. Agreed that you should not ignore it and you should devote energy and attention towards it. However, you should also make a conscious effort to give attention to positive, desirable behavior. Allocate these people some interesting opportunities, discuss with them new initiatives and projects. Highlight the behavior in newsletters, let these people attend conferences. Through doing so, negative energy and resistance can start losing some of its energy.

It works in the animal world when trying to train dogs. They get rewarded and praised for good behavior and told off for bad behavior. Are we saying that IT people should be treated like dogs? No, but it is a recognized psychological instrument used when trying to influence and change behavior.

Motivating

As a leader, or change agent, you must interact with people to try to help them change behavior. To gain their support you must be able to motivate them. To be able to motivate them you must understand a bit about human nature. We are now going to get all theoretical and put people to sleep but it is important to know, so we will write as quick as we can and keep it short.

People behave according to certain principals of human nature. Except technoids who it would appear have a law unto themselves. American psychologist, Abraham Maslow, published *A Theory of Human Motivation* (1943) in the Psychological Review Journal that theorized his 'Hierarchy of Needs' model. In this he stated that people needed to satisfy basic needs before they would be motivated to change at a higher level need. So what? Why is this relevant?

We will just explain the first four needs. If you want to know more look it up yourself. These four basic needs are:

1. Physiological - food, water, shelter and other such types of needs.
2. Safety, free from immediate danger.
3. Belongingness, feeling part of a group.
4. Esteem, the feeling of moving up.

These are important because when people are faced with a need to change the way they work, they may feel threatened. What does it mean to my job? Will I lose my job? Will I get a job I don't like? It helps to know which need is driving somebody's motivation. For example, consider the issue about registering time at the Help Desk from earlier. It may be that one of the intentions was to identify where additional resources and skills were needed so that extra skills can be developed and resources claimed, leaving people with time to do other more interesting and challenging work (basic need 4, above). However if you explain about registering and an employee is thinking "Uh, oh! Control. They want to see who they can get rid of!", then he is thinking and behaving from the motivation at basic need 2. He doesn't see opportunity and chances.

Of course, in our worst practice book we would have said if people show resistance for whatever reason revert to a level 1 motivational tactic. "Do what I say or else….". But as this is a serious, best practice book we won't be suggesting that as an effective motivational intervention!

How do you deal with resistance?

The age old tried and tested strategy of burying your head in the sand and waiting until it goes away is finally accepted as being less than successful in today's working environments.

A certain amount of resistance can be prevented by considering a careful approach. This approach needs to address the following aspects.

Forcefield analysis

Before you consider a change approach and make the selection of a change team (that is people who are going to help realize the change) it may be useful to understand the forcefields in the organization. What is a forcefield? I know it sounds like something from Star Trek so maybe it will appeal to the technoids amongst us. A forcefield is, indeed, like something that Captain Kirk might encounter. You don't see it and you suddenly walk in to it and it stops you in your tracks, slows you down, needs a lot of energy to break through and may even be painful. These forcefields also exist in your organization so it is worthwhile knowing what they are. There are a number of ways of doing this.

We can ask ourselves some assessment questions:

• Which power sources do the key change agents have at their disposal (such as formal position, authority to make decisions and allocate resources, money, information, respect, loyalty, credibility)? For example if a change agent is well respected by the technical specialists they are more likely to be open to his or her requests for dealing with behavior change. If a change agent is not well respected by the technical specialists they may well resist, argue and refuse….. creating kick back and requiring a lot of additional time and energy to overcome.
• Are the key players influential (this can be dependent upon how the power sources are used, do they have a track record of getting things done)?
• Are the interests of those involved aligned? Or do they conflict? Some change agents want the change to realize significant cost savings and control, others may want a focus on innovation and speed of deployment. These may be conflicting interests.
• Is there a relationship of trust between those involved?
• Are those involved in relevant/influential networks?
• What is the attitude and the style of those involved (positive/negative, direct and blunt/ diplomatic)?

By carrying out this analysis, aimed at selecting a change team, you now need to consider what are the most important criteria for selecting those to be involved. Considerations might include diversity of interests, representative and a good communicator, to-the-point and result focused, predictable and thorough, creative and inspirational.

A simple instrument that can be used is the following matrix. You can use this matrix to help you place people from your team, department or organization in your program initaitives. It gives a good idea as to where you can place people in your team and where you need to give more careful consideration.

The trick is to place people in one of the four quadrants. The questions to be asked are:

1. Is the person working with or against?
2. Do I need this person or not?

	I need him	I do not need him
Works with	No problem. Include the person in your team and give them challenging tasks and assignments. Make use of their 'desired behavior', make them role models.	Difficult, try to involve and motivate and look for opportunities to use them.
Works against	Try to get this person on the team. Discuss with them. Try to create buy-in and motivate this person to be in the team. Take care to look out for signs of negative resistance and a negative attitude that may then influence others.	No problem. Ensure that this person doesn't start displaying negative reistance, and trying to undermine or sabotage initiatives.

Another way is to try to get an impression of the members within the department based upon the following:

- Who are the employees who want to get things done?
- Who are the employees who can get things done?
- Who are the employees that help get things done?
- Who are the employees who ensure that things really are done?
- Who are the employees who watch whilst things get done?
- Who are the employees who stand and moan because things don't get done?

Finally it is important to determine if the employees are capable of scoping and realizing the change themselves. In short, have they got the right attitude and behavior required to solve the problem and realize the change, and what coaching and facilitation will they need?

By using the above guidance you will have formed an impression of the employees and how you can best use each one to make a team and realize the change. The change initiative will be successful if there is a sense of ownership and it is deployed using the right forces in the organization.

Discuss the change initiative with these employees, explaining what you expect from each. Give each a role in the team and delegate to them the responsibility and, if necessary, the authority to realize parts of the change.

Ensure that those in a position to authorize and allocate resources are involved, in order to ensure sponsorship and display leadership. They will need to reward desirable behavior and address inappropriate behavior. Ensure they are prepared to 'walk-the-talk' and lead by example. Discuss with them what will happen if people openly undermine the change initiative. What is thet management role in this? You must discuss this and make it clear what 'management commitment' means and explain the possible consequences of lack of commitment and leadership. If managers are not convinced, tell them about a Forrester report which revealed that of the change initiatives that failed to achieve their aims – 52% were caused by resistance.

Develop an approach that the group endorses and is comfortable with
The right approach is dependant upon the following aspects:

- The time available to resolve the problem (urgency). Is there time to make gradual and continual improvements, or does the change need to be resolved within a time constraint for whatever reason?
- The knowledge and capabilities of those responsible for making the change happen. Are the employees capable of realizing and embedding the results of the change in the organziation? Are they experienced in doing this?
- The scope of the change. Is it about installing a support product or a tool? About implementing new workflows and processes, about changing behavior and embedding responsibilities? Does it require using and managing external partner resources in whatever form?

Important criteria for a successful change approach are shown in the box below:

The design principles for implementing sustainable, repeatable working processes:

1. Make use of the personal motivation and ambition of those involved.
2. Make use of individual and group reflection.
3. Make use of a feedback system.
4. Involve people from all groups who will be responsible for the management or delivery of the process in the diagnosis, design, implementation and institutionalisation of the processes, to ensure buy-in, ownership and commitment, Make use of collective diagnostic, design, implementation and embedding.
5. Ensure that there is a shared vision, strategy and objectives for the improvement.
6. Ensure there is sufficient commitment of resources (time, people, money, facilities) to realize the change.
7. Ensure there is sufficient management commitment to address undesirable behavior and reward desirable behavior.
8. Let the desired change happen by changing attitudes and behavior.
9. Use the workplace as a learning environment.
10. Ensure there is room for reflection, evaluationand feedback.
11. Apply learnings to insight, rules and behavior.

(source: Proces verbetering in ICT Service Management)

This approach is explained in more detail in the above publication from Jan Schilt.

Shared perception of the problem and the need
When we work using a 'shared perception' or a 'shared vision' then it becomes clear to all why a change is to occur. It clarifies what problem is to be resolved or what opportunities the change will create. By performing this analysis together with those involved or impacted by the change, such as those who have a form of influence, or those who display negative resistance or behavior, it will increase the buy-in, the belief and the commitment to the change. Try to make sure that all parties are involved at an early stage in the process, this will ensure that the thought processes

are aligned and no group gets a feeling of having somebody else's efforts thrust upon them. This will also help create acceptance. The more that people feel involved in the scoping and decision making processes, the greater the chance for acceptance.

The resistance can be caused by the difference in the thought processes of the various groups. Try to analyse the problem from different perspectives. Analyse the problem from the perspective of the employees, the team or department managers, senior management, the user community. Involve people from each of these stakeholder groups.

Include those involved or impacted by the creation of a solution
Create a team made up of those involved or impacted, based upon the forcefield analysis. Give this team the task of working to create the solution. The role of the consultant/ team leader/ facilitator is to support and empower the team to help them create a soltion that is best for the team. Try, as consultant/team leader/facilitator to bring your own input into the process.

Let employees communicate their own solutions
When a team has found a solution, let them communicate this solution to their peers. Often, the solution is found within the team, but the management will still have to be convinced. It is a great motivator to let the team convince the management. As a consultant/ team leader/ facilitator you can assume the role of mediator by talking to the management about the progress made and to prepare them for the meeting with the members of the team.

The advantage of this approach is that the members of the team are responsible for, and propagate their own solution.

Make employees responsible for solutions
Those involved have to become responsible for carrying out the solutions. This can be achieved by letting them scope and carry out the solutions. Also make sure that they feel responsible for the results of their solution. So, not only let them implement the solutions, but make sure they deal with any criticism. If a solution is not effective they must also learn to solve the problems.

Give credit to the right employees
Do not forget who got the results in the first place. Give employees the credit they deserve.

Make sure results are celebrated
Naturally, results are defined and measured up front. Showing actual results is very motivating and has a positive effect on subsequent actions within the program.

Culture
The culture of an organization can influence the attititude and behavior of individuals. Even if you successfully address individual attitude issues, the organization culture can be a barrier. For example a strong hierarchical culture in which line managers have power and influence and absolute authority can be counterproductive to an attitude of personal responsibility and empowerment of employees.

Adopting 'process managers' in this culture may conflict with managers' 'attitudes'. They will be giving away power, control and influence to process managers!

'Culture' is the word most used during organizational changes. Some examples:

If a change doesn't succeed then it is often because of the culture.

For example a change needs to be made in the way that the second line staff work. They have to work, according to newly defined procedures, documented in a procedures hand book. The procedure is aimed at ensuring that the status of an incident is captured and shared. The implementation manager tries with all his energy to ensure these procedures are followed, but the second line staff more often than not do not comply. The new way of working meets with resistance and the managers decide not to try to force it. The reason is 'it isn't in our culture to work according to procedures'.

Projects begin with a culture change program
Before we begin with an implementation project there is firstly a focus on changing the culture of the organization. There are messages, PowerPoints, bullet point lists developed and workshops given about the new culture. It seems as if that is all that is needed and the culture will be changed within a number of weeks or months.. Really?

What is culture?
This can be described as the accepted ways of working within an organization, the values and standards that people find as normal.

As there are numerous descriptions of what culture is, we will restrict ourselves to a few of the important characteristics.

A way of doing things that is strongly embedded in the organization. This may be seen as 'this is the way we do things around here'.

"If you turn up too late nobody will say anything, so don't worry about it."

There are two aspects of accepted behavior implied in this statement. One is that turning up late seems to be common, and not saying anything or giving feedback is also acceptable. Apparently they are so normal they are a part of the culture.

Shared values in a team of employees
The team believes that 'The customer is king'. This shared value drives everything the team does. People in the team communicate with respect, whenever problems or delays occur somebody always asks "*who is going to inform the users*", Regular pro-active information is sent to groups of users: "*You better do that incident first, the users have got to present those reports tomorrow*".

Ways of doing things are transferred and are a part of hand-overs
Whenever a new employee is hired, people look for the 'best fit'; will that person fit in with our way of doing things. We don't want somebody who will start rocking the boat and trying

to change things. Also, when a new employee is being shown around you can hear interesting insights into company values "They are the specialists…nobody understands them, they are left pretty much alone, we don't want to annoy them….", "This is the directors' floor…..you may see one occasionally", "They're always complaining but nobody takes any notice of them…". It is in these ways of selecting people and of instructing new employees that organizational culture, values and ways of doing things remain as part of the culture.

Culture is maintained

A culture maintains itself. Employees who display accepted cultural behavior or quickly adapt to the cultural way are rewarded. This rewarding can be seen in two ways:

- An employee who comes in too late is greated with "So that must have been a great party last night!", or greeted with a laugh "Oh good afternoon, so we're working part time now….I wish I had your job!". He then grabs a coffee and gets on with work. He was the center of attention for a moment, has grown in status (look at me, I can come in late and everybody gives me attention, and I can get away with it). In this way he is indirectly rewarded for his behavior.
- An employee made a mistake and quickly informed the customer. He apologized and spent time developing a work-around so the user could continue working. The manager from the department goes to the employee and thanks him for his actions. During the team meeting this example is brought up by the manager and the employee is named as somebody showing the behavior we expect.

Culture is acquired

In light of the previous examples it becomes clear that culture is acquired. It takes years of rewarding, punishing, setting examples and development. It will also be clear that changing that same culture needs to be based on the same process of 'unlearning' and acquiring.

Culture is often invisible

Actions and behavior are obvious. Someone does something or someone says something. Culture is often hard to recognize, at least for members of staff.

A striking example:

We were playing a business simulation with a team of project managers (They had to build a pyramid using lego). *Halfway through, the team had developed 50% of the product and it had taken them four additional years on top of the 12 that we agreed on. The question: "How do you feel it's going?"* yielded the anwer: *"Well, we're not dissatisfied"*. Our remark, that we could not understand why the project leader was satisfied with the result, was looked upon very strangely and we were told we were in the wrong. *"This is a good result, end of discussion"*. Further enquiry revealed that the 'culture' was *'the customer must be satisfied when the project is finished, even if this takes a lot longer than agreed'*.

During the second part of the day we tried, as a customer, to make them conscious of their own culture and we acted out a role as customer who got very angry when the project started to lag behind schedule. The final conclusion of the game was *'this game is not realistic'*.

Trainers, consultants and new employees often find out very quickly which cultural aspects are apparent within an organization. They are new and have not yet been sculpted, directed, influenced or indoctrinated.

Example:

We are playing a business simulation at a company. During the intake meeting the manager says: *"Why don't you give me a role that is not so active"*. During the workshop, when participants are free to choose a role, the seats of the difficult roles (incident manager, manager specialists and flight director) remain empty. Our question: *"How come these seats remain empty?"* gets no conclusive answer. And it seems as if nobody realizes this has happened.

Something is going on here. Apparently people are afraid to make mistakes. Possibly, making mistakes is punished. At first sight it is unclear what the cause is, but it reflects some of the culture.

Behavior that is a result of culture is never premeditated
You should not immediately judge behavior that stems from culture. You risk saying something that is perceived the wrong way and this could lead to an awkward situation.

Example:

An organization's goal is to work in a more result oriented way. Two rounds into the simulation game, the results are discussed and are found to be below the norm. However, we do not see any 'drive' to improve the results. No disappointed people, no-one taking any initiative to improve things. We begin the improvement session with the following remark: *"What is apparent to us is that the result is not good and nobody seems to care! I see passiveness and not a single action to improve"*. The group grows quiet and the day turns into a debacle. The group felt attacked and blocked up completely.

It was our fault (as we found out during our follow-up meeting with the customer). The team felt attacked because they interpreted our remark as a reproach; as if they did not feel like improving and were being passive on purpose.

When changes collide with values and standards you will get a reaction. This reaction is often called resistance. Make sure you realize the behavior is a result of this collision.

The onion-model of Sanders and Neuijen
The model shows the different aspects that make up a culture. The closer you get to the heart of the onion, the harder it is to change.

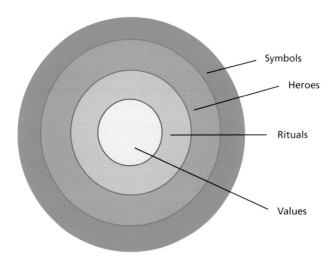

Symbols: words, gestures, jargon. What is said during meetings, during coffee breaks.

Heroes: the employees that show exemplary behavior within the teams and the organization. Also, often the stories that circulate for years about founders and former employees.

Rituals: technically superfluous actions that are necessary to maintain the culture.

Values: which behavior is perceived as good or bad. The values and standards within the organization.

Recognizing or exploring culture

As mentioned before it is very difficult to recognize a culture. The question is what do you need to look out for? We will give you some directions based on the onion-model described above.

Let us take a look at the layers one by one.

Symbols

It is essential to find this out by interviewing staff, team leaders, process managers, managers or customers. Go and find the exact meaning of these words. Who is using them as symbols? When are they used? Are they used cynically or realistically?

Also find out whether the symbols lead to an agreed result. Do they give energy? Are they productive? What are the effects?

Heroes

Who are the heroes? Which employees carry an organization? Again, interviewing staff is crucial. Ask a lot of people within the organization who they think the heroes are and why? Which behavior is characteristic of these heroes?

The explanation as to 'why' employees see their colleagues as heroes also paints a picture of the organization's values and standards. It says something of the culture if someone who is considered a hero always opposes the management.

You also need to examine which heroes, with their accompanying behavior, have an effect on the company's or department's results.

Rituals

These are easy to spot. Look around you, be astonished and marvel. Ask members of staff why things are as they are when you observe them. Example: why is a certain person always last to join the meeting? Who is this? What are the reactions to this? Who is reacting to this? Example: why does someone always have to talk to person X before voicing an opinion? Who does this all the time? Who is person X? Has the opinion changed and how come?

Examine the rituals and discuss them with those involved. Explore the meaning of the rituals. Examine the effect of the rituals. Are they effective or rather the opposite?

Values

This concerns people's convictions. Their opinions on work, life, colleagues, etc. You will find convictions such as whether something is good or bad. or accepting or not accepting something. These convictions are so strongly embedded in who we are that they are almost impossible to change.

You can examine these values and standards by talking to members of staff a lot and by asking many questions, such as "What do you think of this?", "Why do you think so?", and "What would you do in this case?" Examine a lot and, especially, explore a lot. Try to find out the reason behind the responses.

Take into account that many people are not always prepared to speak their true mind. A lot a people do not like answering 'soft' questions like this. But be aware that the information you receive is of great interest.

Working the culture

One of the most important lessons when working the culture is that culture is generated as a result of working on behavior and attitude.

Do not focus on changing the culture

Do not focus all your attention on culture when improving organizations. Use the word as little as possible and focus instead on changing behaviors and attitudes. The long term effect of changing attitude and behavior will be a shift in culture.

Talk a lot to those involved

It is important to create a shared perception of the current characteristics of the organizational culture as well as the desired organizational culture. It is necessary to discuss findings, such as the values and standards, with all involved. What do they truly think of the issues that are apparent within the department? Can they come up with a solution? What is the desired situation? What is important to them in that new situation? Talk to everyone involved, all the heroes, even if this is not always easy.

Develop a joint picture of the desired situation

This is an important step on your way to a new culture. Staff have to become conscious of the desired new way of working. By mapping out the situation with those involved you also create buy-in.

Results substantiate evidence

Many members of staff will want proof that the new way of working is better than the old one. This can be very helpful when changing attitudes and behavior, and with that, later on, the culture.

Exemplary behavior, create new heroes

By rewarding desired behavior and ensuring that people 'unlearn' unwanted behavior, you create new heroes. These heroes will be given assignments, new tasks and new roles. They will also be asked to create new teams in order to spread the desired behavior. It is essential that management also starts to show desired behavior and thus set an example. When managers reward desired behavior and, just as importantly, when they punish undesired behavior, people see that managers are also commited to change and are displaying the appropriate behavior.

Be prepared for resignations

As soon as an organization starts to change, some employees will be unhappy with the new way of working, especially when it is significantly different from their values and standards. If this is the case, so be it. But if that is not the cause of their unhappiness, you have to work very hard to try and keep them.

A model for change

There are many models available in the market to help with change. There is a danger that in adopting a model we display the same worst practice as we display when adopting a process framework, thinking that a tool will solve the problem. Remember the tool, model, framework or whatever is only an instrument to help change behavior.

In this book we will make use of the model 'Learn to Change'. The changing of behavior requires a different approach than that of 'implementing ITIL processes'.

'Learn to Change' makes use of the following aspects:

Learning Based Improvement

Vision, guidance, working processes and problems

Work related problems often arise out of the work processes. These processes are required in order to execute the strategy of the organization, as defined through guidelines and policy. When using this model we will refer back to the vision, the guidance or policy, and the working processes.

Urgency

The advisor or change agent needs to spend adequate time and energy addressing the urgency, or the need for change. The advisor or change agent will work together in a variety of ways with the sponsor and the stakeholders involved in, or impacted by the change in order to identify, recognize and agree areas of pain or bottlenecks. A variety of work forms could be used, such as workshops, team meetings and brainstorm sessions. Without a clearly recognized and felt urgency it will be difficult to motivate people to change, or become involved in the change initiative. Another model that makes use of this, as described in ITIL is that of John Kotter. His first step in leading change is to 'create a sense of urgency'. This goes further than identifying the urgency, he says you need to create it. An example we came across was an IT manager needing to motivate staff to adopt process-based working for the legacy and the new data center operations. The organization had failed to apply processes for a number of years. The IT manager said that if the processes were not at a CMM level, with demonstrated value by the end of the year, then the new data center would be outsourced. This would mean existing IT staff would remain on the legacy systems and would not be involved in learning and managing the new technology and platforms. It was not true, because outsourcing was never an option. However, it created a sense of urgency with the specialists who wanted to learn the new technology - after all a new cyber center has a more sexy image that the antique, dinosaur legacy systems that hobble along, wheezing, croaking and groaning under the strain of business demands.

The advisor or change agent doesn't need to analyse and make conclusions about the cause of the pain, but has to make an analysis of the pain and bottlenecks that are standing in the way of the learning process or change process. The stakeholders involved in the sessions, involved in the processes, or impacted by the processes, are better equipped to identify and analyse the cause based upon cases and experiences and expertise. The ABC card set that accompanies this book is an instrument that can be used in meetings and workshops to identify and recognize 'worst practices'. These 'worst practices' once recognized and agreed, can be discussed to determine the consequences and likely business impact. This can often give new insight into unacceptable attitudes and behaviors and thereby create an urgency to fix them. An urgency, in fact, to change behavior, as seen by the people themselves.

Team
The approach works from the basis of 'creating together'. It is recommended to work in teams. Once the urgency for change is clear (something that has also preferably been established and agreed by the teams) it can be determined who will tackle which pain area and bottleneck, and in which role. In the selection of the team, personal ambitions play an important role. The people in the team and the role they are to play can be determined by asking the following questions:

• Which competencies do we need?
• Where can we get those competencies
• Who is involved or impacted by the need for change?
• Who is willing to help?
• Who can help?

You can use the forcefield analysis to help identify idividuals, personal motivation and ambition, and the power, energy and influence to make change happen.

The customer also plays a part in the team.

Approach
The team is responsible for the approach. The key question is: "How are we going to handle the assignment?". We can make use of the available resources, like the results of an assessment, a customer satisfaction survey, a service improvement plan, charters, PID's, etc. The advisor is working with the team to help them define the approach. It is possible the team will have to go back to stage one (necessity) because it is not yet clear to everyone on the team why they are together. Eventually the plan is presented to the customer. There are no major goals yet, these will be defined during the next phase.

Creation
As soon as the team has been given the all clear regarding the approach, the required results or outcomes are inventoried together with the team. This is an important phase because it might be necessary to sometimes return to earlier phases. Yet it is distinctive of the approach to do this during this phase, as the results that are defined by the team carry a wider acceptance base than when they are dictated from above. The results are communicated to the customer and adjusted where necessary. We only set down to work when the results are clear and agreed to be SMART (Specific, Measurable, Achievable, Realistic, Time related) by everybody.

Thinking
This phase is used to explore, with those involved, the possible solutions that can achieve the goals. Commitment from the department managers, process managers and the process employees

is of utmost importance in order to establish a solid foundation of buy-in and acceptance. People are working in teams using different approaches aimed at stimulating the power of thinking and creating combined solutions.

Realization

During this phase the team chooses the solution they are going to implement. Which one is feasible is dependant upon the goals, the organization (policy, work processes) and other limiting conditions that were described in the *Approach* phase. During Realization, the solution is worked out in detail. For example, creating the process flowcharts, selecting a tool and creating a procedure. The team again thinks about 'how, and by whom can these activities best be carried out with the greatest chance of success?'. It is possible for a team member to create a temporary team that creates an approach and sub-goals by following the same method.

Deployment

By working according to this method the solution is implemented piece by piece, little by little. By working in teams and by guiding them into learning to 'double loop', they will achieve insights that make up the foundation of the final solution. In this phase the <u>solution is established as part of the daily work</u>. Agreements are made regarding the new way of working, old procedures are replaced by new ones, etc. This phase is a success if all participants are able to apply the new solution to their daily work. The double loop learning ensures also that rules, procedures, and even processes, are part of the discussion and may be changed to avoid future errors or improve the performance of the team. Double loop learning can be recognised if people ask questions like 'why......'.

Evaluation

It is important for the total approach that there is an evaluation of the result, and the process to reach that result. This is called 'reflection'. Arising out of this reflection may be new improvements that again lead to a better process, a better service or product. Reflection is one of the important skills of a team. The advisor spends a lot of time teaching reflection skills.

Working on Culture, Attitide and Behavior

Culture is invisibly embedded in the organization in which we are working. There are various ways of describing culture and what it is; 'the way of life, especially the general customs and beliefs of a particular group of people, at a particular time', 'the way things get done around here', 'the combination of values, rituals, symbols, slogans, mission statements'. A culture is an integral part of every organization and is maintained by the people who work there.

According to some experts 'culture is the most difficult organizational attribute to change, outlasting organizational products, services, founders and leadership, and all other physical attributes of the organization.' Whatever definition you use, whatever the experts say, we in IT all recognize its impact on, and importance in, realising ITSM improvement initiatives.

A culture basically exists, it is taken on and assumed by individuals, it is unconsciously learned and adopted, and it is invisible. People's attitudes are often formed by the culture. It is the way people think about things, how they interpret things. Within an organization people operate with a set of rules. These rules can be explicit (defined, documented, visible) or implicit ('that is the way we do things here', 'oh, that is normal around here'). These rules influence people's behavior. It is behavior that leads to results. Good or bad, desired or undesired.

An example:

Culture:	"Just do what is asked and not more, otherwise you set expectations."
Attitude:	"Passive attitude."
Rule:	"If you are asked to suggest ways of improving things, say nothing. It may mean more work and people will start expecting that we all start doing more things."
Behavior:	"Don't make any suggestions when asked if there are any suggestions as to how we can improve things?"
Result:	Delay in project success, no solutions for a problem, no buy-in for an eventual solution, extra money to hire in externals to help improve things, frustration, eventual resistance to whatever gets thought up, because of a 'not-invented here' attitude. There may be numerous undesired results. However nothing has been done, so how can we be resisting? Right? Wrong!

If you want to change the attitude of people then the following diagram may help understand how to approach this.

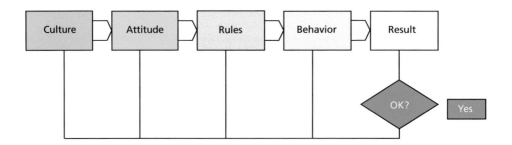

As already said, behavior will lead to a result. This result can be compared to objectives, targets or agreements. If the result is according to agreements made, then everything is OK. However if the results are not as agreed, we have a number of ways of trying to address this:

1. We 'correct' the behavior of people by addressing them on their behavior in relation to an expected outcome. "Next time register what you did to solve the incident!", "Next time you pick up the phone. I want you to be more customer friendly". The result of this intervention may well be that the next time the employee does indeed perform the requested behavior. However, if there is nobody there to control this and point it out, he or she may soon revert

back to the 'old' or 'normal' behavior. The effect on the desired results or outcomes is zero, zip, zilch.

2. Define new rules. 'We will now agree, as documented in the procedure flow that all incident resolutions will be recorded', or 'When we pick up the telephone we will say our name and function and ask how we can help the customer'. The rules have been defined by the manager or process manager, or worse still an external consultant. The rules are by 'them', 'not-invented here'. If the rules are not monitored and enforced, or if there is no buy-in, or acceptance of the rules then they will soon be ignored. The effect once again is zero.

3. We can talk to the team or the people involved and make them aware of the impact and consequences of their actions on the desired, expected or agreed results. The impact on the customers and users, and the impact upon each other and their own work.

We can discuss why things need to be registered, to allow us to deal with things quicker if they happen again, to help us identify new training needs, to help us ensure that the incident is solved quicker, to ensure that the customer can get back to work as soon as possible, to get some respect from the users and create a better working relationship with the users, to influence user and customer satisfaction.

This is hard work for the process manager or manager. You will need to describe the drivers and the vision behind this, you will need to discuss it and try to hold a mirror up to people's attitude and assumptions as to why this behavior change is being requested. You may need to make it clear to people 'what's in it fort them?', 'what value is this going to create? And for whom?'.

If you succeed in getting the group to discuss at this level you can get a shared picture of the attitudes, and can help influence or shift attitudes. Once there is a mind shift, an attitude shift, buy-in, acceptance, understanding, willingness, you can then make the step towards new rules and agreed types of behavior.

Example: "Ok, we think reporting is part of good incident management. You also think it is important to have good registration. Ok, what are we going to do in the next couple of weeks?".

The team gets the chance to issue statements like:

"We agree that all incidents will be registered."

"If we can't manage it straight away, we do it afterwards."

"We answer the phone by saying 'good morning'....."

These agreements now originate from their own consciousness and their own (and not the manager's) rules. The behavior will now stem from their own rules and they can measure the results themselves. The team can be held accountable for the results and be encouraged to make their own corrections.

Tips for working on Attitude, Behavior and Culture
For staff:

1. Ask yourself what you think about certain things, is this what *you* think? Or do you think it is what others think?
2. Ask yourself what you want within the team. How would you like to work? Which achievements do you want to realize?
3. Think of it as your own company, and if you would accept the way things are currently being done?
4. Be critical of the results. If you are not satisfied, start correcting, or start discussing this within your team.
5. Before you say 'yes' to do something, make sure you can substantiate your 'yes'. Otherwise ask for help and resources.
6. Don't nod and say 'yes', when deep inside you are thinking 'no'. It is your responsibility, it will ultimately effect you, say why you think, feel 'no'.

For managers, consultants and service managers:

1. Define the department's or team's desired result.
2. Define the desired behavior within the department.
3. Let the team make up their own 'rules'.
4. Let the team voice their opinions on certain situations. How do people feel about certain situations?
5. Let people compare their results against the norm and let them make their own corrections.
6. If, as a manager or team leader, you want to make people aware of the result of their behavior, use feedback techniques like:
    a. I see that....
    b. The effect from..... is.....
    c. My opinion is....
    d. What do you think....?
    e. What are you going to do about it?
    f. Do you think this is acceptable...?
7. If the team does not make its own corrections when the results are not up to standard, make the corrections yourself. You then have to discuss with the team why the corrections were not made by them.
8. If the desired behavior is not shown, you have to step in.
9. Keep in mind the in-through-out policy of staff. Hire employees that show the desired behavior. Develop employees that like to change, and part with employees who do not want to change. This is obviously easier said than done and requires senior commitment to the change. This will show whether senior managers really are 'committed' to the change and 'walking-the-talk'.
10. Go and look for the attitude behind the behavior. Here you will find the key to change.
11. Be upfront when giving feedback. Do not beat around the bush; be upfront with your feedback to the right person. Have customers or others approach the person that made the mistake directly.
12. As a manager, set tasks. Make sure people accept them.

Chapter 5
The ABC issues in detail

ABC worst practices and practical advice

We asked a range of people throughout world to review our ABC worst practice cards and to pick a card they they feel is the most significant issue that needs resolving, or an ABC card they feel particularly strongly about. Some of the contributors are seen as subject matter experts, some are customers who have struggled to apply IT best practices. We have not only asked them to provide a case study to underpin the worst practice, but more importantly to describe a practical example of how to overcome the worst practice. We hope that their contributions may inspire you and may help you resolve the ABC issues in your organization.

Unfortunately a lot of the actual customers wished to remain anonymous.

The ABC cards

A set of ABC cards was given to each contributor. The suits in the ABC set of cards represent Attitude (Clubs), Behavior (Diamonds), Culture (Spades) and the Stakeholders(Hearts).

The cards contain a series of worst practice cartoons, cartoons that have been prompted by and suggested by ITSM practitioners, and are based upon real life experiences. We have not included the cartoons in the book, but we have described the situation of each card. For each card we have also described an example of what we see and experience, and we have provided some characteristics. These characteristics are in the form of questions you can ask yourself about YOUR organization. The answers will reveal whether this worst practice is relevant to YOUR organization.

It is these types of ABC worst practices that can seriously undermine, and even stop, your ITSM program. Very often people are not consciously aware that these types of ABC issues exist. ABC is like an Iceberg, much of it hidden beneath the surface and yet capable of inflicting enormous damage. Often they are taken for granted or ignored. You should ignore them at your own risk!

Why did we develop these cards? The ABC cards are not just a fun give-away. They have been designed as an awareness and assessment instrument and are intended to facilitate dialogue. There are a number of exercises you can perform using these cards in order to confront people with these ABC issues. They are intended to help identify, recognize and discuss them in relation to your organization and, more importantly, discuss the consequences and risks that these pose to your business.

Identifying and agreeing the worst practices and their consequences is the first step in creating a 'sense of urgency' for doing something about them. Identifying and recognizing them provides input into your service improvement initiatives and helps you identify risks. Risks associated with ABC that must be mitigated if your ITSM initiative is to succeed.

A skeptical look

We also asked the IT Skeptic, Rob England, to pick a card to write about. He was unable to do so. Not because he felt that none of the worst practices were relevant any more. No. Unfortunately too many of them were relevant.

Rob England, IT Skeptic

"'People, process, technology' is one of the most effective mantras for any change in IT. And the people come first and matter most. Focus on ABC is essential to the successful outcome of any IT change, including ITSM improvements.

No one ABC practice stands out as the worst. None of them are universal (for any one ABC card, there are plenty of sites that do NOT do that worst practice), but some of the most common are:

- 6 of Clubs - IT'IL never work here. Or as the IT Skeptic says "IT'IL end in tears".
- 4 of Diamonds - failure to capture the right knowledge. Perhaps I move in the wrong circles, but I feel the whole science of knowledge management is in its infacy: the methodologies, processes and technologies do not exist for effective knowledge re-use.
- 8 of Diamonds - we are going to install ITIL. Despite lip-service to the contrary, too many managers hope to find ITIL OOTB (out of the box) - can I buy an ITIL please? Or they try to do ITIL in their spare time. I guess this usually stems from the 5 of Diamonds.
- 8 of Spades - Plan Do Stop. The real value in an ITSM project is the foundation it lays for ongoing improvement, so failure to capitalise on that is an irresponsible waste of available ROI. Worse still though, failure to have an ongoing activity means that whatever was gained will not just sit still, but go backwards. This stems from organizations ignoring the people part of 'people, process, technology'. Technology won't stick without process and process won't stick without continual attention to the people.
- Jack of Hearts - a process flow and some procedures are all you need. I've fallen into this hole. Process without cultural change, without ABC, is just money wasted.
- Joker - a tool solves all problems. This is just as bad as 'a process flow and some procedures are all you need'. In each case only one aspect of people, process, technology is addressed. On their own, tools do nothing but absorb money.

That initial cultural resistance, the 6 of Clubs – 'IT'IL never work here', is not easy to overcome, but it is one of the best-understood problems with effective solutions available: apply John Kotter's eight steps. I also like to start by explaining WIIFM, (What's In It For Me), the personal interest people should have in ITIL. This can readily be based around two things:

- Executive mandate: align yourself with the way things are going to be done around here. If you disagree with the direction, ask yourself which is more likely to change, you or the organization?
- Job vacancy advertisments: how many want ITIL experience? ITIL looks good on a CV.

I'm sorry to say I don't think I have ever seen an effective fix for any of these. They all seem to require the gradual maturing of an individual's or organization's understanding to the point where they see it otherwise. If they aren't ready they aren't ready, and there is no magic cure."

No respect for, or
understanding of,
customers & users

2 of Clubs

'No respect for, or understanding of customers and users'

Very often people say "We are customer focused", We see boards and slogans stating 'The customer comes first'. Very often a characteristic of this type of organization is indeed 'words and slogans' and not embedded attitude, ownership and visible behavior to support these words. It is all too often not translated into action. We in IT have been saying for the last 10 years we are 'customer and user' focused but still in the Netherlands the need to improve customer service is high in the list of priorities. We still give presentations using this cartoon, 10 years after our first presentation. People still nod their heads in recognition and come up to us afterwards and say "that is our IT organization!". Too little has been done to consciously address this attitude. This cartoon is also the most popular cartoon requested and used in ITIL awareness initiatives.

Characteristics:

- How often do you hear IT staff complain about the customer or user?
- How often is there pro-active communication to the customers and users?
- Are the customers and users asked for their input to improvement programs?
- When people are discussing resource choices, how often is the word 'customer or 'user' mentioned in relation to choices?
- How often is a dialogue openly started instead of continual moaning about the unrealistic demands from the customers and users?
- How well does IT understand the real needs and requirements of the customers and users?
- Are customer and user satisfaction surveys conducted?
- Is it clear who is responsible for improving customer and user satisfaction?
- Does anybody take sanctions or address people for showing undesirable behavior (non user or customer friendly)?

We conducted a mini survey on the itSMF website in the Netherlands using this cartoon. They were shown the 2 of Clubs in which a trainer is explaining to a student "ITIL uses the terms customers and users, what terms do you use?", the student replies "Dorks!". They were then given a statement to vote on: "We are not customer focused enough in IT". **89% agreed!**

We also used the cards in an itSMF roundtable conference. We got people to vote on this same statement. **86% agreed**. We then asked them to write down examples of 'non customers focused' behavior so that we could discuss them, and their consequences. This is what the delegates (60 IT professionals) came up with:

Examples of behavior to support the statement we are not customer focused enough:

- The customer behind the customer needs to be taken into account.
- We need 'round the table' sessions with our customers.
- Grey areas in service delivery (entitled/not entitled to support – the customer is the victim!).
- We have problems realizing 'time to market' of new services and solutions.
- IT is too busy with its own processes.
- We are too internally focused.
- We can keep the end user happy, but not the business manager.
- IT doesn't understand the business.
- There is still no clear, single point of contact for customers.
- Language and communication towards customers is still an issue.
- We don't take the customer seriously.
- We focus too much on technology, ….because that is *SO* interesting (2).
- If we were customer focused ENOUGH we wouldn't need all the models (frameworks).
- Users are poorly represented in IT projects.
- We display a tunnel vision by only involving a subset of the user community.
- IT is convinced *it* knows how the business should act.
- IT thinks it knows best what the business needs (2).
- If you call the help desk you won't get a direct solution.
- Costs of IT are confusing.
- Otherwise we advisors wouldn't have any work anymore!
- Most IT staff have no idea.
- We have a 'blinkered' view.
- The customer is a pain in the …system.
- Is the customer always right?...you might never achieve the customer requirements – we need to think ahead.
- We still need to be more proactive.

When I showed the worst practice set of cards to Sharon Taylor, Chief Architect of ITIL V3 and now Chief Examiner for ITIL training, I asked her the following question:

"We have had ITIL and CobiT and the frameworks for a number of years, still organizations are struggling to improve. In your view which ABC worst practice is the one that needs resolving the most?"

Sharon:

"I believe they are all important, but since I have to pick one, I'll take the 'not customer focused enough' worst practice. Getting in touch with the customers' vision of us is better than looking in the mirror. The effect of truly being customer focused can turn a worst practice into a best practice and demonstrate how our ABCs should look in the mirror. If we are really focused on the customer, then our attitudes, behaviors and culture shifts from making service just about 'IT', to making service about business value, customer loyalty and trust. Think about a person or organization you trust. What is it that they possess that makes you feel that trust? Their ABC reflects their commitment to your needs as a customer. ITIL and CobiT are tools in an arsenal of practices. They work! But only if the commitment and loyalty to them are embedded in our ABC."

A practical tip as to what people can do to solve that worst practice?

Sharon:

"A lot of people in this industry say that the customer is the window of the perception of our service quality. I say, instead of looking through the window, try walking through a door! Spend time with your customer and learn how they use your services. Listen instead of speaking, and view the world from the customer's experience. This does not need to be a major exercise. Something as simple as spending an hour observing your customer using your services, can be extremely revealing. And above all else BE HONEST. Don't offer excuses for a negative customer experience, offer apologies and a commitment to understanding how it affects the customer and how you can change it."

We have also two cases we would like to share:

Case:

Apollo 13 simulation:
Very often teams declare 'We are customer focused', 'We don't need to learn that!'. More often than not these types of teams make the same mistake in each round. They do not involve the customer or user in process design, they do not give pro-active status or communicate issues, they do not prioritize improvements with the customer, they do not know, or attempt to identify, customer satisfiers and dissatisfiers. *They then declare that this is indeed what they do in their own organization*. However at the start of the simulation they were conviced they were user focused. The simulation had helped change their attitudes.

Case:

Another company declared themselves customer focused, they understood the needs of the customer. They didn't see any need for a customer satisfaction survey. They started an ITIL improvement project and improved the service desk and incident management as well as a new service desk tool. This cost a lot of money. Finally we pursuaded them to do a customer satisfaction survey, at least a set of interviews with key business users. The business users were not at all worried about the service desk or the way calls were handled. They didn't understand why the investments were made! Their complaints were: 'not being aware of changes', 'disruptions to work caused by sudden changes', 'not enough training with the release of new software and upgrades'. Release and change management? The IT organization had improved the service desk and incident management. *Is this an example of 'customer focused'?*

In order to find out if your organization really is customer or user focused we suggest you conduct one of the exrcises using the ABC of ICT card set. The Çustomer & User focused exercise. See 'ABC card set – case and example exercises' at the end of this book.

Other cards that underpin this are:

- The Joker 'Unable to specify the VALUE required by the business';
- 4 of Spades 'Internally focused';
- 3 of Hearts 'Helpless desk';
- 7 of Diamonds 'Throwing solutions over the wall and HOPING they will be accepted';
- Jack of Clubs 'Let's outsource the business';
- Queen of Clubs 'No understanding of business priority and impact';
- 10 of Spades 'The superiority complex - we know best!';
- 9 of Diamonds 'Maybe we should have tested that change first!';
- 8 of Clubs 'ÏT thinks it doesn't need to understand the business to make a business case';
- 5 of Clubs 'Neither partner makes an effort to understand the other';
- Queen of Diamonds 'The solution the customer sees isn't the one that IT sees';
- King of Diamonds 'IT strategy's contribution to business strategy (or lack of)';
- Two of Diamonds 'We don't measure our value contribution to strategy';
- Two of Spades 'Them and us culture – opposing and competing forces'.

3 of Clubs

'Knowledge is power!'

In this type of organization there is a general unwillingness to want to share knowledge. Knowledge is what makes specialists valuable. Giving it away reduces value. To who? Not to the organization. I used to be a systems manager and I was guilty of this. I used to get called out in the evening to fix things, I got the batch jobs restarted and I was the talk of the morning shift, having restored things and ensured the online transaction system started on time in the morning. No down time for the important users. Everybody happy. I was the hero.

The cartoon on the card shows a specialist responding to a service desk employee who wants to obtain some knowledge or training. The specialist says "If I told you how to do that then you'd know as much as ME!.....we can't have that now can we!"

Characteristics:

- Are your known error databases and systems often out of date?
- Is the information in work-arounds and known-errors often unhelpful?
- Do specialists complain about not having time to share knowledge or record activities and solutions?
- Do people say they will get around to it later, but never do?
- Do managers say specialists can't share knowledge as they are too busy doing important things?
- Is there an attitude that 'knowledge is power'?
- Do service desk staff often complain about not getting the right information?
- Do Service desk staff often complain that they have seen a particular problem before, but there is no help?

Case:

Colin Rudd, Director IT Enterprise Management Services Limited. Colin is a well known figure in the ITSM community and one of the authors of ITIL V3. He also serves on a number of committees for BSI working together on ISO 20000. Colin selected the 3 of Clubs to write about.

"All too often people keep knowledge to themselves for many different motives:

- To make themselves indispensable;
- To become a focal point;
- To establish power and control;
- To save themselves effort in making it available to others.

The problem with this approach is that it causes inaccuracies, duplication of effort and conflict.

In every organization the people and the information are the most valuable resources.

In one example recently I came across a large company operating in the media and information industry, which effectively had three different data repositories for managing the set of IT services provided. These were the Service Catalogue, within the Configuration Management Database (CMDB), the Business Impact Analysis (BIA) spreadsheet and the Server Portal Database. Each of these data sources was maintained by a different group, each contained valuable information, but the names and the number of services they contained were all different. This meant the use, analysis or integration of the information was incredibly difficult, if not impossible. This in turn led to inconsistencies with both the approach and outcomes obtained from different groups within IT.

An exercise to review, rationalise and combine all of these sources of information was initiated, involving representatives from each of the areas concerned and has been remarkably successful already, even though it has not been completed. The duplication, conflict and confusion have largely been removed and agreement has been established on a common set of business facing services. This has, in itself, bought about a change of culture and attitude within the IT unit along the lines of:

'*knowledge is power, but **shared knowledge is real power**'*

This attitude brings about real value, particularly when linked to a business focus within the unit.

Research shows that in the 1980s an individual's ability to provide an answer to a particular question or issue relied 80% on information recalled from the individual's own memory and 20% on access to reference information. In contrast, within today's environment, an individual's ability to provide an answer relies 20% on memory and 80% on reference material and information. On this basis, only organizations exploiting the benefits of knowledge sharing and knowledge management will be able to gain full value from their people by developing each individual's capability.

This is process is a symbiotic relationship that enables both the organization and the individual to benefit, as illustrated in the following diagram:

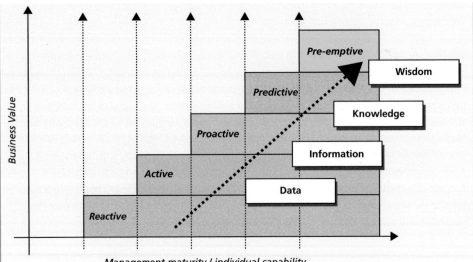

Management maturity / individual capability

If organizations can automate the processes for data collection and analysis, then comprehensive, integrated information sources and knowledge management systems can be developed. These systems can be used to develop and enhance an individual's knowledge, wisdom and the quality of their decision making, increasing their value to the organization. This, in turn, enables an organization to move from a largely reactive one, through the stages of active, proactive and predictive management, to becoming an organization using predominantly pre-emptive techniques and processes.

This whole area of knowledge management and sharing not only benefits the organization, but also the individuals within it by enhancing their job satisfaction, peer respect and self esteem, as well as improving their own personal development and career progression. This has led to a situation where:

*'knowledge is power, but **knowledge management is empowerment***'

Mature knowledge management systems and processes empower individuals to consistently make the right decision irrespective of the team or group within which they operate."

Case:
This is a case from my experience, Paul Wilkinson, ex-technoid.

"When I used to be a systems engineer, or systems manager I was a hero. I used to come in evenings and fix things, I was the saviour. Luckily for them, I could always solve the problems and allow the evening and night shift to continue, and enable the transaction systems to start up on time for the next day.

My boss had learnt about ITIL and about 'work-arounds'. He called a meeting with the operators and asked me to explain how I fixed a number of these issues. He asked the operators if they could also do this with the right instructions "No problem!" was their answer. I was given the task of transfering knowledge. It was painful and I felt less valuable. However more work was progressed and the evening shift managed to finish earlier a lot of times. I lost my overtime hours.

This was realized because my boss intervened and brought me together with the operators. He ensured I transferred knowledge, he got all the system managers and specialists together and made us all come up with a top three list of things to be handed over. I did not want to do it and thought of many lame excuses for not doing it. However my manager was adamant and refused to accept our excuses. Thinking back on this it was only the persistence of my manager that ensured we carried on transferring knowledge.

Do not underestimate the difficulty of getting people to share and transfer knowledge. This will require leadership and sometimes confronting people with their behavior.
One thing that can help to start with is to check with second or third line support staff about what annoying, simple, repeat requests they continually get that they would rather outsource to somebody else. This will give an insight into a number of possible quick wins. A win-win can be created. Specialists get rid of something simple, easy and annoying (they are happy), some problems or questions can be handled by other specialists (knowledge transfer), and a basis exists that this can add value. Step two is the tricky one, actually getting them to give away knowledge that is valuable."

The fact that this needs resolving was confirmed by a mini-survey we conducted on the itSMF Netherlands website. We published this cartoon with the statement: "We are not good at sharing knowledge in IT" – 86% of those responding agreed.

Other cards that may be applicable in this type of situation are:
• Jack of Diamonds 'Saying yes, but meaning NO';
• 9 of Clubs 'Walking the talk';
• 10 of Clubs 'No respect for, or trust in management';
• 4 of Diamonds 'Not capturing the right knowledge for reuse'
• 5 of Diamonds 'No management commitment'.

IT not seen as an added value partner to the business

4 of Clubs

'IT not seen as an added-value partner'

Customers and users are often complaining that IT doesn't understand the business. IT makes changes and breaks the systems, causing down-time and outages. IT changes things but doesn't inform the business in time, causing irritation. IT delivers systems too late and they are not properly tested, things go wrong. IT is always saying it hasn't got enough resources. Any of these sound familiar? Imagine in this environment that the IT organization has discovered ITIL V3. Through which we, IT specialists, have now convinced ourselves we are a 'strategic asset'. Can you imagine from the examples above how the business will react? In order to be seen as an added-value partner we must first gain trust and credibility. Start doing what we promise, start behaving like a business. Show that we really are 'customer' and 'user' focused. Start showing and demonstrating we are capable of managing IT as a strategic asset.

The card shows a CEO interviewing somebody for the position of CIO: "....you can't think in longer term horizons, run around like a headless chicken, no clue about planning.....we've decided to make you the CIO!".

Characteristics:

- Does the business complain that IT doesn't deliver on its promises?
- Does the business complain that IT talks in technobabble, that IT makes business cases focused on technical functionality and not on business value and return?
- Do all IT managers know what the business issues are?
- Do IT people KNOW what the real issues are of customers and users, I don't mean THINK or ASSUME, I really mean KNOW?
- Do people say that IT is unable to demonstrate its added value?
- Is IT unable to demonstrate how it contributes to strategy?
- Do IT reports show KPIs that demonstrate business added-value of IT?
- Is IT hardly ever invited to strategy and decision making sessions?
- Does IT complain that it is always involved too late?
- Does IT complain the business doesn't involve them enough or ask for their advice?
- Does IT complain about unrealistic demands from the business?
- Does IT feel that it is a 'victim' of the business?

Case:

Still a big complaint from many businesses. IT talks in terms of systems and doesn't know how to explain new IT features in business terms. Partly because IT doesn't understand the business well enough. Being a 'partner' means understanding the issues of the other partner. At a large Dutch based global company that has been using ITIL for five years, a senior IT manager told me that the 'business analysts' had been moved from the business into IT. "Is that because, after five years of ITIL, IT is mature and the business wants the analysts to learn best practice?" The manager looked at me for a second or two and then laughed. "No we are hoping these people will help change the attitude and behavior of the IT people, helping them think in business terms, helping them gain knowledge of business processes and business issues". This was obviously an example from a strategic leader that understood a framework (ITIL and CobIT) doesn't automatically make people more business focused. This was also an attempt at slowly trying to change the culture.

Another example was a CIO who hired in new service level managers from business people. He hired in business people into IT job openings so that they could communicate easily with the business and would communicate in business terms to the internal IT departments. When he took over he realized that the IT process managers and middle managers didn't understand the business and couldn't talk with business people. "I recognized the technoid in your book" he said..... "I heard a lot of technobabble and very little business".

Katsushi Yaginuma, ITPreneurs in Japan offered his insights into ABC from a Japanese perspective. I interviewed Katsu via email.

Question: How important is the ABC for ITSM?

"ABC is nice and useful in helping people understand ITSM from the perspective of the daily life people are facing. ITSM sounds complicated to many people, but people can get familiar with the idea by looking at the ABC cards. The ABC cards shows the types of Attitude and Behavior that frameworks like ITIL should help resolve."

We have had ITIL and Cobit and the frameworks for a number of years, yet still organizations are struggling to improve. Which ABC worst practice is the one that needs resolving the most according to you?

"I have chosen two main cards. They are related. The first is 'IT not seen as an added value partner'. A reason for this is the second card 'We don't measure our value contribution to strategy'. As IT is becoming so important for business, IT must add value. When the business invests in IT they want it to improve the business and they want to ensure they do not face risks. When they invest in IT or ITSM they want IT to show what this has achieved for the business."

Do you have any practical advice for resolving this, based upon your experiences?

"Create awareness at senior management level and get them to realize the value of ITSM; I guess in reality ITSM is still owned only by IT people and considered as an 'IT' tool. But it is really about business management, and managers need to understand its value and cost by providing education and using instruments like 'workshops' to get people involved and create awareness and interest. Also managers must start to measure and show what ITSM delivers."

Other related cards are:

- 5 of Clubs 'Neither partner makes an effort to understand the other;
- 8 of Clubs 'IT thinks it doesn't have to understand the business to make a business case';
- Queen of Clubs 'No understanding of business priority and impact'.

5 of Clubs

'Neither partner makes an effort to understand the other'

The relationship is 'them and us'. We looked up the word 'partner' in the dictionary. The description that we found most appropriate in this context was 'a player on the same side or team as another". In this type of organization the attitude is that they are playing on different teams. But what can you do about it? After all we have been trying for years.

As the description of Weill & Ross on IT governance clearly states, it is all about: 'Establishing the decision rights and accountability frameworks to encourage desirable behavior in the use of IT'. As we mentioned earlier, IT organizations focus too much on the frameworks such as CobiT, ITIL andBisL, and not enough on addressing the Attitude, Behavior and Cultural issues.

The cartoon on the card shows the CEO and the CIO sitting in front of a marriage guidance counsellor. Both of them declaring "He doesn't understand me!".

The IT perspective:

- In this type of organization IT complains about the business.
- IT says the business doesn't understand IT issues, they make unrealistic demands, are always changing their minds, they never get involved in specifying requirements, or testing, or roll-out….they make their own changes and do what they like.
- IT says the business blames everything on IT.
- IT thinks the business don't give IT enough resources.
- IT feels that the business don't value IT as much as they should.
- IT moans that the business don't treat us as partners

The business perspective:

- The business complains about IT.
- IT doesn't talk in business terms, doesn't make business cases.
- IT doesn't deliver on their promises.
- IT doesn't demonstrate value.
- IT is inflexible.
- IT has escalating uncontrollable costs.
- IT has unpredictable performance.

The state of affairs reminds us of a married couple. In England this would be the man in the pub moaning 'My wife doesn't understand me'….The wife sitting at a tuperware party complaining… "My husband is useless, he never does what I ask, and if he does anything it's always half finished".

In more than 95% of the cases this will be their lot in life unless they do something about it. Either they sit down and have a serious discussion, or they go and see a therapist to help them. In 95% of cases between business and IT, we suspect this is the same. We sit and moan. How many business and IT marriages tend to hobble along.

However the thing about 'hobbling along' in the business and IT situation is that one of the parties has another choice. The business can outsource IT. IT cannot outsource the business….. this should prompt IT managers to reflect on the possible consequences of hobbling along.

Characteristics:

- Do both parties continually complain about the other?
- Does IT complain about the unrealistic demands from the business?
- Does IT complain about business involvement in IT projects, such as requirements specification? testing?
- Does IT complain about being informed or 'confronted' too late with business decisons and choices?
- Does IT complain that the business sees everything as urgent?
- Does IT feel that business goals are contradictory? Lower costs, whilst at the same time increasing innovation?
- Does the business complain about IT's ability to deliver?
- Does the business complain about escalating costs?
- Does the business complain about lack of control?
- Does the business complain about things being too late, or not right?
- Does the business complain that IT is too unflexible?
- Does the business complain that IT thinks in terms of systems and not in business cases?
- Does the business complain that IT people have no understanding of the business?
- Does the business complain IT people are not 'customer' or 'user' minded or focused

Case:

I saw one business who moved a 'financial controller' from the business into IT as CIO. This person brought along some business people to act as service level managers…..IT jobs went. The business was fed up of IT not performing. They made this move because they didn't want to outsource. But equally they were no longer happy with the status quo.

It is in the interest of IT managers to take the first step. Why? The business is busy running the business, IT is a secondary concern mostly. IT is busy running IT where IT is a primary concern. Business managers spend 95% of their time on business issues and 5% on IT issues. IT spends 95% of its time on IT issues and 5% on business issues. As such, IT is probably a lot more aware of the real underlying issues and concerns that need resolving and has time to think about them.

So how can WE change things? Start demonstrating trust and credibility first. (Just like starting to hoover the house, your wife will take notice.) The next is to develop a plan as to how IT improvements will be made and how these will directly contribute to business value and business continuity (the business will then think "Oh so they do understand what we need!"). Then show facts and figures about IT outages, downtime, changes backed-out as a result of business behavior, relate these to the same business value and continuity issues ("Oh! You mean we may need to change?"). This will help to show that the business is also part of the problem and has responsibilities for the good governance of IT.

I found another great example of this in the Wall Street Journal. An article entitled 'How to tap IT's hidden potential', written by Amit Basu and Chip Jarnagan.

This article stresses the fact that IT should be a strategic asset, confirming ITIL V3's service strategy approach. IT can add enormous value and provide a competitive advantage if deployed effectively. However the articleemphasises that the reason we have failed to do this is 'the metaphorical glass wall between business and IT'. There are five primary reasons for this wall's existence:

• Mind-set differences between management staff and IT staff, (attitude?);
• Language differences, (culture);
• Social influences, (culture);
• Flaws in IT governance - defined as the specification and control of IT decision rights (behavior);
• The difficulty of managing rapidly changing technology.

As we can see four of the top five are all people related; attitude, behavior and culture.

The article gives great examples of common worst practices that we should all recognize:

'Unfortunately, the chief information officer often reinforces this separation. That's because he or she usually is an IT professional chosen to be a director of technology, rather than an executive who is expected to fully integrate IT into the company.'

'IT people use jargon and acronyms that are indecipherable to others. Executives speak the language of business, fully expecting to be understood by everyone in the company. Much is lost in translation, leading to sub-optimal results that IT is blamed for, which causes resentment and cynicism toward management.'

'Another divisive factor is the persistent perception of those who are oriented toward science and technology as 'nerds'. The recent boom in IT outsourcing has worsened this estrangement. Now, IT professionals are almost pitied as dinosaurs whose jobs will soon be sent offshore.'

The article goes on to stress a seven step solution to shatter the glass wall between IT and the rest of a company. I have included extracts of the seven steps below to show how they focus on ABC issues:

'Begin with IT literacy - and commitment - at the top. The impetus for effective IT management must come from the CEO and the board. There has to be a willingness on the part of the CEO and the other executives to know enough about IT to understand its functions and its value to the company, in the same way that they understand accounting, finance and marketing.'

'Hire an IT leader who sees the big picture. The next step is to hire a true chief information officer - not just a technical expert, but a leader who understands the strategic importance and use of IT......'

'Rotate management and executive candidates through IT. A stint in IT must be part of the training for people being groomed as general managers and senior executives. At the same time, IT personnel should be groomed as integral components of the enterprise...... they should participate in management classes, cross-functional training, and rotations through non-IT functions, and should be included on planning and control committees and cross-functional teams.'

'Create demand for IT solutions. Managers at all levels across the organization need to be convinced that innovations in IT-related areas such as knowledge management, business intelligence, information security, change management and process integration are essential to the success of the enterprise.'

'Make sure nothing gets lost in translation. A company must have people at all levels who can translate IT language for those outside that department and translate the language of management for those in IT.......at the same time, IT staff should have a clear understanding of the business role and value of their work.'

'Rationalize IT spending.' Too often, executives sign off on IT spending without a clear understanding of its business value. To ensure that all IT spending makes sense for the business, the executive management of the firm must institute proper IT governance.'

'Create an IT portfolio by evaluating risks and returns. Just as an investor balances risk and returns in constructing a portfolio of investments, management should analyze the costs, benefits and risks of all IT projects to determine how to get the most benefit from the dollars invested.'

Dr. Basu & Mr. Jarnagin can be reached at reports@wsj.com.

I contacted another of the ITIL gurus, Brian Johnson, author of some of the orginal ITIL V1 books and a world renowned and well respected champion of ITSM. I asked Brian the same three questions I put to other industry experts:

How important is ABC to ITSM?

Brian:

"The ABC is as important as any other good idea and just as useless if it becomes something that is used as commandments. All good ideas have a place and many can be used by thinking about how that might work in practice. Too often a good idea is branded as a tablet of stone which denies rational thinking. Dogma has never solved anything, innovation is the only way forward."

Which of the ABC worst practices is the most relevant or the one you feel you would like to talk about?

Brian:

"It is a combination of all of them, because all of them relate to the idea that there is only one answer to a complex question. Even good ideas, such as 'mapping ITIL to CobiT', cause more problems than they provide answers. The easy answer is to follow the map, because the expert provides the answer. That means for every organization, in every country, with myriad different business lines, countless different cultural issues, regulations and complexities - there is only one answer. Wake up. Smell the coffee....

But if I have to pick one card, it is the Five of Clubs, which indicates that the CEO and the CIO don't understand one another. Think about this; IT is critical. Who provides it is not—otherwise outsourcing would not be a business. If the CIO does not fully support the business, kiss the business goodbye. IT cannot dictate 'beneficial' changes. Who do they benefit? If IT wants to save money by automating something, and the business don't want to be automated - who do you think will win? Automation benefits must be sold as improving the business, not the business of IT, so you must understand business needs first before proposing something that makes IT business easier.

Or start thinking about which outsourcing company would be best for the business....."

What about some practical advice for solving the ABC issues?

Brian:

"Think for yourself. If it sounds too good to be true, it is."

Other cards related to this one are:

• 2 of Clubs 'NO respect for, or understanding of users';
• 4 of Clubs 'IT is not seen as an added value partner to the business';
• 8 of Clubs 'IT thinks it doesn't have to understand the business to make a business case';
• Queen of Diamonds 'The solution the customer sees isn't the one that IT sees';

- King of Diamonds 'IT strategy's contribution to business strategy';
- 2 of Spades 'Them and us culture – opposing and competing forces';
- 10 of Spades 'The superiority complex – we know best';
- King of Hearts 'Which part of NO didn't you understand';
- 4 of Hearts 'The best way to improve services is to outsource…..the business!';
- 7 of Hearts 'Demand and give. I demand and you give in!';
- The Joker 'Unable to specify the VALUE required by the business.

6 of Clubs

'ITIL never work here'

Very often we see employees thinking "Oh no!, not ANOTHER management toy, as shown in the cartoon on this card. We have had Baldridge, ISO, EFQM or whatever. Managers always come with their latest good idea about what is good for US. They will soon see it doesn't work, they will get fed up with it and then the next framework or model will come!"

Part of it can be lack of respect for, or belief in, management, or lack of belief that change will really happen. You often hear things like "I'll believe that when I see it", "Let's see management change first". But another important issue here is that this is a normal reaction to change, people don't like change. They need to know what it means for them and what is in it for them, they need to feel they are being listened to and that their concerns are being felt, understood and also addressed.

Part of it can also be genuinely believing that ITIL is all about books of bureaucratic procedures that are wasting time when we should be busy doing IT. A lot of this feeling is relatedto the way in which we have mis-applied ITIL in the past, the stories of ITIL being books of procedures in a cupboard.

Management communication and management reaction to the reactions of employees can positively or negatively impact this attitude – significantly.

The cartoon shows two technoids discussing some kind of report or a new process flow diagram, one says to the other "ITIL!? Just ignore it and it will soon go away....It's just another management toy!"

Characteristics:

- Do people say 'We tried that before....it didn't work then either'?
- Do IT staff think to themselves: 'Just say 'yes' they will soon get fed up and go away?'
- Do people think that ITIL is just a bureaucratic waste of time?
- Do people think that ITIL is just a lot of books of procedures?
- Do people think that ITIL will mean you can't do anything anymore without having to fill in forms?
- Do people think that ITIL is a way for managers to start getting rid of people?
- Do people think ITIL is just a way of letting managers see what people are doing so they can control them?
- Do people think 'I am already too busy I haven't got time for that as well as managing IT!'?
- If people do not follow ITIL procedures are there any consequences?
- Have people tried 'implementing' ITIL and are now moaning about the results it delivered? .... or rather didn't deliver.

One great quote we heard in an IT organization was: "I haven't got time for all those change management procedures, I am too busy fixing the changes that went wrong or suddenly needed more resources, because there was no impact assessment!"

Case:

A lot of attitude or behavior is a direct result of poor communication, not involving people, not engaging with them, not enough two-way dialogue. Very often a 'manager' tells people what will happen and why. The 'why' is usually something that the IT employee doesn't relate to, and he or she sees no immediate payoff 'what's in it for me? Why should I care....I'll see what happens....I'll believe it when I see it....really!' The communication is important for changing attitude. Changing attitude is the basis for changing behavior.

An example:

" We played Apollo at a large US customer. Part of the team consisted of network engineers and third line support specialists. We were told they were likely to be negative and may disrupt the session. They resisted ITIL and thought it a waste of time and effort. We did an introduction round: "Who are you, why are you here and what do you expect to get out the day". The techies sat, leaning back, with their arms folded and totally disinterested looks on their faces and announced "We were TOLD we HAD to come, I don't have any expectations...I suspect that today will be a waste of time"....an attitude that made us as game facilitators feel like we were seen as valuable as......

We played Apollo and let the teams experience the impact of their behavior and ad hoc ways of working on the service level targets....and let them feel the pain and personal frustration of things not working. We reflected on their energy and commitment as they did their best to do everything "It is too much work" they said, "It is just like the office."

After playing four rounds and making significant improvements we reflected at the end of the day. "Was it valuable? What did you learn?" We were expecting to hear what we always hear at the end of an Apollo session and were not disappointed. The techies declared: "Now I understand what this process working is all about and how it made my work easier. ....It's not all about books of procedures and bureaucracy...It is common sense...we were able to agree our own ways of working that made a real difference,....we were able to prioritize and make choices...we were able to escalate and have somebody resolve our issues....we learnt that not everything is OUR problem, managers are there to help resolve priority and resourcing conflicts with the users and the business, I can use this in my department."

Suddenly we had an attitude of 'buy-in', a 'belief' that processes could add value and 'may work'. We are still not there. We still do not have full commitment but now we have the chance to influence behavior change. We had succeeded in changing 'attitude' towards ITIL. These techies became champions back in their own departments. This type of peer group promotion is a lot more valuable than a far removed senior manager saying how wonderful ITIL is."

Other cards relating to this card are:

- 3 of Clubs 'Knowledge is power';
- 10 of Clubs 'No respect for, or trust in management';
- 5 of Diamonds 'No management commitment';
- 7 of Diamonds 'Throwing solutions over the wall and HOPING that people will use them';
- 10 of Hearts '…waiting for the IT organization to improve";
- The Joker 'A tool solves all problems – a fool with a TOOL is still a FOOL'.

7 of Clubs

'My TOOL will solve ALL your ITSM problems'

This is a card focused primarily on suppliers, however it typically also represents the attitude of many IT organizations. 'A tool will solve my problems'. Very often what is created is 'A fool with a tool is still a fool.' However, as one smart supplier said to me: 'Ah, but a fool without a tool is still a fool!',.."Yes I agreed, but now he still has his money to invest wisely in a TOOL that really meets his needs, not a TOOL that somebody convinced him would solve his problem....a problem that he didn't even know he had!"

This type of 'attitide' is partly because of the 'technology level maturity' or the technology culture of many IT organizations. They don't really understand 'processes', they don't see how a 'book of procedures' is going to help. Processes will cost time, effort, energy, they are confusing and nobody will follow them anyway, so why don't we just buy a tool. There are a lot of 'ITIL compliant tools', we'll just buy one of those.

A Gartner investigation a year or so ago stressed that 80% of IT efficiency and effectivity improvements would come from PROCESSES and not TOOLS. However there are numerous car salesmen…er sorry, tool suppliers that are only TOO WILLING, EAGER and HAPPY to sell you a TOOL, "and as you are talking about ITIL" they will add, "…buy this one because it's got all of ITIL in it. We've already put ITIL processes in it, so you don't have to worry about all that process design nonsense….". Does this sound at all familiar?

The underlying attitude and behavior is the fact that neither the customer nor the supplier really understand the holistic approach to 'People, Process, Product'….and now, with ITIL V3 we have an additional 'P'- 'Partner'. Many tool providers were confronted with a need to have some kind of ITIL process expertise in-house, or offer some kind of ITIL training. Some fully 'understand' and offer holistic solutions, some just want to sell a tool. The trick is getting the right 'Partner' to offer you a TOOL as one component of a holistic solution. The attitude of suppliers needs to change, as does the attitude of customers. The attitude of customers needs to be 'we want a holistic solution, and not a tool'.

The cartoon on the card shows an IT director explaining his problem to a tool supplier. The IT manager pictures in his head a hammer cracking open a nut. The smiling tool provider has an image of a worker carrying an expensive jack hammer to crack open the nut.

Characteristics:

- Do people think that a tool will solve their IT operational problems?
- Does your technology provider insist that you need a set of management tools?

- Does your technology provider promote the 4 P's? And declare that a solution is more than just a tool?
- Are process managers and those involved in carrying out the work asked for their input for selecting or customizing a tool?
- Is everybody that uses a tool trained in both the tool and the process?

Another interesting example of this was the ABC roundtable workshop we ran at the itSMF Best Practice conference in the Netherlands in April 2008. We had a number of small teams of participants. Each team was given a set of ABC worst practice cards. Each person was told to select the top three worst practices. This card scored second highest together with a number of other cards.

What to do?

Use ITIL V3 to help you select a 'Partner' who you trust to provide a 'Product' as part of an overall holistic 'People, Process, Product, Partner' solution.

Ask them to provide you with a vision statement or white paper that explains this holistic approach, If the supplier does not have a core competence in one of the 'P's', for example process design and implementation, then ask them which 'Partner' framework they have for addressing this?

Ask for reference sites where they can 'demonstrate' they have done this before. And don't forget the 5th 'P' – 'Performance', ask them for some demonstrated 'Performance' gains, showing added value KPI's that other customers have realized using the TOOL solution. And last but by no means least, ask them for their vision on the ABC of ICT?

What do we mean by this? What has this got to do with a TOOL? Well, consider the following:

- Capturing knowledge and sharing knowledge. Often people don't like doing this and don't do it.
- Often tools become out of date because they are incorrectly used.
- Often tools are not well customized because too few requirements were specified as to what reports were needed.
- Often a tool doesn't meet organizational needs because there has been too little thought to the process flow.
- Often organizations do not have clearly defined 'tasks, roles and responsibilities' to help decide who needs to be involved in customization and who needs what information from a tool, or who needs to use and update the tool.
- Often organizations have no clear view of the KPI's they need to realize, so they are unable to define metrics and measures that need to be captured.

Now we are not tool experts, but these are all examples of ABC issues that prevent the effective selection and deployment of a tool. Tool providers do this ALL the time, so they must know what the common ABC issues are and how to overcome them. If they do not, then you have a danger of a TOOL being 'installed' and 'implemented' that is not part of a holistic ITSM solution that adds value.

Another case was provided by **Martin Andenmatten**, Glenfis. Martin provides these observations followed by the case study from Swtzerland.

"There are still many organizations which believe that IT services can best be managed by implementing appropriate systems management tools. Automation is seen as the key for efficient operations. Automatic workflows replace process activities in such a way that no management intervention is needed.

Organizations with this type of attitude have difficulty in seeing the difference between systems management and service management. Systems have to be monitored and administered. Services are much more complex and cannot just be seen from a technical point of view. In fact, a service is more about cultural behavior and taking care of business and user requests. Good systems management tools are important but will never replace service management processes nor solve problems.

ITIL is a collection of best practices for an IT service management environment and not a cookbook on how to implement service management systems step-by-step. Many managers actually struggle with the implementation of service management disciplines. They would be more than happy to find ready-to-use tools promising to be ITIL compliant or even ITIL certified, and with all disciplines just built or installed out of the box. So why develop processes on their own, when there are tools available that have already been successfully installed in various place? We are often confronted with such questions and have to explain that tools are only one element on how to become an excellent service provider. People and Processes are the other two elements, and now with ITIL V3 the fourth 'P'- Partner has been added. According to ITIL Best Practices it is the combination of all four, aimed at delivering value, or the fifth 'P' – Performance that is the basis for realizing service management success."

Case:

"After having trained a part of their IT operations staff in ITIL Foundation, a mid size private banking institute in Switzerland was confronted with different initiatives in IT service management projects. Whilst one team wanted to start evaluating a configuration management solution, a second focused upon automating systems monitoring combined with an automated workflow tool.

The CIO invited a large tool vendor and ourselves, as an independent consulting company, to submit an offer to support the organization in this challenge. We offered a standard approach which includes a management workshop to build the vision and mission for the project. First of all an initial assessment, based on the process maturity model (PMM), was recommended and executed in order to verify the organization with regard to ITIL service management compliance, or capability. In a second workshop the findings were prioritised to enable the building of the roadmap for implementing the change program. To successfully implement the change program, it is of utmost importance to involve staff and management in order to create awareness and obtain everyone's commitment to the changes.

The tool vendor offered his product as the sole solution for all IT service management processes. They had successfully installed their product at various locations with just some training needed for the administrators. Their ITSM-portal is user friendly and self explanatory, so no further instructions were needed – as they explained. The CIO was overwhelmed and he believed in the vendor's assertions that no further activities and investments were needed. After receiving confirmation from the system engineers that the system requirements of the tool fitted the company's guidelines, the deal was done.

In spite of our concerns regarding the current situation and capabilities, and the lack of clear business requirements as to what needed to be realized, we were overruled."

What was done to overcome this?

"Eight months later, we got an invitation from the CIO to support this project again. The tool had been installed, but it was still a long way from being used. The system engineers, both on the vendor's and on the customer's side were absorbed in scripting interface modules. Somehow they didn't manage to get control over the complexity. In fact, the tool became a hurdle because of the growing dependencies and complexity. Changes to the infrastructure could hardly be handled. Customer requirements couldn't be implemented on time and the operational staff were not able to provide the services because of a lack of knowledge or capabilities.

After an intensive management workshop we were able to convince the management that service management differs greatly from systems management. Services are much more than just a combination of loosely related systems. There are requirements from the users, meaning that the services and change requests have to be handled in a customer oriented manner. Tools are important to automate tasks and to facilitate communication. However, to fulfil these requirements in a service oriented manner skilled people and defined processes are mandatory. This newly formed awareness was the background to build the new vision of the IT organization. Within the next three weeks, we performed the ITSM assessment and agreed with management that building a service desk and improving incident and change management were the most important topics to start with.

The formerly implemented tool could be integrated as well at a later date, but complexity was no longer the problem. The processes, in particular the change management process, enabled the organization to achieve better planning / budgeting and to even become a more reliable partner to the business."

Unfortunately this organization had to first feel the pain themselves before they fully appreciated the need for a holistic solution. If you are trying to sell the 4 P's to your management team but are getting kick-back and the signs are that a tool is all that is needed, show them this case. Find somebody through the itSMF who has run into this problem and suffered. Let your management team visit or talk to another peer level manager who can explain the consequences of failing to address it in a holistic way.

Other related cards include:

- 4 of Diamonds 'Not capturing the right knowledge for reuse';
- 7 of Diamonds 'Throwing solutions over the wall and HOPING that people will use them';
- 9 of Hearts 'OK so the functionality isn't great but look at the flashy user interface';
- 8 of Diamonds 'We're going to INSTALL ITIL…it can't be that hard';
- The Joker "A tool solves all problems – 'a fool with a TOOL is still a FOOL'.

8 of Clubs

'IT thinks it doesn't have to understand the business to make a business case'

The cartoon shows a CEO giving feedback to an IT manager who has just presented an IT solutions proposal. The CEO says: "IT is a brilliant solution…..I only wish I had a business problem to go with it!...".

This card in fact describes two worst practices. There is one underying problem to these, 'not KNOWING the problem to be resolved'. The two worst practices are:

1. We build IT solutions and systems for the business without knowing the business problem to be resolved, or the business added-value to be realized. ITIL V3 Service Strategy explains this.
2. We adopt ITSM frameworks such as ITIL, CobiT and ISO without really KNOWING what problem we expect to resolve by using them, or by defining the value they will deliver for the business. The characteristic of this is 'ITIL is the goal', not what will be different (measurably different) as a result of deploying ITIL. Many IT organizations have a set of 'internally focused' KPI's for ITIL, but not the business focused value indicator.

IT solutions for the business

This results in the business complaining that we think too much in terms of systems and not in terms of solutions, partly because we don't understand the business well enough, partly because there is not enough engagement and involvement between business and IT during the early stages of IT selection. It is also partly because we in IT don't see the NEED to engage with the business. Our attitude is 'IT is an IT solution, and we are IT specialists, therefore we know how best to use IT'. Unfortunately immature business organizations happily accept this. "That is an IT project, let them get on with it, we don't have to get involved....we are too busy running the business!".

There are numerous examples to be found in the press of hugely embarrassing and costly IT projects that are cancelled at hand-over time. A Standish report a few years ago stated that as few as 28% of IT projects actually got into live use, and after two years only 8% were still in use. This is a frightening figure that shows a poor alignment. Recent facts still show that 70% of IT projects are over time, budget or fail to deliver the right quality.

Characteristics:

- Is the business involved in requiremenst specification?
- Is there enough end-user or business process expertise in building solutions?
- Are users not adequately involved in testing?

- Are there adequate go/no-go mechanisms to cancel IT projects when the business case becomes out of date?
- How well does IT make a business case stating business value to be realized by adopting and deploying IT?
- How well are projects managed to ensure, and demonstrate that value is achieved?
- Are all business users given enough training in the use of new systems?
- Does the business say "That is an IT project...let IT get on with it!"
- Does IT leave the business out because the business doesn't understand IT or hasn't got the time to get involved?

Adopting ITSM frameworks without KNOWING the problem to be resolved

Very often we adopt ITIL without KNOWING what results must be achieved. Very often we assume or guess, very often there are conflicting views as to what that success is.

We ask people two simple questions at the beginning of an ITIL initiative. We say "This is costing money, somebody in the business will want to know what was done with the money; let us assume we are going to spend $250.000 'applying' ITIL. Imagine you are the IT person responsible for spending that money. We are now one year into the future and you step into the lift with the business manager whose money you just spent, he says "So you spent $250.000 of my money on ITIL? What did I get for that?"

We will tell you what the most common answer is that we hear, and it is wrong! We'll tell you so that you don't make the same mistake. Most people say: "We have more effective and efficient processes!" (with a smile on their faces to show they understand the key messages of ITIL). As a business manager we would ask: "Give me an example? Give me a KPI? Have I saved money, am I able to do anything quicker, better? What and how much?" If you can't mention any, then your ITIL initiative is a case of 'If you aim at nothing, nothing is what you will hit' and quite rightly at the end of the year many internal and external stakeholders will moan that ITIL didn't deliver enough......
because nobody agreed what it should have delivered.

Characteristics:

- Do people have confused and conflicting perceptions of what ITIL should deliver?
- Do YOU know what ITIL should deliver in terms of measurable value?
- Can a process manager say when his or her process is successful? And who decides that success?
- Do people involved in carrying out ITIL processes know what value the process must deliver?
- Are the users or customers involved in process improvement projects?
- How often are customer satisfaction surveys carried out?
- Does everybody KNOW what the customer or user dissatisfiers are?
- Were these the basis for ITIL improvements?
- At the end of an ITSM improvement initiative can you demonstrate a measurable improvement?

Case:

At the start of an ITIL improvement initiative in one organization, we interviewed people to identify which process improvements were important. We were not allowed to interview the users (we might set expectations, or the users might start complaining - see the 2 of Clubs). One senior IT operations manager we interviewed declared *"Availability is our most mature processs"*. He proudly showed me the KPI's - 99.8% Unix availability. Finally when we were deploying processes I was allowed to interview some users. Their biggest single complaint... availability.

I mentioned this to the IT operations manager. His actual quote was: *"That is because the users don' t understand what availability is, they' re complaining about the application!"*. Indeed the application was so poorly designed and built that the whole transaction processing system had to be taken offline for every update to any transaction user group. As a result the application was up and down like a yo-yo.

Here we see an example of ITIL that didn't provide the solution that the business needed, and an example of 'customer and user focused'.

The IT manager agreed to hold a meeting with IT operations and application development managers about availability. The application managers did not find it worth sending people to the ITIL training or awareness, or getting involved in ITIL.

A user was invited to explain what had happened and what the experiences were. After the session the managers were asked what they thought, whether this was acceptable and what they proposed to do about it. The application managers were forced to involve themselves in the ITIL availability management initiatives.

Other related cards are:

- 2 of Clubs 'NO respect for, or understanding of users';
- Jack of Clubs 'Let's outsource the business – we'd be better off';
- Queen of Clubs 'No understanding of business priority and impact';
- 2 of Diamonds 'We don't measure our value contribution to strategy';
- 3 of Diamonds 'Too little business involvement in requirements specification and testing';
- Queen of Diamonds 'The solution the customer sees isn't the one that IT sees';
- King of Diamonds 'IT strategy's contribution to business strategy';
- 2 of Spades 'Them and us culture – opposing and competing forces';
- 4 of Spades 'Internally focused';
- 10 of Spades 'The superiority complex – we know best';
- Jack of Spades 'Avoidance culture';
- Queen of Spades 'Not my responsibility';
- 4 of Hearts 'The best way to improve services is to outsource…..the business!'

Walking the Talk

9 of Clubs

'Walking the talk'

This is one of the characteristics of poor IT leadership. One of the characteristics that shows that real 'commitment' is lacking. Procedures are for OTHER people to follow, procedures are OK unless they get in MY way. Managers who bend the rules just THIS ONCE. Employees are told of the importance of procedures, the importance of following them, they will be punished if THEY do not follow them. When managers start to break down the commitment to follow procedures it opens the dam for the rest of the organization to do the same.

The cartoon shows an IT manager strangling a technoid and declaring: "....Don't do as I DO.....Do as I SAY! .....".

Characteristics:

- Do managers declare the importance of procedures but are the first to break them whenever convenient?
- Do managers say procedures are important.... but this project is more important?
- Are jokes made about people who follow procedures?
- Do people declare "I'll belive procedures are important when I see it happening"?
- Do managers avoid confronting people who don't follow agreements?
- Do senior managers fail to intervene in arguments between process and line managers?

Case:

How often have I heard IT managers declare that they recognize the ABC issues and cartoons. But when confronted they are unable to say what initiatives they have undertaken to break through this ABC worst practice. Often at a conference I present these cartoons and people nod....I then ask "Whose job is it to break through this? The business? The CIO?"

Usually it is still before somebody says "the business?", "the CIO!". Father Christmas or Harry Potter is what I am thinking to myself. They are waiting for somebody to come and give them a present or wave a magic wand that will make it go away...."

"You" is what I tell them. Anybody who is an 'IT manager' of any description. Hoping that the technoids will change themselves has as much chance of happening as hoping that all the countries will reduce CO_2 emmisions because they are bad. "The CIO and the business aren't here listening to this" I say. "The techies and IT employees who need to change aren't here listening to this. You are the only people aware that these ABC worst practices are there and need breaking down otherwise we will fail. If YOU don't consciously do something to fix it then NOBODY else will do it for you!". That is another aim of this book, to give you some concrete examples of how these ABC worst practices can be changed. How real behavior change can be realized.

Other related cards are:

- 5 of Diamonds 'No management commitment';
- 10 of Diamonds 'Never mind about following procedures….just do what we usually do';
- 3 of Spades 'Hierarchic culture. The boss is always right even when the boss is wrong';
- 8 of Spades Plan, Do, Stop….no real continual improvement culture';
- Queen of Spades 'Not my responsibility';
- 8 of Hearts 'The buck stops anywhere but here'.

10
♣

"We've to put toilet paper in the IT managers Printer....his reports will be useful for I thing at least."

No respect for, or trust in, IT management

OT
♣

10 of Clubs

'No respect for, or trust in IT management'

Now relate this to the example above. You as a manager now go back to your organization and tell everybody THEY need to change. What will people think?

In just about every branch, people will complain about their managers. Just like kids complain about their teachers, men complain about women and women complain about men, employees complain about managers. However there are certain symptoms of complaints that are indicative of a serious lack of leadership, or problems that will prevent change happening.

The cartoon on the card shows two technoids standing by a printer. Toilet paper is coming out of the printer. One of the technoids says: "We've put toilet paper in the manager's printer.... that way his reports will be useful for one thing at least!".

Characteristics:

- Do you see examples of the 9 of Clubs. Managers not 'walking-the-talk', or showing poor 'example' behavior?
- How well are the aims of change programs communicated? A memo or statement from above?
- Is there enough commitment to change initiatives? Allocating time, effort or resources to ensure they work?
- Are there effective reward or punishment mechanisms? Reward good behavior in memos, notes, quotes, actions? Saying what good, effective behavior was and praising it so that people can see and feel appreciation of what they have done. Addressing senior managers who do not behave in line with the goals of adopting and deploying ITIL. Making examples of poor behavior that can no longer be tolerated.
- Are people supported in adopting new ways of working? E.g. given time to learn new procedures, given help and training, provided with tools to support new procedures?.
- Do managers try to motivate and inspire people to perform?
- Do managers back-up IT staff and say NO to the business?
- How often do people actually give feedback to managers about their behavior?
- How often do managers ask for feedback from the employees?

Managers are often blind to their own shortcomings. You could give them a set of ABC worst practice cards and say to them. If we gave these cards to our employees and said which cards apply to your managers, what cards would they choose? This will force managers to look at themselves as others may do.

Other related cards are:

- 5 of Diamonds 'No management commitment';
- 3 of Spades 'Hierarchic culture. The boss is always right even when the boss is wrong';
- Queen of Spades 'Not my responsibility';
- 8 of Hearts 'The buck stops anywhere but here'.

Let's outsource the business
-- we'd be better off

Jack of Clubs

'Let's outsource the business – we'd be better off!'

This is another example of not understanding the business or not attempting to resolve differences. An extreme form of this is when IT has an attitude of being superior. IT works against the business. No respect for, or trust in, how the business manages IT. IT starts dictating toward the business…. 'IT knows what is best for the business, the business will take what it gets'. IT often needs to try to adopt standards to help ensure compatability. This needs to be well agreed with the business and should be part of a well chosen architecture, or design principals, with an eye on business flexibility. Not on some ad hoc IT decision to make life easier for IT.

This is often the type of attitude we see when IT feels a 'Victim' to the business. We poor long suffering IT people. The business doesn't understand us, they ignore us, they tell us off. They are the cause for all of our problems. The Victim attitude becomes one of anger and frustration reinforcing the 'them and us' feeling. The anger and frustration translates itself into IT centric behavior.

The cartoon on the card shows an IT manager giving a presentation. He explains: "80% of problems and changes are caused by users. The best way to increase the quality of service is………. user free IT!"

Characteristics:

- Does IT decide what is best for the business?
- Do IT managers complain about the business?
- Is IT locked down because it makes IT management easier for IT?
- Are IT standards there primarily to make life easier for IT?
- Does IT see that the business isn't changing, so IT will do whatever it can to get its own way?
- Has IT given up trying to convince and change the business because they refuse to listen?

Case:
In one IT organization the IT director used some of our cartoons at the start of a presentation to senior IT managers.

'You can fool some of the users all of the time'
'You can fool all of the users some of the time….'
'But our strategy for the coming year is to fool ALL of the users ALL of the time…'

Jokingly, he said that he was surprised by the emphatic nodding of heads and the 'yes'! However, he did admit that this was an eye opener and indeed expressed the feelings and frustration of his IT managers.

What IT needs to remember is if any of the partners is capable of outsourcing the other it is the business. They can outsource IT but IT can't outsource the business. You can sit and moan about business and HOPE they will change. Like we have in the last 10 years. The only way this will change is when IT takes proactive measures to break out of the 'victim' syndrome. The way in which IT can make the business take notice is first to gain trust and credibility. This can be done by demonstrating that IT can and does deliver value. You can also ask each IT team. What do we need to do to gain trust and credibility with the business......you could also ask the business but hey! Let's no go THERE!

Other related cards are:

- 2 of Clubs 'NO respect for, or understanding of users';
- Queen of Clubs 'No understanding of business priority and impact';
- 2 of Diamonds 'We don't measure our value contribution to strategy';
- 3 of Diamonds 'Too little business involvement in requirements specification and testing';
- Queen of Diamonds 'The solution the customer sees isn't the one that IT sees';
- King of Diamonds 'IT strategy's contribution to business strategy';
- 2 of Spades 'Them and us culture – opposing and competing forces';
- 4 of Spades 'Internally focused';
- 10 of Spades 'The superiority complex – we know best';
- Jack of Spades 'Avoidance culture';
- Queen of Spades 'Not my responsibility';
- 4 of Hearts 'The best way to improve services is to outsource…..the business!'.

"...here are the emergency updates to the onboard navigation software!"

No understanding of business priority & impact

Queen of Clubs

'No understanding of business priority or impact'

This is another symptom of not understanding the customers or users, of not having an understanding of the business and the business needs and drivers, of IT and business not having an effective relationship. IT projects are poorly prioritized, IT problems and resolution is poorly prioritized. Often when the business demand for both on-going maintenance activities and structural improvements increases, IT decides itself what it will handle first. Without actively engaging with, or agreeing, short, middle and longer term priorities.

Often IT doesn't have enough insight into potential business impact to make the call. Often you see IT people running around trying to do everything at the same time. Total commitment, energy, dedication, professionalism wanting to do everything..... but failing in some without fully understanding what they should do first and what the impacts of the failures are.

The cartoon on the card shows a technoid handing a floppy disk to a Nasa launch engineer. In the background you can see the Shuttle already lifting off from the launch pad. The technoids says: "Here are the emergency updates for the onboard navigation software!"

This worst practice can often cause IT to do too many things at the same time with limited resources, and before long an unacceptable failure WILL occur. When it does who will the business blame? In our view, quite correctly, it will be IT. Why, quite correctly, we hear the indignant IT people call out. 'We keep telling the business we need to prioritize but they won't listen!'. We agree. We know because we have been there. But let's ask another set of questions? We are now going to get all philosophical, just to warn you, so you can skip the next bit if philosophy isn't for you. Imagine you are sitting on the ground with Confuscious the well known and respected Chinese philosopher. He takes time out on his busy agenda of doing nothing, because as he says: "When you do nothing, nothing gets left undone". You explain your dilemma of trying to get the business to prioritize. He asks you: "So you know what the consequences are when the business does nothing?'

"Yes!" we say, "but they don't listen!"

"So" says Confuscious "the business does not understand? We have a saying in China, a hungry, blind man must stand a long time on the top of a hill before a chicken will fly into his mouth. A business manager who does not understand will not find understanding himself.....somebody who understands must help him understand; if someone who can help a suffering man does not do so, but instead lets the man suffer, what do we say of such a person?"

After we let that sink in, we then say, "No, no they do understand but they don't care….they will let it happen, knowing we will fail!"

"Soooo?" says Confuscious, twirling his moustache between his fingers, "If a man deliberately does the emperor harm, what would the emperor do to such a man, after the emperor has been kind enough to give the man safety and shelter, and the man betrays him with such treachery that he wants to harm the state and all who live in the state?"

Basically the emperor will be severly unchuffed and will give the person a good kicking………. but as most of you are by now totally confused as to what the moral of all this is, we will explain. If you don't help the business change, nobody else will, and if the business won't change and this starts impacting business continuity, then you can be fairly sure that when the CEO or CFO hear what IT behavior is doing to the business there is a good chance that the butt kicking will come from the CFO or CEO and you won't need to…..we think.

If business behavior is impacting business performance and causing delays, down-time, lost opportunities, wasted money as a result of poor governance of IT then IT should make this visible. Believe us, no CEO wants to see or accept business risks as a result of poor governance of IT.

Characteristics:

- Who determines impact, urgency and priority? Is there adequate involvement of the business in defining or using these?
- Does IT decide priorities when there are project and resourcing conflicts, without notifying the business of decisions and consequences?
- Is there adequate business dialogue and engagement to determine priorities?
- Does the business says everything has high priority?
- Do IT managers respond to the business person who shouts the loudest?
- Does the business align its own internal priority mechanisms for balancing IT decisions?
- Does the business ensure governance mechanisms exist to protect the business and reduce the risks and consequences of poor decision making?

One example:
"….I am now a business user of IT. I use PowerPoint all the time. If I am preparing a PowerPoint presentation for an itSMF conference that is in six weeks time, how important is a PowerPoint failure to me? It is inconvenient but at this moment it doesn't have a serious business impact. However, if I am putting together a PowerPoint presentation that I need to give tomorrow morning to the board of directors of a large multi-national company to secure a large deal, how important then is PowerPoint? Who can best decide the business impact? Our IT support organization felt it was in the best position to make this call and said I'd have to wait. I had to escalate this all over the organization before this was given the right priority. Who was right? Me, as a business user who made a call on business impact? Or the IT organization with its 'Compass – mature IT organization' stamp, ISO certified and compliant processes? You tell me!

All I know is I voted to outsource the IT support when I saw the questionnaire arrive on my desk."

Here is a small example of using the ABC cards to identify that this worst practice was an issue in the company. We used the cards at an itSMF conference workshop. We started the session by having people put the 2 of Clubs on the table:

> ITSM best practice trainer teaching people about ITIL. "ITIL uses the terms Customers and Users, what terms do you use?" The technoids in the class reply "Dorks!"

People then voted on the statement: 'We are not customer focused enough in IT'.

- In the itSMF website vote **89%** agreed with the statement and gave examples of behavior that needed changing, many of them directly related to the ABC cards.
- At the itSMF best practice conference **86%** agreed.
- The itSMF Academy workshop scored considerably lower. Only **75%** agreed with the statement.

We walked around the teams at the workshop to get a feel of their 'attitude'. This is what we saw and experienced:

- By one table there was 'irritation', and the 'crossed-arm, head-shaking' negative body language, implying that it was a mistake attending this session.
- "So you obviously don't agree?" we asked.
- "Now...yeah. Listen, **of course we are customer focused! We are IT managers at this table and we talk to customers all the time**, if you talk about the support teams and the techies then you are right....what do you want us to vote? Of course we can make your figures look high!?"
- "Vote as you perceive it", we said. "The idea is to recognize worst practices that need fixing..... you obviously don't have any.......**as managers.**"
- Their attitude was WE don't need to change. WE have no worst practice BEHAVIOR.

For the next task we put the 'customer' card on the table. The task was:

"Imagine that end-users or customers are sitting here at the table and we give them the pack of worst practice cards. We then ask them to select three cards that apply to your organization, which cards would they choose?"

Each participant chose three cards. This task was aimed at forcing them to think from a different perspective, try to take time out from the daily operation to think from the perspective of another stakeholder. The stakeholder that we run our IT systems for,, in fact!

The next task was to discuss all of the cards chosen and select, as a team, the top three. Should we choose the cards that were selected the most? We told them to choose using the following criteria, related to ITIL V3 Service Strategy and 'value'. Value talks about 'fit for use' and 'fit for purpose'.

"Look at each card and discuss the consequences to the business. Think in terms of 'wasted money', 'lost revenue', 'delayed projects', 'down-time and non-availability of critical systems', 'solutions that fail to deliver business value'." This created new discussions and new insights.

When the teams were finally finished, we asked them, including the team of 'customer focused' managers, to present their findings. we call this team the A-Team for obvious reasons; heroic champions capable of aligning business and IT single handedly.
These were the results:

- The A-team (as well as three other teams) chose the card the Queen of Clubs 'No understanding of business impact & priority' as the top recognized worst practice.
- Example behavior was:
  - The business won't invite us to discuss business needs, we are too late in the process;
  - we try to tell the business but they won't listen;
  - we allocate resources and start a project portfolio and then find they are no longer important;
  - we have business users declaring that solutions don't meet their needs.
- Example consequences were:
  - failure to solve 'real' business problems;
  - delays in business projects;
  - lost business opportunities and business revenue;
  - not enough testing, causing downtime and additional changes;
  - unpredictable services and project performance;
  - increased costs;
  - business dissatisfaction;
  - IT frustration.

We then asked the team, "Is this an acceptable business risk?"

The answer was "NO!"

Then the 64 million dollar question, "Now that you recognize that this is what you, as an IT organization do, and that it is an unacceptable business risk, IS THERE ANYBODY ACCOUNTABLE IN YOUR (IT) ORGANIZATION FOR RESOLVING THIS?"………

There was a moment of silence…. "No"

"So let me just summarize then, to see if I understand. YOU, as IT managers, are customer focused enough…..however you accept that your current behavior causes unacceptable business risks, and you also accept that you don't need to do anything to ensure that this business issue is resolved….is this an example of being customer focused enough?"

The A-Team vote was now 100%. "We are not customer focused enough."
"What are you going to do now?" we asked.

"We are going to perform this exercise in our organization.....more people need to be confronted with the consequences of our attitude and behavior."

Other related cards are:

- 2 of Clubs 'NO respect for, or understanding of users';
- 4 of Clubs 'IT is not seen as an added-value partner to the business';
- 5 of Clubs 'Neither partner makes an effort to understand the other';
- 8 of Clubs 'IT thinks it doesn't have to understand the business to make a business case';
- 6 of Diamonds 'Everything has the highest priority...according to the users'.

A case was also provided by **Ken Turbitt**, *President & CEO, Service Management Consultancy (SMCG) Ltd. Ken was, until recently, with BMC.*

"Imagine that your business depends on the overall success of a space shuttle flight. 10..9..8..7..6..5..4..3..2..1..The spacecraft has just taken off, but the crew needed an emergency update, two hours ago, for its onboard navigation software. And they had to have this update before launch. Let's say your IT department got a request for the update to the navigation software, but didn't know how critical it was, and didn't understand its importance or its impact on the launch. After all, IT staff members get many requests and all are deemed urgent from the requestor or user's perspective. IT might have put off responding to this incident to deal with incidents ahead of this one on the basis of following the standard of first-come, first-served. That strategy would have created a disaster for the flight and the crew.

That's why it's essential for IT, and indeed all involved parties, to understand the complexity and criticality to the overall business or project, or launch. In the case of the space shuttle this would include knowing the functions of the components and how they all worked together – the criticality of one over another in relation to the overall goal. At the same time, you need to be able to understand the implication of these solutions and processes and how they are used in support of business objectives.

Communicate, communicate, communicate
Communication is critical. The business must communicate its priorities to IT, and the IT team needs to listen to their priorities to determine the best way to support them. When you understand priorities, you can respond to them in a timely manner. As in the example cited earlier, fixing the navigation system software before the launch should have been a number-one priority. It's the same with your business. You should focus first on what's most critical to your company's success, usually anything directly impacting the customer or client, revenue generation, or cost saving initiatives. It should not be up to IT to decide what has more priority than another request – it's the role of the business to decide and communicate this information, remembering that it's time sensitive, what was urgent yesterday, may not be today.

When the business and IT work together, focused on business priorities, they can achieve strategic, operational, and tactical alignment and integration in both directions – from the top down and from the bottom up. The business can learn a lot from the IT side by understanding the potential solutions and capabilities that new technology can provide, and interpreting these in relation to new business offerings that could be developed or improved services that could be offered. Think of eBay, few people previously went to auction houses to buy or sell things, now millions do so around the world, in many cases generating new businesses within businesses.

The CIO needs a seat at the board room, because his organization's technical capability and know-how can be used to advise business about what new applications, software, or capabilities are technically feasible and achievable.

IT organizations must understand the architecture and infrastructure that they are supporting and maintaining, and how these relate to the business functions that they are supporting. The business needs to understand how their business processes are automated and how the integration of business and IT would enable both sides to know the impact of any decision that's being made.

That's where an ITIL best practice approach comes in. ITIL (v3) recommends that the business and IT are not only alignedbut integrated, they use the term Business Service Management (BSM) as an approach. This approach includes integrating ITIL-processes across the infrastructure in support of the business and its priorities, taking a business perspective on IT.

The business processes need to be automated and supported by IT, in a way that, until now, has not happened. IT is a support function of the business, just like Finance, HR and Marketing, and just as critical. We all know the impact of an IT outage on the business, this has a far greater impact on the customer, revenue and profit, and reputation than almost any other business function.

That's why ITIL bought into the Business Service Management (BSM) approach. The name itself already creates a shift in attitude from IT service management to business. This approach focuses on understanding the business processes and priorities aligned to the overall goals and objectives.

Attitude: as highlighted, communication is key and involves an attitude change. Saying "It's not my job to talk to the business or to IT" is just not good enough. We all need to review our attitude, understand the business and work to one goal, after all it's the business that pays your salary which funds your home and family.
Behavior: We need to stop playing with the latest gadgets, persuading the business to buy the latest tool, unless we can justify it as 'fit for purpose', fully utilize it as 'Fit for use', and ensure a return on value from it. Our behavior influences our attitude and vice-a-versa. If we start to behave like professional adults focused on the goals of the business, then we start to show value back into the business by understanding the priorities and impacts of our decisions, work and results. Treat the company money as you would your own.
Culture: With the 'A' and 'B' in focus, a cultural change will start to occur. Yes, it needs to be given direction from the top, but it cannot be dictated. Some people lead and others

follow a culture – they cannot be forced into talking. The overall change needs to be focused around communication and joint understanding; these are the two critical elements for success.

So, next time you're given a task to perform, communicate and ask all the relevant questions, starting with the importance or impact that this could have on the business, enabling you to understand and prioritize from a business perspective, not from your own. Let's all ensure we take off with all we need to succeed and not discover too late that we failed to communicate, failed to deliver and failed to survive."

King of Clubs

'ITIL is the objective....not what it should achieve'

In many organizations ITIL is implemented with a primary focus on customer satisfaction. Often we ask, "Have you done a user or customer satisfaction survey?". In more than 75% of the cases no survey is done. A few senior users were listened to when they complained. Often the IT manager says, "We don't want to ask the users, we will set expectations..." or "...they will then tell us eveything that is wrong". Worse still, in the example driven from a 'superiority complex' (the type of IT organization described by the Jack of Clubs), "the business will get the improvements they deserve...". This to us is one of the major reasons why ITIL has failed to deliver and why many ITIL initiatives go wrong. Too often ITIL is 'the goal' rather than what it should actually achieve. This is also very similar to the 'value' Joker card towards the end of this section.

The cartoon on the King of Clubs card shows a technoid holding a book of procedures. An irate, angry user is smashing his fist on top of his screen display. The technoid says: "I don't understand. I followed all the ITIL procedures.....according to me you are now a satisfied customer!"

Characteristics:

- Did the IT organization conduct a customer or user survey to determine improvement needs?
- Was the survey actually used to make improvement decisions?
- Do IT staff KNOW what makes users unhappy or makes them satisfied?
- Do ITIL procedures actually deliver value? Do you KNOW what that value is? Or is ITIL just a lot of books of procedures?
- Who decides if an ITIL process is working successfully?
- Is the business case for an ITSM improvement program linked to business outcomes or value?
- Does the ITIL business case describe key measures that show the value to the business? Or the ROI?
- If you ask each employee in your organization, "What is the goal of ITIL?" what would they say? Would they all give the same answer?
- How many people could ACCURATELY answer the above question?

Case:

At a large international transport company based in the Netherlands it was decided to adopt ITIL to improve customer service and satisfaction. It was decided to invest in call center software and improve the service desk, incident and problem management.

This time I didn't even ask if we could do a customer satisfaction survey. I had by now changed my approach, I simply asked, "What is the reason we don't want to do a customer satisfaction survey at the start of a project aimed at improving customer satisfaction?". They all looked at me like I was an idiot. One answer was "It'll take too much time and we want to be finished within this years budget!", "the other answer was, "We already know, we have a good relationship and understanding. We are customer focused and have been for a long time."

OK. Once again, at roll-out time I got to interview a large group of users. We explained about the updated service desk and incident handling procedures to speed up resolution and improve business availability. "I don't know why they spent so much effort on that" declared a group of senior users. "What we are dissatisfied with are the changes. They change things without telling us, or they roll-out new upgrades to office systems or SAP modules without any new documentation or training. Sometimes this happens at really bad moments in business planning. We'd like them to improve the roll-out of new IS systems!". So that was a great example of customer or service minded attitude. That was a great example of, "We followed all the ITIL procedures....you must be a satisfied customer!"

Other cards that may be related to this are:

- The Joker 'Unable to specify the VALUE required by the business';
- 2 of Clubs 'NO respect for, or understanding of users'.
- Jack of Hearts 'A process flow and some procedures are all you need';
- 8 of Diamonds 'We're going to install ITIL. It can't be that hard'.

Ace of Clubs

'ITIL certification means I know what I am doing.....
22 points means I can change the world!'

This is one of our personal favorites. Our whole book is focused on the need to change ABC to get ITIL or ITSM improvements to work. The people responsible for deploying ITSM best practices in the market place also need to change their own ABC.

ITIL deployment to the market is facilitated through new 'best practice' publications - such as ITIL V3. It is also facilitated by ITIL training, endorsed through a certification system. It is also facilitated by the itSMF and other industry recognized, knowledge sharing platforms. In our view the training and certification scheme doesn't go far enough in helping people learn how to address the ABC issues. The best practice guidance doesn't address the needs and experiences gained in the last 10 years, and we don't believe that conferences spend enough energy or attention on the ABC issues. It is getting better, but more can be done.

The cartoon on the card shows an ITIL consultant talking to a business manager. The consultant says: "....I have 22 points. Therefore I am fully certified in ITIL, therefore I am right.....therefore you must be satisfied!...."

The worst practices we see are organizations sending employees on ITIL certification and then assuming they are ready and able to instigate a program of organizational change! They are let loose in a live, production IT environment to 'install' and 'implement' books of ITIL procedures to technoids who thinks processes and procedures are a waste of time, to technoids who don't like to read technical literature, let alone procedural handbooks. They are let loose in an organziation where most managers display an attitude of 'don't do as I do, do as I say'.

What does ITIL best practice say?

ITIL challenges and risks

These are hidden at the back of the ITIL books, so there is a good chance they will be overlooked. They do indeed cover just about all the various issues we are addressing in this book. However, below we have added, in between brackets, some quotes and questions. Questions that the ITIL books and ITIL training currently do not answer. Questions that customers should ask to any provider trying to sell them an ITIL V3 solution, whether that is training, a tool or some consultancy.

Strategy:
- The more you try to change them, the more they resist. (*So what should we do about managing resistance, especially as 52% of those that fail are due to resistance?*)
- Reacting to events and trying to predict them in place of learning from them.
- Need for shared views of outcomes.

Design:
- Understanding business priorities and having these at the top of the mind. (*....What about ANYWHERE in the mind.*)
- Lack of knowledge or awareness of business needs and priorities. (*Indeed this is the TOP most commonly chosen worst practice card so far in three workshops played with IT manager groups.*)
- Involve as many people as possible in the design.
- Gaining commitment from managers and staff. (*What is commitment? What is the difference between 'involvement' and 'commitment', what does commitment look like? How do you know you have gained it?*)
- Poor relationship between business & IT. (*What poor relationship? We don't trust them, they don't trust us, we ignore their needs, they ignore ours, they don't like us, we don't like them, they know how we feel about them, we know how they feel about us....sounds like an understanding relationship to me!?*)
- Insufficient engagement and commitment from applications functional development. (*Which book explains how to engage and get commitment from applications functional development? This 'throwing it over the wall' has been an issue for years, what advice is given to break it down finally? Does ITIL V3 address the needs of the applications group? Will they buy-in to this ITIL?*)

Transition:
- Establishing & maintaining stakeholder buy-in & commitment. (*How do you establish this and how do you maintain it?*)
- Developing a workforce with the right service culture. (*What is a service culture? What does it look like? What does it sound like? How do you know when you have one? How do you develop this workforce?*)
- Ability to appreciate the cultural environment..... (*Sorry I missed which element of ITIL training covers the subject 'What is a culture, how to appreciate one, how to develop a service culture?'....If this is a critical success factor, I am hoping for some help from the training and certification scheme to give me the capabilities.*)
- Establishing a culture that enables knowledge to be shared freely and willingly. (*......like we have in the last 15 years? In an environment in which technical knowledge is rewarded, therefore knowledge is personal value, therefore knowledge is power.*)
- Defining clear roles, accountabilities and responsibilities. (*What about making sure everybody knows what these are and making sure they are adhered to?*)
- Risks. Alienation of some key operations and support staff. (*What should we do do address this?*)
- Resistance to change and circumvention of the processes due to perceived bureaucracy. (*So what should we do to convince them otherwise? What guidance is there and advice to managers?*)
- In the book: Knowledge management: 'The Service Transition Team will soon become familiar with the need to change attitudes and the operation of converting culture. For them it is a routine task, holding no threat'. (*!!!! ..... Which book helps this become a routine task? Which*

ITIL training tells how to convert culture as a routine task? .... it must be five minutes on the first day. I must have missed that block. We've had the one minute manager, now we have the five minute culture change!?)

- Managing change: Effective leaders and managers understand the change process and plan and lead accordingly........ (*What is an effective leader? What does one do? What does one look like? Which training covers this? Or better still, which particular can do I have to open in order to pour out a dozen effective leaders? How many managers understand the change process?*)

Service operation:

- Senior management must provide visible support during the launch of new service operation initiatives. (*What does visible support look like? More than turning up for the first two minutes and saying "this is really important…thank you, I have to go and play golf now!")*
- Even worse are senior managers who support the initiative verbally, but abuse their authority to encourage circumvention of the service operation practice.
- Senior managers should also empower the middle managers who will be directly responsible for service operation. (*Empower? Is that more than saying you are now responsible and you will get the blame if it goes wrong? What does empower look like?*)
- Middle managers should go out of their way to make their support known, not just by their words but by their actions and adherence to the organization's agreed processes and procedures. (*Very often they don't, they don't 'walk-the-talk' or 'lead by example', they display the attitude of 'don't do as I DO....do as I SAY', what should senior managers do to address this? What training covers how you deal with this?*)
- It is equally important that the business understand, accept and carry out the role they play in service operation. Good service requires good customers! (*So let's outsource the customers and get some good ones.*)

The ITIL books make a clear reference to the importance of ABC. Service Transition does actually mention many of the issues raised in this book. Chapter 5 in Service Transition should be read by ALL IT managers and people responsible for making the change happen, not just by a select few new 'Transition' roles. All of the core books should refer to this chapter to ensure it remains 'top-of-mind' and doesn't get ignored or forgotten. However, although the Service Transition chapters identify and recognize the need to 'manage the organizational change', at time of publishing this book, there is little formal ITIL training or certification to help address these challenges.

We also asked other industry experts and ITIL champions to give their views. Here are three cases from Aidan Lawes, David Wheelden and Paul van Nobelen. Sharon Taylor also gave her input and explained how ITIL certification will help address the issues of ABC.

Aidan Lawes. Aidan was, for a number of years, the CEO of the itSMF UK and International and is now a self proclaimed 'service management evangelist'.

ABC issue: Attitude towards certification (qualifications)
"In my view, one of the biggest issues facing organizations is differentiating between holding a piece of paper and competence. Organizations need to employ staff, or engage

external resources, who are competent at performing a specific role or set of tasks. This means considering far more than whether the individual holds a certificate of some kind. Other factors, such as practical experience of applying theoretical knowledge, are just as, if not more, important.

Organizations need to implement service management solutions, not ITIL, and hence require people who can adapt and adopt the 'best practice' guidance for particular circumstances and cultures.

As an example:
I have shared speaking platforms with a multitude of senior executives, primarily from vendor organizations, who proudly proclaim that they have 'n' thousand 'ITIL certified staff'. If one added all these numbers together they would exceed the number of candidates who have passed a manager's level exam by a factor approaching triple digits. Therefore, they clearly count people who have managed to pass the Foundation certificate as being 'ITIL certified'.

The Foundation certificate is exactly what its name states – a foundation for building upon. It is designed to be passed by the majority of candidates – hence the pass rate of approaching 90% - and many of the people who hold the certificate would be the first to admit that it qualifies them to <u>do</u> virtually nothing.

Even when we consider the higher level of qualification such as the manager's qualification, the situation is still often not rosy. Candidates can retake either or both of the papers and thus attain the certificate. Accepting that some candidates just don't perform well under written exam conditions, there are clearly some who eventually pass, who struggle to demonstrate a sound grasp of the principles involved.

On the other hand, many smart young graduates have successfully passed the exam, despite the fact that they don't meet the strict entrance requirements in terms of experience. If they are attuned to sitting and passing exams, the whole process is easier than for someone who hasn't practised the art for many years! In such cases, the knowledge is all too often pure theory."

So what should we be doing?
Aidan: "If an organization is embarking upon a service improvement program based on ITIL, they need to think about their human resource needs. Successful organizations define the roles they need to fill in terms of knowledge, skills, attitude and experience. ITIL knowledge alone is not necessarily all that is required; other skills may be needed.

While each enterprise's requirements will differ, some generic competencies do offer themselves readily. For example, many consultants and most architects and designers will probably need: capabilities in requirements capture, analysis and articulation; good expressive skills (written and verbal); empathy in dealing with multiple authority and responsibility levels; technology knowledge; the ability to see both the macro and the micro picture; persuasiveness and willingness to listen to other views; good understanding of the business and its drivers; and so on. Many of these attributes are innate abilities or skills learned through experience.

Once the criteria have been defined, the enterprise can perform a gap analysis on their existing staff against them. From this can come a sensible education program for current internal staff, which will take into account the individual and the needs of the program. People need to be trained in the right timeframes, i.e. when they will be able to apply any theoretical knowledge in practice, and at the right level for their specific involvement. It is also important to recognise that people who have recently acquired new knowledge or learned a new skill, typically will not be as productive as someone who has practised those skills for some time.

If new staff or temporary external resources are required, candidates can be assessed against the same broad set of criteria. As can be seen from the above example, whether or not they hold a particular qualification is just a small piece of the jigsaw; whether they have other attributes and skills, and most importantly, whether they can demonstrate practical application of them, is usually far more relevant to selecting the right candidate.

In summary, ITIL qualifications are important, but not the whole story."

David Wheelden, HP. *David has been helping organizations improve using ITSM best practices for years. He was an author for ITIL V1 , ITIL V2 and ITIL V3 and is an experienced ITIL practitioner and champion of ITIL.*

"Why the Ace of Clubs?. It's pretty obvious to everybody now that IT is becoming increasingly important to business operations, any business. That is one of the reasons that ITIL V3 declares that ITSM capabilities are becoming a strategic asset. What this means is that when we adopt ITSM best practices such as ITIL we can no longer afford to fail.

We must demonstrate that we can bring IT under control and manage the availability and continuity demanded by the business. As a result of the increased demand for ITIL, there is also a corresponding growth in the amount of 'ITIL certified' consultants."

Is this a worrying situation. If so, why?

David: "The current ITIL certification schemes end up giving somebody a certificate. However a certificate alone doesn't necessarily mean that the holder has the capabilities, skills and experience for successfully deploying ITIL. Having a certificate doesn't in itself turn you into a strategic asset! It concerns me to see the amount of supposed 'certified' ITIL experts that have no real experience in how to manage the organizational change that adopting best practices entails. It is a risk and a danger to let some of these people loose into your live environment."

My advice to customers wanting, or needing, to employ external ITIL expertise is to go beyond looking just for qualifications. In addition, look for proven experience and involvement in actually having applied ITIL. Also look for how the consultant or the consulting firm addresses the management of change issues that arise as a result of the decision to use an ITSM best practice framework."

David fully supports initiatives such as the ABC card game and business simulations such as Apollo 13. Why is this?

David: "These are a great way of getting the message across. A great way of 'involving' people and 'engaging' people in the change program. Instruments such as these help create awareness, gain buy-in and involve people in suggesting improvements to their own work. We in HP often use our own business simulation during ITIL programs specifically for this."

Paul van Nobelen, *Director Suerte*, a Dutch based company. *Paul works often in the Scandinavian countries and related this case.*

"In the northern part of Europe ITIL is becoming increasingly popular every day. Under the pressure of the last economic downturn, the big outsourcing providers moved into the prosperous economic fields of Scandinavia and the Baltics. And they used ITIL, at least they said they had ITIL. This caused the local players to ITILize themselves. It also ignited the large telephone company, who were outsourcing and off-shoring their IT services to providers as far away as India. ITIL is spreading like a fire on a dry, windy summer day. Of course, to really understand the implications and consequences of the framework is one thing, to assess a partner's ITIL capability is something else. This worst case is an example of 'He who says he is ITILized, may not be really be aware of what this is about'."

Case: Fool me once, shame on you! Fool me twice, shame on me
"A large Scandinavian telephone company decided to outsource their maintenance (incident management, change management) to an Indian partner. One of the criteria underpinning the decision to select a partner, was that the partner must be 'ITIL compliant'. So, during the RFP process the partner showed some ITIL certificates, these indicated that somebody had done something with an ITIL course and had achieved some level of ITIL certification. The contract was closed, and the operation started. Service levels were agreed, (# calls per category and response times), reporting was agreed and procedures exchanged. It soon became evident that these service levels did not cover all the parties involved. It appeared that there were more parties in the chain than were actually covered by the contract. Subsequently, the involved parties had differing interpretations of response time. On top of this, calls dispatched to other parties were not monitored. Needless to say, the idyllic partnership between the hot blooded, yet modest, Indian dream princess and the, cool, enchanting, Scandinavian prince started to show some dents. A solution was sought and found! If the

amount of calls exceeded a certain level, they would undertake a service review to look for the root causes, just as the ITIL doctor ordered!!

After examining the results of these reviews, they found that it was very hard to determine root causes, since there was no proper registration to enable investigation. Furthermore, it no longer seemed very important to the management of the Telco. They had already moved their attention elsewhere to another part of the operations, because the objective of outsourcing was to focus on the core business. Therefore whatever was outsourced was not core business and did not merit attention."

What to do about it:

Paul: "For a while, the manager responsible for this outsourced service did not quite know how to deal with the situation. On the one hand there was this problem of services that were not achieved according the agreements, on the other hand nobody seemed to care. It nagged her until she went to take the ITIL service manager course. And by building knowledge and insight into the relationships between the processes, she started to understand how to ask the proper questions to both management and the outsourcing provider. She also understood that the processes of the two departments within the same service needed to be aligned. She realized that ITIL is not a general, 'one size fits all' solution. She grasped the essence of incident management in relation to problem management, and the significance of a proper call registration.

She understood the importance of a realistic, relevant and measurable service level agreement. But most of all she learned that there is not such a thing as 'ITIL compliant'. So, after asking questions about the ITIL compliancy of the outsourcing partner, she was shown a couple of foundation certificates of people who may, or may not, be involved in running the service for her company. She discovered that the certificate doesn't necessarily mean that people know how to successfully USE ITIL procedures to really manage the service, as opposed to be able to write procedures that don't add value, or procedures that are not followed. She has learnt that, in future outsourcing deals, the selection on the evidenced ability to deliver according ITIL practises is much more important in the negotiation and transition phase. The outcome is that a qualified (which may not necessarily mean the same as certified) service manager is now able to conduct an assessment on the delivery teams of the partner. By having this assessment it truly shows if the partner is 'talking the walk' or 'walking the talk'."

We also conducted a mini survey on the itSMF website using this card. Our statement was 'ITIL training and certification does not adequately address ABC'. 94% of respondents agreed. Admittedly, as Sharon Taylor pointed out, the survey was hardly a proper one, it served more as a way of showing the perception of the ITIL public. Those wanting to adopt and deploy ITIL, currently perceive ITIL training and certification as inadequate.

Sharon Taylor, Chief Architect for ITIL V3 and Chief Examiner, responded to this worst practice issue and explained what the future holds for us.

"I think that the survey shows people that ABC is very critical to the success of ITSM. Where it falls down is in making broad assumptions about V3 training when no respondent has knowledge of the outcome in this regard, since it isn't being used yet. The passing quote demonstrates nicely that the level of awareness about how much content IS in the guidance has not yet reached mainstream awareness.

Let me clarify how ABC will be dealt with. There are two ways that ABC's are dealt with in V3 Qualification:

1. Firstly through the curriculum – the syllabus and examinations cover ABC through learning modules for organization and culture. Your survey respondents are perhaps not quite familiar with all the core books, since each covers organization and cultural practices, and the syllabi and exams will cover this at the intermediate and higher levels. Particular focus is paid in ST and CSI in the lifecycle, and RCV in the capability, but all deal with it to some extent, because it is so important.
2. How training is delivered in the classroom. The V3 scheme, will help improve the focus of ABC in curriculum delivery by mandating specific criteria for what is delivered, how it is weighted in the syllabus and the hours trainers are expected to spend on the topic. This is new to V3, and is a more rigorous standards-based approach than we have seen in past.

Each module will undergo its own CSI cycle (the Foundation is preparing for its now). This will allow the scheme to evolve and grow with customer needs....So even if surveys are flawed, and most are, perception is still important and the qualifications can respond and improve."

So we can see. The experts also agree having a certificate is one thing, but proven ability to realize organizational change is something else. The good news is that ITIL V3 training and certification will eventually address ABC needs. Ask your training provider how they will help you with ABC!

Other related cards are:

- King of Clubs 'ITIL is the objective....not what it should achieve';
- Jack of Hearts 'A process flow and some procedures are all you need';
- 8 of Diamonds 'We're going to install ITIL. It can't be that hard'.

2 of Diamonds

'Measuring our value contribution'

Despite what we profess, we are still poor at measuring our value contribution to strategy. Take a look at the example in the 8 of Clubs. A recent Parity report also declared: *'Only 27% of IT managers have directly measured the return on investment from ITIL implementations, and under half measured the value that IT service management delivered to their business.'*

A Compass report entitled *Can the CIO justify the investment in ITIL?* also revealed in response to the question 'To what extent are you able to able to express the relationship between ITIL maturity and IT performance' that 72% of respondents declared having some form of measures but no linkage.

The cartoon in the card shows the CEO talking to the IT director about the 'key performance indicators', particularly the KPI 'reduction in the number of incidents'. The IT director displays his graph which clearly shows a significant reduction. The CEO says "....closing the Help Desk between 09:00 and 17:00 isn't what I had in mind!...."

There is a lot of text now in this section to describe this card and give examples. Why is this? In a recent workshop at an itSMF Best Practice conference, teams were asked to select the top three worst practice cards that applied to their organizations. The results of all the teams were consolidated. There were two, equal top scoring cards. One was ***this card***.

Van Haren Publishing also conducted a poll in its own website, at the same time, on the following statement:

"The senior business management in my organization understand and act on our IT metrics reports."

72% disagreed and **28%** agreed.

This also shows that this worst practice is in serious need of resolving. Two other high scoring cards in our ABC workshop were:

• IT not seen as an added-value partner.
• Neither partner makes an effort to understand the other.

This confirms for us that before we can successfully 'demonstrate' we have IT under control, we must resolve this measuring and steering dilemma. Before we can resolve this, we MUST enage with the business. However, first we must create an attitude of 'trust' within the business, and to create that trust we need to eliminate the worst practices within our IT organizations.

The results above undeniably show that we implement ITIL without a clear idea of how it will contribute to value. In one of our worst practice articles we also took a slanted, simplistic look at service design. We know, we know! Service Design does go on to talk about measurement design.

> **"Many designs fail through a lack of planning and management....Preparing and Planning the effective and efficient use of the four P's." (ITIL V3)**
> People, Process, Product and Partner. It then struck me. We missed a 'P'. A bucket full of expert authors, an advisory group, a football stadium full of QA experts, all missed a small power point ball that, when introduced in ITIL V2, received worldwide QA acclaim as finally getting the point and being seen as added value. Indeed the Service Strategy book labored the point. ...the P for Performance (value), the why.

We suggested that the model of the 4 P's indeed missed the additional ball that should be first.

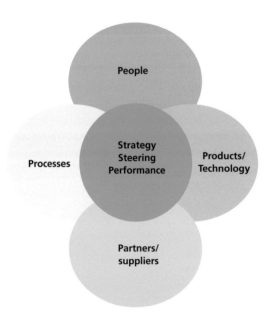

What this diagram reveals is before you change any of the 4 P's you should firstly go through the 'Performance' ball. The value. The 'why are we doing ITIL'. It should then cascade down and give a clear shared set of goals to those involved in the People, Product, Process or Partner initiatives.

In our worst practice article we set a challenge to the readers. We declared we still suspect there is no shared view amongst management teams as to what 'value' ITIL should be delivering. If you wish to prove us wrong then try the challenge. OK, so what is it? Take the following Joker card and try the challenge with your IT management team, or any other IT team for that matter. (See example exercises in Chapter 7, ABC card set case and examples.)

Challenge:
This is the one of the Joker cards from our new card game. Get all of your senior IT managers together in a room. Put this cartoon on the table. It is the CEO card from our game. Get each manager at the same time to write down on a piece of paper what he KNOWS that the business is demanding as a result of applying ITIL. Not what he thinks. After five minutes discuss the findings.

If everybody came up with the same answer and it really is what the business wants, then nominate yourselves to be a speaker at the nearest itSMF event and tell everybody how you achieved this. If all the answers are different and you conclude you don't really KNOW, then do something about finding out what it is the business wants. **This is another great attitude we have. We THINK we know what the business needs. And if we don't KNOW, then what are we currently measuring?**

Characteristics:

- There are numerous KPI's being reported on, does anybody know who uses them?
- Do you KNOW who uses the KPI reports?
- Can you give examples of actions taken as a result of any KPI reports?
- If action was taken, was a check subsequently done to ensure it had the desired, measurable and demonstrable effect?
- Can you demonstrate a link between IT KPI's and business goals and business strategy? Can anybody in IT? Ask the senior IT manager to tell you the link.

And if you still don't believe us, here are some cases from practitioners in the field, who felt an urge to elaborate upon this card.

The first case is from **Gary Case**, Pink Elephant, one of the authors of the 'Continual Service Improvement' book. This example comes from Canada, The second case is from **Stephane Vleeshouwer**, Senior Consultant IT Service Management", CTG, Luxemburg.

Gary Case:
"ITIL says that we must do reporting, so by golly we will. Unfortunately this is the attitude many organizations take when implementing ITIL. There is no thought process around what should be measured to show value and how IT is supporting the organization's strategic goals and objectives.

One organization had 22 incident management reports that were produced each month and distributed to a group of senior managers. There was never any follow up or discussion around what was being measured, or even on the performance of the incident management process. The monthly process was simply, measure, create report, ship report and ignore, to be repeated 12 times each year. There was no comparison of achievements, service level breaches or anything. No analysis was performed to understand trends, or if the trends were good or bad.

One organization that this consultant worked with even had recipes and cartoons buried in the middle of their reports because they knew no one read the reports. Well maybe they read the recipes if they were any good......

Reporting is one of the strategic decisions that is required as part of any ITIL journey. Measuring and reporting should provide an organization with the ability to make strategic, tactical or operations decisions based on the information reported. This means that the reports actually have to be looked at and someone has to be prepared to make decisions.

Some key questions to help move in this direction are:

• What information do we need in order to show that we are supporting the business goals and objectives and enabling business outcomes?
• What information do you need to plan for the next 6 – 12 months?
• What information do you need to ensure compliance to following the process?
• What information do you need to coordinate your team around coordinating the work schedule, identifying new training requirements etc?
• What information do you need to ensure that our process is both efficient and effective?

Many organizations create a single report that goes out to all the various stakeholder groups, such as the business, senior IT management and IT managers at different levels. One large financial organization would create a 50-plus page report each month that all of the above groups received.

Each group will have their own set of interests. The business is primarily interested in whether IT provided what they said they would provide in a cost effective manner. Senior IT management will be interested in the same information, but also in seeing trends, what led to the results, what improvements can be made to improve service delivery, and the management of IT costs. IT managers at different levels will use reporting information to make operational type decisions such as scheduling, coordinating, training, or review of key volumes such as handling of change requests and incidents."

So how do you get it to work?

"Process owners and process managers need to take ownership on the development and implementation of the management information framework that will include the monitoring, measuring and reporting of metrics. They also need to work with the business to truly understand what is important to them as well as the senior IT leadership. A well thought out and implemented management information framework will help the IT organization to understand how they enable business outcomes and can be linked directly to supporting the business strategy, goals and objectives. It will also allow IT to continue to monitor and improve the overall health of the IT processes.

If you find it difficult to get the business or senior IT leadership to define what is important to them, than here are some tips you can pursue:

- Get the process owner to define three to five key performance indicators, and only report on these.
- Only report on what is in an existing SLA. For incident management this often isn't much more than a response time, repair time and perhaps system / service availability. However, I would encourage you to report in business terms and not in IT terms, i.e., number of outages, duration of outages, instead of 99.996%.
- Quit sending the reports for one month and see what the reaction is. Perhaps this will open up the discussions.
- Remove one report per month until someone says "didn't we used to get…", now you have something to discuss.

Of course before removing reports it is best to get agreement with the business and senior IT leadership on what are feasible and valuable key performance indicators and activity metrics. Since an organization may be used to getting lots and lots of reports, you may need to have a game plan on how to respond when the business complains about not getting the same volume of information that they used to get. Some techniques you can use:

- Provide a cost summary of what is required to measure and create the reports each month. In terms of man hours and technical requirements, this can be substantial. Some organizations will spend many days preparing reports that are basically ignored.
- Be prepared to discuss with the business and senior IT leadership how they use the report information.

A Government organization reviewed the current incident management reports and, working with the steering committee, got agreement on what the top five measurements were at the time. It really wasn't that hard to get agreement on the top five, as everyone recognized that there were far too many reports that were not being managed at all. It was simply taking time each month to create the reports.

The decision on what were the top five reports was focused around what was important to the business. The Mean Time to Repair (MTTR) report, which was based on the different priority levels, was one of the first reports created. They always had a MTTR report, but it wasn't broken down by priority. They quickly saw that they were doing pretty well with three out of the four priority levels, but that they really needed to improve in one level where they were consistently experiencing issues in terms of meeting the service level objectives. Another report was specific information on service level objective breaches.

The steering committee was made up of a Deputy CIO, IT directors and representation from the business.

The incident management team would provide the steering committee with an overview report that focused on key trends, actual results against KPI's, a description of what led to the results and any actions, taken or planned, designed to improve performance.

It is always a struggle to get management to buy into the concept that sometimes less is more and this is true with reporting, especially when you are first getting started. As stated before, when management understands the amount of effort and cost associated with measuring and reporting, they will have a tendency to agree to cut back. Selecting only a few KPI's will help an organization to focus on its ability to monitor, measure and report. As the organization becomes more proficient at these few items, they can continue to add more on as the process and organization matures. However, it is important to show the cost of monitoring, measuring and reporting on many items in relation to the value this brings. As with many decisions in IT, it will often come down to a cost benefit analysis.

In order to be able to measure and report on how IT contributes to the business strategy and provides value, it is important that IT actually understands the business strategy, goals and objectives. Sadly, this is still missing today in some organizations."

Stephane Vleeshouwer, CTG

"In most of the ITIL projects I have worked on, there was no IT value analysis framework in place that allowed positioning of the project against the value drivers of the company.

The only positioning was a statement and small speech by the project sponsor at the kick off meeting, telling everybody how convinced he was about the importance of the ITIL for the IT organization, and claiming he would follow the project closely. So, there were no quantified objectives, no specific link to any business value driver, and no translation of the 'importance' into KPI's that could make people aware of their value contribution or actually demonstrate that value.

Quantifying the contribution of an ITIL implementation to the enterprise bottom line is more tricky than for a front office application like a new B2C (Business to Customer) portal. An ITIL support process, for example, has only an indirect contribution to the business and then, often in combination with other processes like incident and change management. To decide if a process performance is 'key' to the value of IT for the business depends on the service architecture; to put it roughly, no service architecture, no IT value measurement.

Let me give an example

A customer had been advised by an audit to improve its incident and change management processes together with the implementation of a CMDB and problem and release management processes.

The scope had actually been defined by the audit, and the company had translated the audit recommendation into 'a product centric" project': "we need a migration of our current system to a tool including a CMDB".

Reaching the end of the second project iteration, the following conversation took place:

Customer project manager: "Good, we are well on track for the implementation of the ITIL support processes, the workshops gave us the buy-in of our support staff and the iterative tool customisation done in parallel convinced our service management organization with concrete business cases. Can you now provide us with 'some KPI's'?"

CTG project manager: "As you know a reporting phase is foreseen in our planning. But the content is not out of-the-shelf, your reporting needs are supposed to be analysed."

Customer project manager: "I understand, but I have a directors' meeting next week and they asked me to explain how the money we spent on the ITIL processes was going to increase the customer satisfaction of our critical business services."

CTG project manager: "I see, you're talking about quantifying the value not only of the processes freshly implemented, but from the IT functions and activities supporting those business processes. We will firstly have to draw the architecture linking all our ITSM artefacts (configuration items, processes, functions, customers, roles…) to this business service."

Customer project manager: "What are you talking about? 10 minutes ago you showed us several reports straight from the tool, can't you simply put this in a presentation and make it 'directors' board understandable'?"

CTG project manager: "Hum…I suppose I can do that, but…"

As in many ITIL projects, the business management buy-in had been neglected. The customer project manager assumed that the obvious metrics generated by the system management tool automating the ITIL processes was good enough for business KPI's, while those are only 'indicators' of a particular process.

What was done to break down this ABC?

To overcome this potential conflict on the business-focused KPI's and the outcome of the ITIL deployment, we had to balance the work done in process design, training of the support staff and tool customization, with a conceptual model of a metrics hierarchy to enable the management to trace the performance of their support and delivery organization against its contribution to the business.

Such a model is all about building a **common language** for all of the stakeholders, from the network engineers to the customer account manager. It cannot be taken 'off-the-shelf' and is more a journey, **involving a wide range of stakeholders**, than a one shot.

We took a pragmatic approach which looked at the complete value delivery chain (network, server, application, database, IT service, business process), defining for each layer the objects (configuration items, services, events…) concerned, their relationships and the process metrics (incident, alarm, service breach, availability, critical operations messages…) attached to each object type.

The definition of the objects and their properties was constructed iteratively during several workshops, involving all of the stakeholder groups, allowing us to build a semantic network from top to bottom of the stack; one that had **buy-in**, **understanding** and **commitment** from all groups.

Once we had reached a simplified model focusing on one critical business process, a Cognos specialist from the customer staff was able to construct the first set of reports based on the extracted data from the system management tool database. A few KPI's based on a hierarchy of metrics were made available to a management team that were now well aware of their significance and the connection with the metrics and events all down the IT stack.

Each function (service desk, availability, capacity) was also provided with indicators and their contribution to the upper KPI's result. In this way all staff were made aware of how their roles and activities contributed ultimately to business value.

Lessons learned
Whatever methodology you choose (Balanced Scorecard, Economic Value Added, home tailored improvement dashboard…), keep in mind that the goal of IT valuation is to draw a direct line between the IT investment in ITIL processes and the enterprise bottom line. In fact every project should be managed in line with these success factors.

When the customer has no clue about a method for measuring IT value, check with the project sponsor what he has in mind in terms of 'producing some KPI's' and act on it.

When one talks about improving the performance, defining a baseline data against which to measure progress is part of the project! Also, it means ensuring that all involved in the realization of value need to know what it is and how their tasks and activities contribute to that value."

Other related cards are:

- 2 of Clubs 'NO respect for, or understanding of users';
- 5 of Clubs 'Neither partner makes an effort to understand the other';
- 8 of Clubs 'IT thinks it doesn't have to understand the business to make a business case';
- Jack of Clubs 'Let's outsource the business – we'd be better off';
- Queen of Clubs 'No understanding of business priority and impact';
- King of Diamonds 'IT strategy's contribution to business strategy';
- 2 of Spades 'Them and us culture – opposing and competing forces';
- 4 of Spades 'Internally focused';
- 4 of Hearts 'The best way to improve services is to outsource…..the business!';
- 7 of Hearts 'Demand and give. I demand and you give in!';
- 8 of Hearts 'The buck stops anywhere but here';
- The Joker 'Unable to specify the VALUE required by the business';
- The Joker 'IT as a business enabler & differentiator (not)'.

Business users....making
the most of the technology
available to them!....

Too little business
involvement in requirements
specification & testing

3 of Diamonds

'Too little business involvement in requirements specification and testing'

A Standish report from a few years ago is obviously outdated as far as percentage figures go, but we are prepared to bet that the figures are still embarrassingly high. The report back then said something like 28% of IT development projects get into live use and, after two years, only about 8% are still in use. One of the reasons for this is lack of business involvement during design and testing. The business is too busy to spend time on these tasks, the business is too busy doing important 'businessy' things that business people do....obviously more important than throwing millions of dollars away on wasted IT investments.

Any CIO who can capture and demonstrate the amount of down time, unproductive hours and wasted money resulting from these badly run business-related projects has a good business case for improving IT governance. This is, after all, poor IT governance from the business. The business must also change its attitude and its behavior in the responsible use of IT and the IT budget. The cartoon on this card shows a computer screen with various 'post-it' stickers on it. Showing a lack of 'use' of the system to support the business workflow and decision making.

Characteristics:

- The business doesn't have time to be involved in requirements definition, that is IT's job!?
- The business doesn't have time for all that testing!
- IT projects are for IT people, the business only needs to be involved when IT has made a mess of IT!
- Does the business have a mechanism for agreeing the priority of IT projects and initiatives?
- Are IT projects evaluated to include business and IT success and fail indicators? Does this reveal lack of business involvement?
- Can you identify costly, embarrassing cases where lack of business involvement has caused massive wasted costs or downtime? Is the CEO aware of this?
- How often are systems backed out or urgent changes required because of insufficient business involvement and testing?

We have two cases here. One is based upon feedback given to us by a customer. The second case comes from **Dr. ir. Walter Servaes**, Senior Project Manager", CTG, Belgium.

Case:

"One CIO from a large global sports-related company was getting frustrated by the way business demands and business involvement, or rather lack of it, was damaging business performance. This was what made this CIO somewhat of a unique creature in my experience; everything I heard him say as he explained the situation was in terms of business production outages, business supply chain problems, time to shop delivery of new goods. This was a CIO who understood the business consequences and business risks. However business unit managers would override his initiatives to structure the demand side, so that IT could effectively manage business risks and help deliver business value. "We are the business, we know best, you work for US!"

The CIO gathered facts and figures relating to IT outages caused as a result of poor business prioritization and business involvement. He translated this into wasted costs, lost revenue and unproductive business hours, as a result of continually reprioritizing projects and resources, and the amount of down time and post implementation changes that could have been prevented by user involvement in testing. He presented this, in business terms, to the CEO who was shocked. They say a picture paints a thousand words, you can also say 'facts and figures, in terms of business revenue and business risks are what make business managers work'.

The facts and figures caused the CEO to make changes to the ownership of business applications, to make changes to the way in which IT project were prioritized, and the way in which systems were accepted, rolled out successfully and with lower wastage of IT costs. The CEO said to each of the business unit managers: "Any IT project with the highest priority comes first to my desk to be signed off. If I don't see how this fits with our company strategic priorities we will have a serious discussion." The amount of urgent IT releases reduced from more than 80 to 11.

This shows that the CIO got buy-in because he understood and communicated in business terms and not IT terms. He managed to get the trust of the CEO by demonstrating an understanding of how IT contributes to value and how risks of IT need to be mitigated."

Case:

Walter Servaes of CTG describes a case from Belgium.
"A medium-sized financial development bank decided to simplify its major business processes, namely the handling of loans and contracts. The entire lifecycle from the creation to the final agreed contract was very complex and labour-intensive due to a lot of manual input, mismatching systems and inconsistent reporting tools. Since the company was growing fast and the current way of processing was no longer suitable and profitable, the need for an automated system became apparent which would ease the process of collecting and processing data. After several missed and lost contracts it became clear that a major process reengineering could not be postponed any longer. Further delay was unacceptable and could seriously harm business affairs and reputation.

The IT department became responsible for the entire project. A steering committee under the presidency of the IT director sat together every two months. Only the managers of the departments were involved and the IT project manager would attend this meeting regularly. In-house developers and some 'friendly' users would be involved in the development and testing process, for which only aging technology was available. Specialists were hired to develop a new CRM package and install a common reporting tool, with the creation of no more than 40 standard reports. Users should be able to design their own reports.

For insiders it was obvious that this project was doomed to fail and several warnings to the company's management lead to nothing. After three years of struggling with old hardware, no commitment whatsoever from the user team (no time, on holiday, sick leave, no interest), two new IT directors and six new project managers, several budget reviews and too many discussions later, there was no doubt this project was a big 'fiasco'. Working for IT in those days was like living in hell. The only progress made was in a new CRM-package and a common Business Objects Reporting tool.

With the appointment of a new CEO things started to change very drastically. After some very heated discussions in several management meetings the decision was taken to immediately stop the ongoing project and to start all over again under very strict conditions. A very good decision was taken to start the new project from a business perspective and no longer solely as an IT concern. A clear vision on establishing user requirements, user involvement and full commitment of the company's top management ushered a totally different approach, which finally resulted in a successful project closure.

A steering committee was formed, with all involved parties under the presidency of the CEO. A project business task group was created reporting directly to the CEO, and several project leaders for the distinctive development, testing and acceptance phases, became responsible for the whole project. Reports on progress had to be delivered regularly as a result of bi-weekly meetings. A user task group with members from the different departments became strongly involved in the designing and the testing process. Testing, acceptance and production criteria were strictly formalized and documented. The development and testing teams consisted of more than 40 developers and key users. Standard reports were built and the users were no longer allowed to build their own reports, except for a very few key users under strict change management rules. Strictly followed migration procedures and schedules, solid agreed milestones and GO/NO-GO moments were the key success factors for this project.

A direct, strictly orchestrated and completely different project approach, heavy business involvement and the strong commitment of senior business managers, users and IT, and a very thorough change and release management process all combined to result in a project success and closure within 10 months. Some minor issues were handled in a follow-up period of three months."

Both of these cases show CEO commitment is necessary to change the way the business behaves in respect to business demand management and business involvement. In both cases it takes visibility into the negative consequences to stimulate the business to take its own governance role seriously, and in both cases the business implemented some governance mechanisms. The governance mechanisms alone were not enough to bring success, it required an attitude change and leadership to make it happen.

Other related cards are:

- 5 of Diamonds 'No management commitment';
- 6 of Diamonds 'Everything has the highest priority…according to the users';
- 7 of Diamonds 'Throwing solutions over the wall and HOPING that people will use them';
- Queen of Spades 'Not my responsibility';
- King of Hearts 'Which part of NO didn't you understand';
- 7 of Hearts 'Demand and give. I demand and you give in!'.

4 of Diamonds

'Not capturing the right knowledge'

The good news is that knowledge management is a new ITIL V3 process. The bad news is that the attitude and behavior we now display to knowledge capture and sharing isn't working, and there is little in ITIL V3 that addresses how to change this.

We were going to remove this cartoon from our presentations until a manager came up to us afterwards and said, "That happened to us last week, a financial system went down and was down for two hours. This was highly visible and very costly...It had happened before. The IT people looked in the system for the previous incident and the resolution captured in the tool was 'Fixed', not what was actually done..". This is a small example of not recording. Another example is when support people stop filling in fields in a tool and there is no reaction! "Nobody does anything with it so why bother recording it!" was the statement. This is an example of how a tool was installed and customized without finding the owners of the information or processes. It was never really defined what the tasks, roles and responsibilities were. What information was required, by who, to do the tasks and carry out the responsibilities and then ensure the information was made available in the tool to support the tasks and the decision making responsibilities. It is all common sense, We know. But you will be surprised at how many tool implementations and customizations are based upon "That is what ITIL says we need to record, so we'll record that", or "This is what the tool implementation built."

The cartoon on the card shows a technologist sitting in front of a keyboard. He has received a task to record something he KNOWS that will help his colleagues, He types something in and then proudly reads back what he has recorded: "Let the telephone ring long enough and the users will eventually give up and stop bothering you!.....".

Characteristics:

- Is the knowledge that is often captured in tools inadequate?
- Does everybody use the available tools to record knowledge?
- Is anybody responsible for defining what needs to be captured?
- Does anybody feel responsible if knowledge is out of date or inaccurate?
- Is the capturing knowledge only done when there are no other tasks open?
- Do people see this as a waste of time?

Other related cards are:

- 3 of Clubs 'Knowledge is power;
- Jack of Diamonds 'Saying yes but meaning no':
- Jack of Spades 'Avoidance culture';
- Queen of Spades 'Not my responsibility'.

5 of Diamonds

'No management commitment'

No management commitment

This is another of our favorites. This is also one of the most widely asked for cartoons in our set, together with the 2 of Clubs. This is the cartoon that often gets pinned up on the notice board somewhere in an organization. It has a lot to do with 'leadership', managers 'walking-the-talk', about 'making change happen', 'facilitating so that change can happen', 'when the going gets tough the tough get going…..right out the door!'.

There is a difference between involvement and commitment. Ken Wilson had a great quote about this is the early days when he was Director of Pink Elephant in the UK. "Commitment and involvement is just like a fried English breakfast of bacon and eggs!"…..The audience looked at him as if he was cracking up. "The chicken was 'involved' (laid the eggs), the pig was committed (gave up its life for it)". The point is that commitment means sometimes giving things up, feeling pain and suffering, being there in good and bad times.

The cartoon on the card shows an IT employee having just made a proposal to the IT manager for an ITIL improvement initiative. The manager replies to the request: "You have my full commitment,. Apart from time, money, effort, and just so long as I don't have to be involved."

Characteristics:

- Do managers present for two minutes at the start of an initiative and are then never seen again?
- Do managers enable and empower people to really adopt and deploy ITIL? E.g adequate resources, time, attention?
- If people fail to follow procedures or work against the change, do managers openly address people and confront them with their behavior?
- Do managers avoid conflict and take the easy route?

We have four cases to support this. The first is from Sharon Taylor, well known throughout the whole ITIL community. The second one is from Ken Wendel, well known in the States and in itSMF international. The third is from Bartosz Górczy ski, a founding champion of ITIL in Poland, and now chairman of the itSMF. The fourth is from David Bathiely Fernandez, a champion for ABC in Spain.

Sharon Taylor, Chief Architect of ITIL V3 and Chief Examiner, who also provided a short piece in response to the question about the importance of ABC.

"...Likely more important than any system, tool, framework or method. The best practices in the world don't work if people are not committed to them and do not espouse the ABCs that are needed to bring frameworks, tools and systems to life. ABC is simply human behavior and there are many examples in life of how we sabotage the usefulness and value of best practices. Here's one: The fitness equipment market has done their ABC homework! Statistics show that most people who invest in fitness equipment never get an ROI on that investment, because after the initial exhilaration wears off, the equipment collects dust in a dark corner. Why do we see marketing campaigns for diets and exercise programs increase in frequency around the holidays? This plays to our ABC, and of course the wallets of the marketeers! Think of a service management framework as gymnasium. Everything in the gym has the potential to make you fit, healthy, and increase your life expectancy (your ROI). But never using the gymnasium or committing to the changes it requires of you to use it will provide no benefit. Commitment to the program improves the chances of success and renders a by-product of a changed ABC!

Now we all fall off bicycles occasionally and because we are human we have to sometimes coerce ourselves to get back on. In service management this is continual improvement; recognizing the realities of how good or bad we are at riding the bicycle, and learning how to improve it. That also improves the 'fitness' of our ABC."

Other cards that are relevant to this are:

- 9 of Clubs 'Walking the talk';
- King of Spades' '(not) Empowering people';
- 10 of Clubs 'No respect for, or trust in management'.

This can arise as a kind of naïve, or gullible belief that ITIL can be easily 'installed or implemented'. The following cards may be symptomatic of this:

- 7 of Clubs 'My TOOL will solve ALL your ITSM problems;';
- 8 of Diamonds 'We're going to INSTALL ITIL…it can't be that hard.

Ken Wendle, Client Engagement Manager, HP Education Services and a well known and respected member of the ITSM community. Member of the itSMF International Board of Directors.

Ken took some time out of his busy schedule to share some of his insights into the ABC of ICT. I asked Ken a couple of questions. The first was, "How important is ABC to service management?"

Ken: "It's important, but I guess it's no more important for IT than it is for good business practice overall. Excellent companies facilitate creating the right attitude, rewarding customer focused behavior and creating a culture of personal responsibility. Historically, however, we in IT have fallen short in creating a customer focused attitude and of rewarding behavior. As far as personal responsibility and accountability is concerned, well, let's just say historically it's not been one of IT's greatest strengths.

Fortunately, ITIL V3 has brought out more than V2 did, especially in regards to the need to choose the right metrics to help reinforce direction and correct behavior. V2 focused on all kinds of metrics and things to measure but not the 'why', with V3 we are now forcing people to think about the 'why' and shifting our attitude towards the business and business value.

I also believe in the power of rewarding good behavior. With metrics you have to be careful about what you reward and what metrics you use. Peter Drucker said that "what gets measured gets done".

Tom Peters took that a step further, stating that what gets rewarded REALLY gets done. It's no secret that getting people to buy-in, change their attitudes and behavior is difficult, at best. Management has both the carrot but also the stick; that is, rewarding people for desirable behavior and punishing people for undesirable behavior when necessary. Let's not forget undesirable behavior, such as failing to follow agreed change procedures, can have severe, unacceptable business consequences and create business risk. Sometimes I ask, "how many people do you have to fire for not following, for example, the established change process?" The answer, of course, is "only one", however you need to use the stick sparingly. It's better to use incentives, and often the best incentive is the pride of doing the right things and doing them well."

I then asked "Which ABC worst practice springs out as being the one that most needs resolving?"

"Let me think about THAT…The card that really caught my eye was the 'commitment' card. The senior manager saying "you have my FULL commitment, apart from time, money, and just so long as I don't have to be involved!". This is one I instantly recognize. 'C' level commitment is a major issue, so little top executive buy-in, they fail to see how far-reaching an ITSM initiative is and what it can deliver to the business."

I then asked Ken "What about a practical tip for resolving this?". Many of the readers will instantly recognize this and say "I have been banging my head against a brick wall trying to get our executives to buy-in, how do YOU do it?"

"I'm a great believer in keeping things simple, hand them a pocket book, or slide it under their door…sometimes simple things work because you've got to remember that 'C' level managers get a lot of sales reps and people demanding their time, they tend to protect themselves, but sometimes when trying to protect themselves from the 'bad' they also fail to get the 'good' ideas. Another issue is where the message is coming FROM. If it is an internal IT person trying to sell the idea, companies often don't listen to their own people, so sometimes it's a good idea to bring in an outside 'expert' with credibility…Let them do the sales pitch and then endorse your ideas. There is an old saying that 'an expert is somebody from out-of-town carrying a briefcase'. Getting an external expert with recognized credibility can help, even though they are saying exactly the same things you are saying."

I asked Ken to respond from his position within itSMF International about the importance of ABC, and how itSMF will help its members recognize and address this.

"I believe we in the itSMF need to help people focus on the fundamentals, the basics. You need to be able to walk before you can run. ABC is part of the basics. ABC is something we need to be aware of, something we need to do and something we need to do well."

Bartosz Górczyński, Partner CT Partners and chairman itSMF Poland. Bartosz was a champion and promoter of ITIL in Poland from the very beginning when people asked 'What is ITIL?'.

"We like ITIL V2 and ITIL V3 because they give a holistic approach combining People, Process and Technology, balanced to achieve quality and effectiveness for IT organizations. However 'People' is key. You can have perfect technology, that is easy. There are many great solutions. There are many highly competent consulting companies ready, willing and able to develop and implement processes. Many IT organizations are capable of doing it themselves. But neither of these will work without motivated, well trained and happy People.

A key element in helping companies successfully adopt and deploy ITIL in our approach is Apollo 13. This enables us to create a big change in ABC. It creates buy-in, helps show how behavior impacts positive results and helps shape a culture change when played with all IT employees. Why Apollo 13? It not only helps transfer knowledge about ITIL but also lets people see, feel and experience what it means and what ITIL can do.

The ABC cards are also an effective instrument. Why? We can make an actual case relating to each and every card. We come across these types of ABC issues in every ITIL project. The cards help us to address ABC challenges and worst practices in a more interactive and attractive way.

I was asked to choose the most important card in the set. After Paul asked me which card is key from my perspective, I spent two hours thinking about this. Plenty of the cards show really big IT issues. But at the end of this I decided to select that the 5 of Diamonds. 'No management commitment'."

Case:

"This card shows the most difficult situation we observe in IT departments. One possible scenario is when the IT manager shows this behavior in front of his team who are proposing improvements and initiatives. We see many IT managers who pretend they care about employees' opinions. The IT manager manages the organization personally without any input, advice or suggestions from the employees. They demonstrate no trust toward their people. They do not motivate, cut the employees' development budgets, think only about their careers.

The second scenario is the behavior of business people who are not really involved and committed. This leads to a lack of IT-business understanding, ultimately to a 'them and us culture' and IT is seen as the 'administrator of the infrastructure' not as a 'value creator'. The result is total misunderstanding on the part of both parties, blaming each other, no communication and no common efforts. At the end of the day both IT and the business are unhappy and the level of support that IT services deliver is really low."

How can we overcome this particular worst practice?

"All of the above are related to the 'People' element of ITSM. Key elements are:

- Selection criteria for IT managers. IT manager selection should be based upon a modern manager, happy to work with the business and his people.
- Business leaders who see value in IT services and are open to discuss the role of IT and the levels of services they expect.

Everything starts at the Board level. They should govern the company, deciding on the roles and department strategies, and the selection of managers able to align IT and IT people with those governance decisions.

Then we need time to create the team work spirit, communication between employees, to select the right people or to change them, time to discuss the ways and levels of cooperation.

So what would be my advice for the IT manager? Spend 60% of your time on the communication with the business, teach them and create the right relationships. Spend 35% time on communication with your people, in an open way, closely, friendly, but based on clear rules and expectations. The last 5% is yours."

David Bathiely Fernandez ,Telefónica Soluciones, Spain

David was unable to make time in his hectic schedule to write a piece. However, after numerous attempted telephone calls and emails we managed an interview.

How important is the ABC for IT Service management? (Many people think it is all about frameworks or tools.)

"It is simply crucial. The most common mistake is indeed to assume that implementing the right framework will solve all problems and make us better.

This is quite simply unrealistic! The right tool in the wrong hands is soon rendered useless. A quote I particularly like from the ABC cartoons is "A fool with a TOOL is still a FOOL!". It is true not only for all these wonderful management tools we are so fond of in IT departments, but also when it comes to put into practice any process- oriented service management system.

ITIL, as a self declared best practice framework, often warns about the importance of senior management commitment and cultural change, the first thing that needs adjustment is leadership, senior management need to initiate cultural change and follow-up. Attitude and behavior are a direct result of upper management behavior.

In short, no process, no framework, no tools are going to sort out our problems or allow us to improve if the people actually performing don't understand the cultural change, and don't adopt a different attitude and behavior."

We have had ITIL and CobiT and the frameworks for a number of years, still organizations are struggling to improve. Which ABC worst practice is the one that needs resolving the most according to you?

"In large organizations it is often easy to come across most of the "worst practices" in the cartoons. However, the first issues we need to face in our organizations are with no doubt the "Not my responsibility" generic response and the fact that "Process managers have no authority".

Spain is a country where hierarchy is not just mere a word. The chain of command is the central component of the organization; moreover it is essential to comprehend it if you want to be able to simply perform your daily tasks, or even to obtain relevant information for your job. It is not uncommon for people to refer to different areas of the organization by the name of its head: "Pablo works with/for Juan Gonzalez" instead of "Pablo works in the legal department" or "Jose is with Pedro Alvarez" instead of "Jose works in the network department". Fundamentally, people are much more important than the organization itself, which is an excellent thing, to a certain degree; the problem is that only people above a certain position really matter.

From that point on, it's easy to understand that a functional organization, where process managers can retain some kind of responsibility or 'power', as it is seen, has little chance to survive. At the same time, process owners/managers can't feel responsible for the outcome of their process when the ones who hang on to the responsibility are the line managers.

The next worst thing is probably "Management commitment". As demands rise from the market, customers and potential clients requesting ITIL processes, or even ISO 20000 certifications, pressure grows internally for implementing processes and, at the same time, reducing costs, without a real understanding of the implications of such a project.

We tend to pursue the wrong objective: get the ISO 20000 and not improve our service quality or reduce our operational costs."

"If You Don't Know Where You're Going, Any Road Will Get You There." - Alice In Wonderland by Jack Donohue.

What practical advice can you give for resolving this, based upon your experiences?

In one word: COMMUNICATION.

"The first costume a service manager has to jump in is that of a salesman. What we achieved in our organization has been firstly the fruit of a long campaign aimed at senior management, so that ITIL, and any other framework for that matter, is understood for what it is: a tool that will help us improve, showing us the way and helping us avoid mistakes others have already met and dealt with.

Secondly, we decided to get ISO 20000 certified, as a strategic objective for our organization (outsourcing of IT services), we got the commitment we needed.
Aside from the direct benefits of the certification for the business, the 'quick wins' along the way have been widely communicated wherever possible.

Where the business had no idea whatsoever why an incident represented such a high cost for our services, they now know what's involved in that price tag and even identify ways to reduce these. Where it was impossible before to tell why we needed so many employees in our service desk to resolve such a low number of incidents per agent, we now know that apart from incident resolution, agents perform many other tasks for the business. Now, not only the business appreciates it and can make use of it, the agents themselves feel their work is further recognized.

The only way to make change happen is through leadership. For senior management to act on the matter at hand, it really needs to see the benefit from a business perspective. Another key factor often ignored is time; in our dynamic business world where time seems to shrink and where we need everything done by yesterday, we tend to forget that the greatest achievements in humanity were not accomplished from one day to the next.

"Rome was not built in one day" - John Heywood."

Other related cards are:

- 9 of Clubs 'Walking the talk';
- Jack of Diamonds 'Saying yes but meaning no';
- Queen of Spades 'Not my responsibility';
- Ace of Spades 'Blame culture';
- 8 of Hearts 'The buck stops anywhere but here'.

6

"...I know I say everything is urgent.....but this time I really mean it.....honestly!"

User

Everything has the highest priority... . according to the users

9

6 of Diamonds

'Everything has the highest priority according to the users'

This is one of the symptoms, in fact, of poor demand management. The business demands that everything be done immediately. Everything for them has high priority, everything for them is instant gratification. I want it, and I want it now. Their attitude is that IT works for them, so IT is there to do whatever it is they want, when they want it, regardless of the impact that has on IT, regardless of the impact it has on other business units. Unless the business is made to recognize this 'attitude', the corresponding behavior of 'demanding priority' and the consequences this brings, they will not change. The consequences need to be made visible and will generally be related to 'additional costs', 'increased delays' for some, 'additional downtime' as a result of conflicting choices. The consequences should be made visible in business terms and be consequences that the business finds unacceptable.

Consequences such as "…your behavior means that we in IT have too much to do…..we have insufficient time for testing…..we do not have enough resources so….." is hardly likely to impress the business or cause them to change. It is more likely to stimulate a reaction of "Do I look like I care!" and they will carry on. More likely to impress is a business case along the lines of "We were unable to deploy the new sales transaction system, resulting in additional man hours and costs to process sales transactions. This delay was due to the fact that the project resources were claimed by business unit 'B' for a higher priority project".

The business needs to be aware and decide which business project is the most strategic. A business sales manager who is losing revenue and incurring costs because resources are put on a less strategic initiative is likely to start asking the CEO and other business managers about 'priorities' and the need for a consistant mechanism.

The cartoon on the card shows a business user speaking into a telephone. The user is sitting in front of a smoking computer that is about to explode. He says into the phone: "…I know I say everything is urgent….but this time I really mean it….honestly!"

Characteristics:

- Do the business users always insist everything is urgent and must be done immediately?
- Are process priority mechanisms actually agreed with business units?
- Are priority agreements actually known by users?
- Is the business aware of the consequences of their behavior?
- Does user behavior result in incorrect prioritising of work and high risk delays or outages?
- Can IT demonstrate the impact of this type of behavior?

Jeremy Hart, an IT service manager relates a case from a large financial institution.

"I used to work for a Fortune 500 financial company in the United States. At the time we were struggling to break free of the worst practice depicted by the 6 of Diamonds card. A lack of a consistent and agreed priority system had led to very minor incidents and service requests being handled with the highest priority. Of course, the crazy thing is that this model was fostered and nurtured by IT. The great misconception was that immediate and vigorous response to every incident equals excellent customer service.

One manifestation of this was that the entire data center team was notified by email every time an incident was logged. This approach required everyone on the team to assess the incident and whoever had the expertise was supposed to then own it. This legacy 'process' forced everyone on the team to treat every incident as the highest priority and then downgrade it after assessing it. With no agreed priority system, the team members were obliged to downgrade incidents in the subjective context of how it compared to the priority of the other work on their plate, instead of the true business need. What this really meant was that if the business truly had a priority request, there was no way for the team to accurately assess it and provide appropriate service. An informal poll of this team placed their reactive work at 80% to 90% of their work day. The team was frustrated and morale was at a low ebb.

Fortunately, some in the organization were starting to realize the folly of this approach. They developed a Technical Service Catalog and started to define expectations around the delivery of some services.

Additionally, the incident manager started taking a closer look at the priority system and escalation protocols. The big step yet to be taken is to meet with the business in order to understand their true needs and to agree to the prioritization system. The team is enthusiastic about this effort and is eager to move in the direction of less fire-fighting. They have begun to see that true customer service involves managing the business needs and expectations consistently."

This case revealed the impact on morale within IT when priority mechanisms are not agreed and, even worse, the risks faced by the business. It also shows a worrying situation faced by many IT organizations. Many IT companies do not have the relationship, or the trust of the business to raise and discuss these types of issues. Even in this company, in which IT is crucial, the relationship is characterized by 'the big step yet to be taken is to meet with the business in order to understand their true needs'.

Other cards that may be related to this are:

• King of Hearts 'Which part of NO didn't you understand';
• 5 of Clubs 'Neither partner makes an effort to understand the other';
• 7 of Hearts 'Demand and give. I demand and you give in!'.

The more of these cards you recognize in your organization, the higher the risk that the business faces; and the greater the impact on business operations as a result of these risks, the greater the need for good IT governance.

7 of Diamonds

'Throwing solutions over the wall and hoping we will use them'

"...here are the procedures we produced for you...."

Throwing solutions over the wall and HOPING people will use them

This is similar to the 8 of Clubs in one respect. That is, it can be related to how we deliver new IT solutions to the business, and how we deliver the results of ITSM improvement initiatives. We will focus on the second issue.

Very often ITSM improvement initiatives are project-based. The project will deliver a number of products or deliverables. In ITSM improvement initiatives these are usually IT tools to support and manage the workflow, and books of process flows and procedures to describe the new way of working. In many IT improvement projects teams of consultants lock themselves away in rooms and design process flows and books of procedures without little involvement of the people who need to use them. Very often these are then 'handed over' to the organization. A common response is the 'not invented here syndrome', where there is no buy-in or commitment for the new ways of working, even if they are good. If there is no management commitment to ensure they are accepted, they can soon be dropped or ignored.

The cartoon on the card shows somebody carrying five enormous, thick books of procedures saying: "....here are the procedures we produced for you..."

Characteristics:

- Does a project team design the procedures and hand them over (throws them over the wall) to the operational organization and people who will need to use the deliverables?
- Are those who have to use the procedures involved in the design teams or asked for their input?
- Is the business or user community involved in agreeing procedures?
- Do books of procedures disappear into cupboards never to be seen again.....until the next audit?
- Are there training sessions to teach all employees about the new ways of working?
- When an improvement project finishes, do the designers go back and do whatever it is they do, leaving the operational organization to pick up the pieces....or to drop the solution like a hot brick and ignore it?

As we said, people don't like to change the way they work or behave, procedures and new ways of working are not welcome. This naturally means that delivering new tools and procedures will be met by an attitude characterized by resistance, time and effort will be needed to address this, and time and effort is needed to ensure the new behavior becomes accepted and becomes the normal way of doing things. If not enough energy, attention and effort is given to this, then people may be inclined to revert back to old ways of doing things, and if the project is disbanded and the processes not embedded or owned, then there is a chance that nobody will feel ownership for ensuring people do not revert to old behavior. John Kotter, professor of leadership, in his eight steps to successful change also stated the need to 'institutionalize' the change. To embed it into the way of doing things.

Paul Leenards, Senior Business Consultant, Getronics PinkRoccade.
Paul gave a lot of QA feedback on the ITIL V3 publications and also wrote a thesis on the experiences of numerous ITIL implementation projects, focusing upon the success and fail factors.

"When implementing a new process, an ITIL consultant should understand the culture of the organization he/she is trying to change. When the new way of working is almost 180 degrees opposed to the current way, it takes a lot of effort and determination to explain the 'why' and the 'how'. It is not uncommon for ITIL consultants, external or internal, to keep the hard core IT specialists at a distance. The ITIL consultants do not understand how the IT specialists think, and the specialists feels that the ITIL consultant is all talk and no action. Without some mutual respect, as opposed to mutual suspicion, the ITIL consultant will have no chance of making any impact on the IT department.

Case:
At an Internet Service Provider based in the Netherlands the decision was taken to divide the IT function into two separate departments: the developers, who created and built the infrastructure, and the administrators, who will be responsible for maintenance and on-going operation. The internal developers were looking at the administrators as their personal slaves and bottle washers. The management, therefore, decided to out-task the administrators to an external party. This party accepted the challenge under the condition that ITIL be implemented to improve the level of professionalism. A couple of external ITIL consultants were hired to implement the basic processes, like incident and change management.

The developers were a law unto themselves; they worked when they wanted to, used a whole range of self-built tools and were self confessed hackers. These were not people who were willing to document anything, let alone willing to keep an administrative list of their change requests. The third party administrators were a little bit intimidated and were not in a position to take over control of the daily operations quickly. The ITIL consultants were also discovering that the developers were not impressed with ITIL procedures and process flows. After some months the implementation of ITIL was turning into a stalemate. The consultants were working hard on handbooks and had hopes of the management team of the company forcing the procedures on the developers.

The only way the administrators knew that a change in the production infrastructure had taken place was when they discovered the empty pizza boxes the next morning.
One of the goals of the ITIL framework itself is to control the way changes are implemented, to make this more transparent and predictable, and to improve the stability. For the

administrators it was often impossible to link service outages or degradation to changes made and this had a direct negative effect on the customers using the service.

Clearly this was a situation that could not continue for much longer. The handbooks of the ITIL consultants were growing larger in size without having any clear effect on the daily operations. As the new manager of the administrators, I needed to change this approach in order to show that ITIL was not an useless concept and that we needed some sort of change control.The first thing to do was to have the CFO admit that he was not willing to put the handbook for change management on the agenda of the management team. This made the strategy of the ITIL consultants worthless and the handbooks were placed in the archive cupboard.

The next step was to set up a meeting between the managers of the both groups, the developers and administrators. Instead of trying to create meaningless procedures that were never going to be followed by the developers, it made more sense to start talking with them on what their needs and ideas were. As the manager of the administrators I had a good chance of initiating the meeting. Both sides agreed that having a weekly meeting to discuss the ongoing business was useful. So there was some buy-in for this first step. The manager of the administrators asked the unofficial change manager-designate to keep minutes of the meeting. At the next meeting the administrators brought these minutes and the developers asked if they could get a copy as well. Sure.

Two weeks later the administrators experienced some performance issues in the network that could be related to an unknown change that had taken place. This led to a discussion in the weekly meeting which resulted in an important decision; the developers should announce their planned changes at the meetings in order for the administrators to take the appropriate measures (like keeping an eye out for possible disturbances, etc.). The developers bought into this because they realized that the administrators could give them useful feedback on the effects of the change and this feedback can only be given to them when the administrators know more about the change itself. They started to see that the administrators were their peers instead of their friends, with different responsibilities and similar interests. The meeting minutes were used to record and communicate the change plans. If the change was not in the minutes, it was not announced by the developers and was therefore an 'illegal' change.

And so the meeting turned into a weekly Change Advisory Board with the minutes used as the change calendar. Soon the developers started to send emails with change requests to the unofficial change manger so he could keep track and prepare the weekly change meetings. The implementation of change management was accomplished to the degree needed bearing in mind what was possible in the circumstances.

Reflection

A lot of ITIL consultants tend to focus on handbooks, the proper procedures and, mostly, on the correct registration of process inputs. This brings a lot of frustration to both the ITIL consultant and the victims of their mission to implement handbooks. Hoping that higher management would want to enforce these handbooks is underestimating the power of management, as well as failing to understand that procedures are not high on the agenda of a management team.

The positive effect of the bottom-up implementation described above is mostly because the focus shifted to the desired outcome or results of the implementation. The question answered was how to ensure that the developers shared their plans on changes before the act, instead of finding out the hard way afterwards. This question is fundamentally different from the question of how to enforce the developers to adhere to the ITIL procedures.

Fundamentally it is first about setting the goals and about sharing the reasons to set and reach these goals with all involved. Think of Kotter's steps 'creating a sense of urgency' as well as his step 'sharing of the vision'. These two steps should ensure that everybody knows 'why' we need to adopt and deploy some ITIL best practices. When there is enough commitment to the goals, then we can focus on how to help the staff to reach these goals. What is needed in terms of resources, money, tools, etc.? Which obstacles have to be removed, like organizational boundaries or obsolete systems?

Implementing ITIL should, therefore, never be about actually implementing ITIL but about reaching a goal and using ITIL as guidance."

Peter Lijnse, CEO Service Management Art. Peter is an experienced ITIL trainer and practitioner. Peter has provided a case from a large financial institution in Canada.

"The ITIL project at this company involved not only the implementation of new processes, but also the merger of different IT organizations. This of course made it all the more interesting from a management of change perspective. After we had developed the process documentation for the customer, we ended up with three different responses from the different groups:

- Great job. More documentation than we have right now. Let's go.
- Good, but we do not see that much different in this documentation than we have at this moment.
- This is not good. There is not enough detail in this documentation.

Not something we had expected at that time... we thought we were doing a great job! The realization sets in; different groups have different perspectives on how much documentation is necessary around processes. We needed to get the different groups aligned so that they would accept the documentation in order to be able to move forward.

We were victim of the worst practice; just develop some documentation and the customer will love it, without actually understanding their documentation requirements based on their culture, skill levels and technology. Now the challenge - how do you prevent this?

The first thing is to ensure that there is a clear understanding of what documentation is required. There are four levels of documentation:

1. Framework
   What process framework is being used? ITIL, CobiT or something else. Most people ignore this step; at the very least get acceptance on what framework you will use as a base for your improvement activities.
2. Process guides
   Every process will need to be defined in terms of roles, enabling technology, inputs, outputs, activities, goals, metrics and audit criteria. This document will provide guidance for the process managers on how the process is defined in the organization.
3. Procedures, templates, decision matrices
   This level defines the activities in more detail. This level of documentation is used by different participants of the processes. These are the supporting documents that make this process happen.
4. Work instructions and more detailed documentation
   These are specifically developed for staff to make sure they know how to do their job. For instance, for this change, fill in these fields with these parameters, use the category table to fill in this field, etc.

Before you start developing reams of documentation, THINK! How much documentation is enough? Can we stay at level 2 for some processes, how much detail is necessary? Do you understand what the organization is looking for in detail in the process documentation? Is it dependent on skill levels, or is it what they are used to...

REMEMBER: Just enough process documentation.... Overdo it and you will have a lot of maintenance on your hand. Not enough and your process might not be accepted.

It is an art."

Other related cards are:

- King of Clubs 'ITIL is the objective....not what it should achieve';
- Ace of Clubs 'ITIL certification means I know what I am doing';
- Jack of Hearts 'A process flow and some procedures are all you need';
- 8 of Diamonds 'We're going to install ITIL. It can't be that hard.'

"We chose you for your promise to implement all of ITIL in 3 months!"

We're going to INSTALL ITIL...it can't be that hard

8 of Diamonds

'We're going to install ITIL. It can't be that hard!'

This is similar to the 7 of Diamonds. Thinking that a book of procedures is all we need, thinking that if we say ITIL is important, everybody will find it important, thinking if we say everybody will use the procedures they will, thinking that "I am the boss, if I tell them to they will…". Because many IT companies are technology focused, they are used to 'installing' and 'implementing' things. Therefore all we have to do is 'install' or 'implement ITIL' and it will work. Right!?

Another symptom of this is people going on ITIL training and believing that all they have to do is go back and impart their new found superior knowledge, develop some procedures and hand-them over to the organization. There is a naïve belief by management that it will be easy, that it will be painless, and that as they are such good leaders it will happen because they say it will happen.

The cartoon shows an IT manager talking to an ITIL consultant. The IT manager says: "We chose you for your promise to implement all of ITIL in 3 months"

Characteristics:

- Do people think that ITIL is all about writing a set of procedures?
- Do managers think that ITIL can be 'implemented' in a number of months?
- Do people talk about 'installing' or 'implementing' ITIL?
- When people talk about ITIL, is the immediate reaction 'we need a tool', or 'which tool do we need'?
- Is there likely to be resistance to having to work with procedures and following rules and agreements?

Implementing ITIL is the same as starting a management of change program. There will be a need to change attitude, behavior and probably the culture of the organization. The following diagram shows the type of emotional phases and resistance that will be met before people's attitudes change and the new way of behaving becomes accepted. Accepted as 'the way we do things around here', with the new attitude and behavior embedded in the culture.

We have three people providing a case or commenting on this card. All three are actively engaged in the itSMF.

Case:

Alexander Kist, ex-Director of Education at Getronics-PinkRoccade, now Director of Newskool and active itSMF international member. Alexander has had years of ITIL experience.

"Ever since ITIL was first introduced in the 1990's, organizations have wanted to 'implement ITIL'. Often driven by the long–felt need to achieve better management control over the IT department, managers both inside and outside of IT respond enthousiastically when they hear about this 'methodology' for managing IT called ITIL. Typically they have been looking for a way to fit IT in a system of gauges and dials (dashboards) for some time and, when they find out about ITIL, they think they have found it.

The issue is worsened by self-appointed 'consultants' who are taking advantage of the opportunity. Often they don't know what they are talking about at all. Their major driver is to make a load of money and, to achieve that, they say things they think will make the customer sign on the dotted line. They have read an ITIL pocket guide, maybe they have taken a Foundation course and they think 'how difficult can it really be?'.

Often there are very real organizational issues in and around the IT department, such as a need for more efficiency and better control. The performance of IT needs to be made more measurable and manageable. Adopting *Best Practices* is undoubtedly a good approach to achieving such goals. The best practice guidance for IT (service) management that ITIL provides is sometimes referred to as the 'Encyclopaedia of IT Manangement'. A manager claiming to want to implement the Encyclopaedia Brittannica in their organization would probably be fired on the spot!"

How not to implement ITIL
In a leading multinational bank a manager with no IT background was made responsible for 'IT infrastructure'. At the time of her role change 'IT infrastructure' was task-oriented and managed hierarchically. The users' perception of service quality was generally poor, but it was not measured formally.

At some point (no doubt triggered by the 'i' for 'infrastructure') she stumbled upon ITIL and soon found out that 'they did not have ITIL' in their organization. Further research convinced her that the way forward was to 'implement ITIL'. She bought a set of ITIL books and sent a number of managers to a Foundation course. They came back confused but enthusiastic about the ITIL methodology. It was decided to engage the firm where they had taken their training to help them 'implement ITIL'. One of their consultants was hired to assume the role of project manager. It transpired later that, even though this person possessed the ITIL Managers' Certificate, his main experience was as a project management in software development.

The consultant mounted an implementation project within 'IT Infrastructure' only. Negotiations with customers and suppliers were considered a second phase. A blueprint of the new departmental organization as well as processes and procedures were drafted. 10 process managers were appointed and staff members assigned to processes. The building phase went smoothly but overran the timeline by more than 100% because the daily work kept interfering. That, together with the sharp increase in user complaints were accepted as unavoidable side-effects of the ITIL implementation.

After the organizational changes were in place, an 'awareness campaign' was executed to inform stakeholders about the implementation of ITIL and all the good things that it was going to bring. Six months later the project had a formal evaluation point. It turned out that the number of staff had been increased by 25% to cover the extra workload 'caused by ITIL'. The user's quality perception was now measured formally, with dismal results. SLA's, OLA's and UC's were in place but generally not met. Suppliers complained bitterly and some even cancelled their contracts. Something needed to be done."

How to fix it?
It was decided that even though support for ITIL was at an all time low, it was felt that there was no way back. However, a major change of direction was required, so a plan was put together for a 'culture first' approach to adopt *best practices in IT service management* across the entire organization. Because of the damage that had been done, they even avoided the use of the term ITIL in their formal communications. What did this actually mean? They started with a stakeholder analysis, finding out what all the key stakeholdesr actually needed. This made IT think in terms of other perspectives, not just their own. They started 'marketing' ITIL and what it could do for the stakeholders to create 'buy-in'. Key to this was

marketing and communications skills, enabling the IT people to learn to speak in customer value terms and business cases. Soft skills training was given to customer facing staff so that they could learn to communicate in customer terms and empathize with customers, which created a better awareness and understanding of customer needs as well as helping to gain trust from the customers.

All managers in IT and related disciplines were subjected to 'IT service management essentials' training. All IT Infrastructure staff were required to pass the Foundation exam and then went on to the relevant Practitioners'. Department heads, regional managers and senior management in IT Infrastructure progressed to the service manager level. The training was also used to communicate the company goals and the way in which ITIL would help support these goals. People were then better able to place the ITIL training in the context of their own situation.

The help of the bank's Communication department was enlisted to completely redo the awareness campaign. This time different level information was given formally and informally to different stakeholders. That helped to slowly improve the general attitude within IT Infrastructure toward ITIL. This eventually led to the formation of one IT division for the entire bank. Some years later the manager who initially introduced ITIL was made CIO. ITIL played a major role when they made some strategic acquisitions and had to integrate the IT functions of those companies into the bank."

We also want to add a piece provided by **Arjen Droog,** CEO of itSMF in the Netherlands and an experienced ITIL practitioner. Although Arjen did not specifically choose this card to write about, his contribution clearly focuses on the problems of managing organizational change.

ABC for organizational change

"Successfully changing organizations. This phrase expresses the assumption it can be done. Sure, to change 'departments' in 'business units' is relatively easy. But real change goes beyond these changes on paper. Every time a management team decides that an organization has to change, a new organizational scheme is drawn up. But what they actually want is to change the attitude and behavior of the organization. And it is nearly impossible to change the culture, attitude and behavior of an organization by simply presenting a new structure. Central in this piece is the question: can the ABC of an organization be changed, and how? In other words, is it nature or nurture?

Nature or nurture

The nature or nurture debate is something scientists argued about for many years. In both cases the perspective is always the individual: Is criminal behavior in one's genes, or does it originate from one's social environment? These same questions can be reflected on organizations. Is bureaucracy nature or nurture? And how about customer focus, nature or nurture?

The general opinion about organizations is that nurture is dominant to nature. At least this could be concluded if you look at MBA programs, management literature and managers' ambitions. But as organizations are just a large groups of individuals, it is interesting to translate this general opinion to an individual perspective. John B. Watson was an American scientist who was often referred to as 'the father of behaviorism'. He said in 1930: "Give me a dozen healthy infants, well-formed, and my own specified world to bring them up in and I'll guarantee to take any one at random and train him to become any type of specialist I might select: doctor, lawyer, artist, merchant-chief, and, yes, even beggar man and thief, regardless of his talents, penchants, tendencies, abilities, vocations, and race of his ancestors." Today this sounds foolish, but it is the way most managers look at their organizations. Professionals who survived multiple reorganizations probably will recognize that most managers are wrong.

Attitude and technology
A great deal of help in order to successfully change an organization comes from ABC, but at the same time ABC makes managers more aware of the difficulties and complexity of organizational change.

The influential thinker Carl Gustav Jung defines attitude as: 'readiness of the psyche to act or react in a certain way'. So attitude is a type of readiness, creating behavior. Often wrong or even bad behavior is a symptom that needs to be improved, but focusing on the symptom will never solve the problem. It is very interesting that scientists see two possibilities for solving a problem:

• Attitudinal fix;
• Technical fix.

The attitudinal fix refers to solving a problem or resolving a conflict by bringing about an attitude change. Persuasion, mediation, diplomacy, and consciousness raising campaigns are ways of doing this. A technical fix is something that refers to changing the physical environment and structures. Most problems need a combination of an attitudinal fix and a technical fix. For organizational change, the attitudinal change is dominant. So managers as well as organizations that are used to solving problems with technical fixes might be unsuitable to lead an organizational change. What does this conclusion mean for IT managers and IT departments (or IT suppliers) that are involved in organizational change more and more often, or even becoming responsible for a process of change?

Cultural dimensions
There are many ways to categorize the culture of organizations. A particularly useful one has been created by Geert Hofstede. He describes five cultural dimensions for societies (slightly simplified and adjusted for organizations). Briefly, these dimensions include: 'power distance' - how power is distributed and used, whether there is consultation or democracy or whether it is autocratic; 'individualism versus collectivism' - whether the individual and self preservation leads, as opposed to group survival; 'masculinity versus femininity' - with clear distinctions between men being assertive and tough and women being modest, tender and concerned, or a feminine organization in which both men and

women are modest, tender and concerned; 'uncertainty avoidance' – the way in which people feel threatened by uncertainty; and 'long versus short term' – which describes an organization's time horizon.

These cultural dimensions can be very helpful in establishing the present culture of an organization and the gap between that and the ideal situation. Insight is very useful, but because of the difficulty in changing the culture of an organization, it might be more useful to accept the culture and look for opportunities to use it to your advantage. On the other hand, cultural change is not impossible. If the continuity of an organization is at risk, or huge business advantages are at an arm's length, it might be worth it. But be fully aware that the risk of failure is high. To manage this risk, it is useful to look at change fundamentals drawn up by a change guru like John Kotter - behavior and image

In recent decades, the behavior of organizations has had a growing influence on the image of an organization. This goes for large enterprises (e.g. Shell and the Brent Spar), but also on smaller scale within organizations. An IT department that isn't able to meet user expectations will suffer from image damage. The same goes if the IT department, for example, decides to limit network, server or internet access because of security reasons. The public opinion is always right, and so are the users. Making changes, technically or attitudinal, is risky business. But since change has become a continual process, organizations, managers and employees have to be well prepared. Just like people, organizations can be addicted to certain behavior. And it can be quite a challenge to overcome such an addiction.

Conclusion

ABC is most relevant when viewed from the organizational perspective. The organizational attitude, behavior and culture shape the character and capabilities of an organization. Too often people have a naive belief that changing their organization is possible. I am not saying that it isn't, but it is usually underestimated. The question of nature or nurture isn't easy to answer. Behavior is the result of the attitude and culture of an organization. Nature and nurture aren't necessarily opposites. In general you can say that the (unchangeable) nature of organizations is underestimated, and managers usually exaggerate the nurture possibilities of an organization. Also, the characteristics of an organization that are nurtured might become nature over time. It is uncommon to make an assessment on whether instead of seeking to change an organization, it wouldn't be more economic in terms of time and money to use the characteristics of the organization as a starting point and as an advantage. But in a rapidly changing world, this might be considered being very old fashioned."

HP Suen, Chairman, itSMF, Hong Kong also confirmed how addressing ABC will help to overcome this type of incorrect view of how to apply ITIL.

"The ABC card set reminds IT professionals that the reality that IT service management is about managing business service, not about putting IT in service. ITSM has been in Asia for only a few years and the main challenges are in understanding the theory and avoiding mistakes. The ABC card set describes the DO's and DON'Ts in the implementation of ITSM."

Other related cards are:

- King of Clubs 'ITIL is the objective....not what it should achieve';
- Ace of Clubs 'ITIL certification means I know what I am doing';
- Jack of Hearts 'A process flow and some procedures are all you need';
- 7 of Diamonds 'Throwing solutions over the wall and hoping we will use them'.

9 of Diamonds

'Maybe we should have tested that change first...'

We in IT are excellent at changing things and breaking them. We have turned 'not testing' changes into a fine art. In a recent BITA Planet survey this ranked as the number one issue that still needs resolving, with the number two issue being 'culture'. These two, of course, are very closely linked.

The cartoon on this card shows two technoids standing next to a skeleton sitting on a stool in front of a computer screen. One of the technoids reads the message on the screen: "....it says a short wait will occur!"

Characteristics:

- We don't have time to test changes because of business priority.
- It is often too difficult to test changes, we don't have the infrastructure.
- Often the test and acceptance environment is different to the live environment...but who feels ownership for changing this?
- Users don't have the time...or willingness to spend time on testing.
- There are too few testing and acceptance demands, and if they exist, they are often ignored.
- Nobody insists that testing occurs.
- There are no sanctions for not testing.

Mats Berger, CEO of Westergaard CSM AB, Sweden, organiser for the leading Help Desk conference in Denmark since 2002, experienced organizational change consultant.

"I have seen during several implementations of the change management process that there is great resistance in adhering to that process. This is because it is very much a control proces and people feel that we do not trust them or acknowledge their competence. The comment I often hear is: "I can't understand why we have to introduce this process. I know what I am doing, I am good at it, so why do you need to control my work – it is my every day job to make amendments and changes to the systems I am responsible for."

To explain to technical staff why the introduction of change management still might be a good idea – we introduced a role model game to be used in a workshop. It is very simple:

- Select a couple of people from various roles within your organization (4-6) e.g. Help Desk agent, CIO, database administrator or user and write these roles in large letters on pieces of paper.
- Take a rope or any other lengthy pliable object and make a circle on the floor.

- Take another rope and put it on the floor to divide the circle into pieces of cake (the number should fit the roles you identified).
- Place one of the pieces of paper with a role name on it in each of the cake segments.
- Get the target group to team up two and two – one is taking the role, the other one writing down what that persons says.
- Introduce the assignment:
  - You will now try different roles.
  - The statement you are going to brainstorm is the following: "We are going to introduce change management within our organization. This means that all changes must be under control and, therefore, authorized and documented before released".
  - One of you will start in the role as Help Desk agent and brainstorm what this introduction of change management will mean for him/her and your team partner will take notes of what you say.
  - If you need help as to what to think of, you can use the following questions as prompts:
    1. What benefits/challenges/problems might change management bring to me?
    2. How will my team and myself be affected in other ways?
  - After two minutes you switch roles and move on to the next role in the circle.
  - Having tried all roles, you step out of circle and your partner steps in.
  - Your partner then rotates through each cake segment and gives his or her input.

After everybody has tried to be both inside and outside of the circle, and in all roles, perform a plenary exercise to review the lessons learned. Here, everybody shares what they have said/written in the different roles. In this way it becomes evident what the benefits are for other roles in the organization, and the technical staff realize that having a change control or change management process is beneficial to the whole organization. It will also become clear what possible resistance there is – and what exactly that resistance is. Discussions can help identify how the resistance can best be resolved."

Simply said, "It is a piece of cake!" according to Mats. This is a great intervention that helps identify and change peoples' 'attitude' towards applying best practices.

Another case from Erna van Kollenburg, EducaSimula, in the Netherlands. Erna describes a case relating to a change management initiative.

"A consultant developed an implementation plan. But the IT department knew that everyone, including the IT employees and the business, wanted their changes to be carried out in an ad hoc fashion. This was not only a problem for IT but in the long term, also for the business. This ad hoc way of managing changes gave the feeling of being adaptable and flexible but, in reality, it was a risk to the business. There was no working together and there was no common goal for the change management process and what it should achieve.

The organization didn't want a new ITIL course, but a refresher course on the change management process. This was not only for the IT staff, but also for all the business people involved.

The aim of the training should be not only to learn the ITIL theory but to try to gain buy-in and commitment for adopting, and sticking to, a change process. One that wasn't seen as overly bureaucratic.

They selected a 'change management' game because the innovative way of learning corresponded with the new approach to 'open and transparent' collaborative working that was to be adopted in future, and because it allowed people from all the different departments to work together and see the interdependencies within the change process and how everybody needed to work together. The change management process was a critical part of the 'open'and 'transparent' way of working and must be seen as a success.

In the game people were confronted with the business and the associated impact of any changes. They learnt it isn't only the one who has the highest management position or the one who shouts the loudest that gets their changes through. The conclusion from the students was that this helped to 'bring the wall down between design and transition'. One network employee, who was skeptical of the change process declared, "The game, it was the talk of the day!", whilst the functional application manager commented: "Now I could speak the same language and understand IT and why they prioritise the rfc's the way they do."

Other related cards are:

- 2 of Clubs 'NO respect for, or understanding of users';
- 9 of Clubs 'Walking the talk';
- 3 of Diamonds 'Too little business involvement in requirements specification and testing';
- 6 of Diamonds 'Everything has the highest priority...according to the users';
- 7 of Diamonds 'Throwing solutions over the wall and HOPING that people will use them';
- Ace of Diamonds 'Process managers without authority';
- 7 of Spades '9 to 5 culture';
- Queen of Spades 'Not my responsibility';
- 7 of Hearts 'Demand and give. I demand and you give in!';
- Queen of Hearts 'Of course we will finish on time and within budget'.

Never mind about following procedures.... just do what we usually do

10 of Diamonds

'Never mind about following procedures, just do what we normally do'

This is similar to the attitude of 'ignore ITIL, it'll soon blow over'. Saying yes and meaning no is another similar symptom, or 'I am an expert I know better, I will do it my way'. Another example is 'it is more important to get things done than to follow procedures and document things'. Often the attitude has an element of truth in it, it is better to get the system working, the user happy, the business process available, the business people working.....rather than documenting things, filling in forms, following cheklists. Right? However, it is only by making the consequences of not documenting and not following procedures visible that attitudes can be changed.

For example, a senior manager admonishing somebody for not following agreed procedures will have an impact on the attitude of others, especially if the result of not following procedures is downtime or an unacceptable business impact. A manager making an example of somebody and telling them off, or even firing them has an impact. It may seem harsh and confrontational but it shows that old ways of working are no longer acceptable and reinforces the commitment to new procedures and new ways of working. Leadership is vital to breaking through these worst practices. Without this level of leadership and commitment there is a danger that new ways of working will be unsuccessful.

The cartoon shows a technoid repeatedly smashing his fist on top of a broken screen and saying: "it's just a question of knowing where to hit it!..."

Characteristics:

- Are procedures ignored or circumvented regularly?
- Are people used to following procedures and rules?
- Do people complain that procedures don't work and are a waste of time?
- Is anybody responsible for reviewing and improving procedures?
- Is anybody ever told off for not following procedures?

Other cards relevant to this are:

- 6 of Clubs 'ITIL never work here';
- 9 of Clubs 'Walking the talk';
- King of Clubs 'ITIL is the objective....not what it should achieve';
- 5 of Diamonds 'No management commitment';
- 7 of Diamonds 'Throwing solutions over the wall and HOPING that people will use them';
- Jack of Diamonds 'Saying yes but meaning no';

- Ace of Diamonds 'Process managers without authority';
- Queen of Spades 'Not my responsibility';
- 6 of Spades 'Hero culture'.

Saying Yes but meaning No

Jack of Diamonds

'Saying 'yes', meaning, or doing 'no'

This is similar to the 10 of Diamonds. However the 10 of Diamonds is more symptomatic of active resistance. This is more symptomatic of passive resistance.

Often at the start of an ITSM improvement program, a presentation is given to the employees to explain the program, the goals and the importance of ITIL. When the moment comes for questions or feedback there is often none. It is assumed that people agree. As soon as they leave the room, the comments and dissent begins. Often as procedures are handed over, people declare that they will follow them but don't. If nothing is done to address this, then it becomes an accepted way of doing things…. ignore the procedures or don't follow them as there don't appear to be any adverse consequences and, if they really are important, surely somebody would say something?

It is important that this type of behavior is addressed. Ignoring it will make it worse. Managers have an important role to play in this, particularly line managers. Often when new processes and process management roles are developed, employees find it difficult to understand that they may work for a line manager or department manager but a process manager can also assign work to them. In the beginning employees may ignore or undermine process managers and fail to follow agreed procedures. If this happens, line managers must address this behavior to show they are committed to process working.

Process managers also have an important role to play in this. The impact and consequences of not doing something need to be made explicit. The reason for new procedures also need to be clear, why are they necessary and important. Not doing something may be a sign of lack of 'buy-in', lack of 'commitment'. It is important to try to identify the underlying cause of this type of behavior.

The cartoon on the card shows two technoids sitting in a session in which the new ITIL processes are being explained. The process managers says "…So these are the new ways of working agreed?". The two technoids both mumble "Yes" but are thinking "No".

Characteristics:

- Do improvement initiatives or projects get delayed because promised activities were not carried out?
- Do people change priorities without informing other people?
- Do people leave things undone until somebody starts complaining or asking about it?
- Do managers often overrule priorities?
- Do people fail to turn up to meetings because of other, urgent issues?
- Do people often apologize for not doing something because they had too much work?

Other related cards are:

- 6 of Clubs 'ITIL never work here';
- 10 of Clubs 'No respect for, or trust in management';
- Jack of Spades 'Avoidance culture';
- Queen of Spades 'Not my responsibility';
- 5 of Diamonds 'No management commitment';
- 9 of Clubs 'Walking the talk'.

The solution the customer sees isn't the one that IT sees

Queen of Diamonds

'The solution the customer sees isn't the one that IT sees'

IT people are highly technical and have a clear view of the possibilities and limitations of technology. If the business is not 'technically savvy' they will be slower to comprehend, they will not understand the reasoning of IT proposals. This can be a symptom of IT speaking too much in technobabble, speaking in terms of systems and not in terms of business solutions. It can also be a symptom of the business not getting involved enough in understanding the technical possibilities and limitations and the choices they need to make, the level of involvement they must commit to, so that both are looking at, and agreeing, the same solution focus.

The cartoon shows a frustrated IT manager presenting an IT proposal to the business for web services. The CEO responds: "It says in PC NERD world for dumb ass business managers 'FREE INTERNET!' so how come the IT department wants $200.000?"

Characteristics:

- Do IT project proposals have a 'real business case'? One that the business understands, one that describes business value and the results to be achieved?
- Does the business get adequately involved in IT requirements specification and planning?
- Is there adequate and timely testing and acceptance as IT development projects progress?
- Does the business see the need to be involved?
- Do business people make an effort to understand how they need to govern IT?

Other cards related to this are:

- 2 of Clubs 'NO respect for, or understanding of users';
- 5 of Clubs 'Neither partner makes an effort to understand the other';
- 8 of Clubs 'IT thinks it doesn't have to understand the business to make a business case';
- 7 of Diamonds 'Throwing solutions over the wall and HOPING that people will use them';
- 10 of Spades 'The superiority complex – we know best'.

King of Diamonds

'IT's strategy contribution to business strategy' (or rather lack of)

A report we saw a year or so ago stated that more than 70% of IT organizations had a clear strategy and deployment of that strategy. However less that 30% could demonstrate strategy realization and did not steer on strategy.

In the light of this, it is somewhat surprising that the organizations who use the ABC cards in workshops and agree that the following cards apply to themselves:

- 'IT not seen as an added-value partner';
- 'No respect for or understanding of the customer';
- 'Business and IT not making the effort to understand each other';
- 'Throwing solutions over the wall';
- 'No shared view in the IT team as to the value that the business needs'.

are the same ones that say, "We have a good IT strategy-making process". You have to ask yourself the value of the strategy and the alignment of the strategy with the business strategy. This card is different to the 2 of Diamonds "We don't measure our value contribution to strategy", in that the 2 of Diamonds may imply that we know what the strategy is and how we should deliver value, but we don't measure or steer it. This card, the King of Diamonds, is symptomatic of IT organizations that don't get involved in time, or at all, in the strategy making process, often because IT is NOT seen as an added-value partner, or IT has too little trust or credibility. Examine the other related cards to determine why this card applies.

The cartoon on the card shows an IT manager presenting a process model; in response to a question about a line that goes around in a circle he replies: "…that circle? That is the IT strategic plan….it goes around in circles before disappearing up its own rear end!"

Characteristics:

- Does the business complain that IT does not adequately support the business strategy?
- Does IT complain that it is not involved on time with strategy decisions?
- Do business people complain about the value that IT delivers to the business?
- Does an IT project always have a business case showing how the project relates to business strategy and goals?
- If you ask any IT employee how does IT support the business strategy, would any of them know?

We received three cases for this card. One is from Vernon Lloyd, a well known and respected figure in the ITIL community. The second case is from Martin Ng, a director of Deloitte Risk

Services based in Kuala Lumpur, and an experienced ITIL practitioner. The third is from Jack Bischof, who is also an experienced strategy consultant and ITIL expert.

Vernon Lloyd, director of consulting Fox-IT and ITIL V3 author. Vernon is also active on the board of itSMF UK.

"ITSM doesn't work without the ABC. I remember, 18 years ago, drawing for the first time on a board three circles and filling them with the words 'People, Process and Technology', and explaining to the class back then that processes and tools are great but they won't work without the right people, attitude, culture, team working, management commitment, buy-in....But people are still so wrapped up in designing processes and documenting wonderful Visio process flows, that they forget to spend the effort on the roles and responsibilities and the organizational structure. I recently had a customer doing exactly this. They were designing some new change management process. I asked who the change manager would be. "We have somebody in mind, we'll hand this over to him when his role is clear....." they said.
"So the change manager isn't involved in designing his own process? He will have something dumped on him...here you are, this is how you need to manage YOUR process?....that is a great way of gaining buy-in and commitment" I replied.".

Why is this? Why do we still focus on processes?
"In ITIL V2, we (the authors) tried to emphasise the need to design and manage people as well as processes but if you asked most people what ITIL was about, the response was normally, "Oh it is that process framework for operations" so perhaps the point wasn't made forcibly enough. We have tried with V3 to raise it to being more strategic and focused on services. Unfortunately, as yet, I haven't seen a real attitude change. People still focus on processes, "how many processes are in ITIL V3? 21? 23? 26?" they ask....The question is, 'does it really matter?'. They NEED to know so that they can start to design their processes.

I tried explaining again to one customer the need for people. The answer from the management team was "we know all that....we know we have to focus on that...but let's get back to how the process needs to work." I could see a lack of commitment, time, effort and energy to work on the people side. They said "I am a manager, if I tell them this is what we need to do, they'll do that won't they?"

But it isn't as black as you paint it in this book, things are slowly changing. Admittedly not fast enough, but they are changing. I have one customer who has three people in their ITIL program, all responsible for the management of change, addressing the culture, gaining buy-in, marketing the program. People with no knowledge of skills in ITIL or IT service management. They know the importance of changing attitude and behavior."

Which card is the one that most needs resolving?
Vernon had a whole list of cards he thought he would be allowed to talk about.
"I have the Queen of Clubs 'No understanding of business impact and priority', which

should be 'lack of', I have the 2 of Diamonds 'We don't measure our value contribution to strategy', I have the King of Diamonds 'IT's strategy contribution to business strategy'…."

I told Vernon I wanted one card only. Which one did he feel the most strongly about? Which one needs resolving the most?

"But I have a load more I want to talk about that are relevant!"

Reluctantly he agreed to choose one. The King of Diamonds. Why?

"IT strategy is not integrated into business strategy, IT people don't understand the impact of the IT strategy on the business. We generally don't get it. I'll give you a typical case. One customer told me "We are busy with a technology refresh, new desktops". "Oh!" I said, "and how many more insurance policies will you sell as a result of this investment?". "What do you mean?" is generally the answer. We must be able to specify for any investment in IT or IT processes how it will impact business performance or help the business mitigate risks. Another customer said "We have reduced the average resolution time of incidents", "OK so how does that add value to the business? Does the business agree?". IT people need to take it that step further, the impact on which business unit, process or operation? And understand how the business gains value. Very few IT people can make the link to specific business results and value.

I have an analogy to describe the way IT works. I was in Denmark presenting at a conference. I put my card key in my hotel room door it bleeped three times and opened. I thought to myself, if you showed this to an IT person they would think about this and come up with a solution to make it bleep twice and then proudly declare we have improved performance by 30%. As a business user I would say, "Do I look like I care? Does that add value to what I need? I can still open my door?"

IT often claims to have made improvements, but the question is does it really matter? Is this going to really improve the business? Nobody bothers to ask these questions. "We have made the web page refresh 30% quicker", "Really, and what does that mean? Did the users want that? Is it annoying them now, the speed of pages refreshing? Had anybody asked if that means increased visitors? Increased transactions?"

What advice can Vernon give?
"Obviously the typical answers are 'communication' with the business and IT people, steering groups to better align decision making…all the books will tell you this I KNOW. Let's stop all this 'talk' about business and IT alignment and which framework or process will help. Get out there and find out who the players are; HR, Finance, Sales, IT. We are all on an equal playing field FOR the business, what are we all doing? And what needs doing. If I tell this to customers they say "That makes sense, but IT staff say to me that we can't communicate with the business, they don't understand us, they don't KNOW what they want, they can't tell us what they want…"

What can you do? At one organization we started introducing focus group meetings, IT people and business people. Cheese and wine events, relaxed setting. People turned up, started chatting, opened up and started discussing things, away from the formal meeting structures. Both gaining insight into each other's perspectives.

Another great intervention are the Sims, (the simulation games). Getting people from the business and IT together to play a Sim. After the first round it is like reality, players are at each other's throats, arguing and blaming each other. At the end of the Sim they are a team working together to solve a common problem or achieve a common aim. One group, during the lunch break, agreed that one of the simulation situations and areas causing them to fail was the same as the daily reality. They agreed to schedule a meeting, get together to discuss and resolve it. It was great seeing how they changed attitudes? They both felt it was now worth communicating with the other party, it changed behavior, they planned a meeting to discuss a problem and find a solution TOGETHER.

Why was it effective? It brings people together and shows the benefits of doing things together. One of the big issues we have with the business is lack of trust and credibility. This helps create trust, they can see how we really want to work together to solve problems. This is a first step in gaining trust and credibility and a willingness to talk about real business needs, business value, business risks that IT can help solve."

Martin Ng, director of Deloitte Enterprise Risk Services, is based in Kuala Lumpur. He is currently IT governance lead for South East Asia and he heads the Centre for Risk Intelligence for the region. Martin has had extensive experience in helping IT organizations adopt and deploy IT governance and service management best practices within Asia Pacific.

"Going through the cards made me realize how completely indifferent we have become within IT. I share this view based on the dozens of projects I have been part of, and I can only agree that the most basic of elements has been neglected – that being the **people** behind and also beyond IT. Gartner rightly puts it – in that 78% of all issues that arise from IT are not technological issues but of people and processes. The people factor can be the bane or boon of any organizational change and, in most cases, they are not adequately managed or allowed proper development.

Observing successful multinationals such as GE, Motorola, Intel and many others, these organizations have made people development a cornerstone of their success globally. At the same time, they ensure that people understand and recognize how they contribute to customer satisfaction and ultimately to business success. In IT this cannot be neglected. The need for the right competencies, the right talent, and an understanding of business and customer expectations is essential to bringing better agility, ingenuity and adaptability in response to the business. Failure to address these issues brings more fear to change, less willingness to adapt and an inability to succeed.

The other related element that is often misplaced is IT value, IT value and how it is aligned to business In business demand today, there is surprisingly little qualification of initiatives (or projects) and their contribution or returns to business objectives. This clearly relates to IT-enabled projects which normally attract a significant amount of investment. The key discussion in most management boardrooms today is to have better visibility into these investment project portfolios and their associated risk in meeting business value and goals. In short, there needs to be better alignment to the common goals and purposes of the business and its customers.

The following case focuses on a business whose strategy for growth and success was predicated on customer satisfaction. It is meeting and exceeding customer satisfaction that drives growth and creates success.

Case:

No business strives to be the worst in what they do - they are either open, or not open, to change, and are bold or foolish enough to make a stand either way. I have seen cases of leadership in the organization spew out lofty plans with very little understanding or appreciation of their teams' abilities to execute; leaders who on another extreme are so operational that the vision and direction of the organization is disjointed and weak. I have been frustrated by divisional heads battling to protect their boundaries, insisting there is nothing wrong within their kingdoms as the fault lies without. I have been engaging with project teams whose managers suffer due to unclear empowerment, weak planning and resource management...and the list can go on. These are all typical issues that plague an organization, even within IT. What clearly is not understood is the customer that has to pay for it in the end. But customers being customers, once bitten, twice shy, and if they have a choice, they may well opt for other choices that will offer the better value.

I was involved in an ITSM project in Hong Kong in which the organization had a very candid approach to driving better alignment and service excellence.

The organization has a strong history in quality and good practices. The leadership culture within the organization has always believed in doing the right things right, and this has permeated throughout the organization. Hence achieving quality standards and applying best practice has ensured an efficient operational expenditure and effective services to its customers in Hong Kong. Being an organization that tests new policies, approaches with products that support better housing management and development, the strong culture of excellence has won it accolades in customer satisfaction.

The measure of excellence has even crept into IT and its operations. Having instituted performance management within IT since 1994, the organization has since measured IT as part of its customer satisfaction (CS) index. Compounding this, the IT organization began a variable-pay system in 2002-2003 whereby the CS index became a true annual key performance indicator which the entire IT organization is strictly measured on. In simple terms, if the index drops a point, the entire IT organization feels it in their pockets.

This meant that the entire IT organization would need to live and breathe on how well they performed, based on the CS survey results. The struggle began over the period from 2003 when complex systems were being implemented and there were many challenges to maintaining good quality end-to-end services. The IT organization was operating too much in silos and it failed to understand or see the customer as the one that mattered.

These CS results were used to convince the organization of the need to adopt standards for IT service management (ITSM). After an extensive search for a complementary framework and practice, the CIO embraced ITIL and became a true champion, even achieving the Service Manager's certification. Starting with good awareness, and planning, the CIO understood the need to address change and manage it during the implementation. Organizational change issues were tackled through education and communication which eased transitions and facilitated the improvement. The CIO clearly understood that the need to create buy-in, commitment and embed the standards into daily behavior was vital. All this cumulated in results that led to an immediate increase in the CS index! Now how many IT organizations out there would dare stake this as their key KPI? "

Jack Bischof, senior manager with Accenture. Jack was also a contributing author to the ITIL V3 Service Strategy book.

Service Strategy problem

"Firms routinely operate their IT organizations along the lines of technological 'stacks' in order to maximize skill development and functional accountability within the organization. This approach is the logical result of a 'manufacturing mindset', and originates from the assembly line approach to building products. The assembly line approach enables each worker to specialize in their respective skills or task set and, ultimately, to enhance both product quality and completion speed. This methodology has been highly effective in building complex products such as cars, aircraft and computing devices.

However, this approach to structuring skills, work and organizations does not necessarily represent the most effective and efficient method for developing, packaging and supporting business services that rely on technology at their core. Building and supporting a business service requires an understanding of articulated and un-articulated desired business outcomes, which should be based on: customer desires (identified value elements that maximize customer outcomes, reduce access barriers, and are valued at price points that enable product strategies); go-to-market and product strategies (e.g. differentiating speed-to-market and value composition alternatives); and company realities (such as financial structures and competing opportunities). In this services-based scenario, a different approach can often yield superior results.

A case in point is one of the largest companies within the financial services industry. During an IT restructuring exercise it initially began to shuffle accountability between VPs based on geography and functional skill sets (e.g. 'all database and infrastructure skills within the U.K.'). After months of internal effort the company realized that it needed to adopt a service-based strategy, and cited two critical points of failure in their current initiative that would inhibit the success they could achieve:

- The structure being created would not improve the performance or internal accountability related to specific business services that were the 'bread and butter' of the company, and would only perpetuate some of the historic problems facing the IT organization in terms of accountability and interoperability.
- The proposed structure and processes lacked business integration and the ability to industrialize the service lifecycle for the purpose of creating and supporting new and emerging business services (as a capability) in the most effective manner and thus promote and support innovation into the future.

As a result, the company held a 'Service Strategy Summit' with all of its IT executives as well as key business executives that represented critical business domains and geographies. The summit was intended to change the strategic path of IT, and to begin the process of integrating IT and the business so that IT could begin to act and be perceived as a critical-path partner for business service enablement. The summit was facilitated by a global vendor-agnostic third party provider to the Fortune Global 500.

Through the course of the summit, two realizations materialized. The first emerged as critical business partners stressed that the inability of IT to understand the fundamentals of what services the business offered in the market, and to shape its practices, services and structures accordingly, created a vacuum that the business often went elsewhere to fill. This practice was found to exist at many levels, not just across lines of business, but similar behaviors were found to exist even within IT.

As a result of this discussion, the group came upon the second realization and began to understand the unintended outcomes of their behavior that were slowly handicapping the firm in terms of time-to-market, transaction costs, net revenues, competitive and cost efficient innovation etc… Jointly, the key stakeholders within the firm began to realize the degree to which it had disparate IT organizations, purchasing habits, labor pools, support organizations, duplicative systems, governance methods, 'shadow IT' and other deviations. Cumulatively, these deviations had already begun to have a noticeable negative impact on business performance and returns. The group made a strategic decision that going forward they would seek to leverage common resources wherever possible, and to alter their operating model and practices to promote this desired behavior. The process of demand management was selected as the focal point for driving much of this behavioral change."

Other related cards are:

- 2 of Clubs 'No respect for, or understanding of users;
- 4 of Clubs 'IT is not seen as an added value partner to the business';
- 8 of Clubs 'IT thinks it doesn't have to understand the business to make a business case';
- 5 of Clubs 'Neither partner makes an effort to understand the other';
- Queen of Clubs 'No understanding of business priority and impact';
- 2 of Diamonds 'We don't measure our value contribution to strategy'.

Process managers
without authority

Ace of Diamonds

'Process managers without authority'

Very often when adopting and deploying ITIL, the new role of process manager will suddenly spring up within the organization. You can either make a line manager a process manager, or you can create a separate role and give somebody the job of 'process manager'. This second option is often the case. However, what we then generally see is that the process manager has insufficient 'authority' and, as a result, they often struggle to get people to follow processes and procedures, or battle with line managers to try to get resources to carry out process activities, such as solve incidents, investigate problems and assess change impact. If process managers are NOT given authority, or line managers do not fully support process managers, then the process manager ends up banging his or her head against a brick wall all day…. people do not take the role seriously and soon ignore processes and procedures, resulting in complaints such as 'see I told you ITIL doesn't work'.

The level of authority given to a process manager is a good indicator of the level of commitment to ITIL within an organization. One of the common reasons for not adequately assigning authority is the misguided conception that you can 'implement ITIL', all you need are some 'processes and tools' and some 'ITIL training', forgetting that it is all about behavior, roles and responsibilities.

This can certainly end up as an issue when line managers begin to realize that various process managers are making claims on the line manager's resources, and the line manager is suddenly losing control. This is when you discover that line managers find ITIL a great idea so long as it doesn't get in the way of their own goals.

The cartoon on the card shows two managers fighting over a person. His clothes are being ripped as the two managers pull him in different directions. One says: "I need him for my process!", the other replies: "I don't care…I pay his salary and I need him for my project!"

Characteristics:

- Are the requests from the process managers always taking second place to the 'real work'?
- Are process managers seen as those people who 'write books of procedures'?
- If a process manager asks for resources, is he or she always being told "you'll have to see my manager" or "I've got more important things to do…..like playing cards"?
- Do line managers find their work more important than 'processes'?
- Are there RACI matrices for each role that show not only responsibilities but also authority?

ITIL mentions the RACI model. Responsible, Accountable, Consulted and Informed. Unfortunately it doesn't address 'Authority' levels. A process manager may be made Responsible, but if the process manager has no authority to claim resources or override priorities then they may be unable to fulfil their responsibilities.

Other related cards are:

- 6 of Clubs 'ITIL never work here';
- 7 of Clubs 'My TOOL will solve ALL your ITSM problems';
- King of Clubs 'ITIL is the objective….not what it should achieve';
- 5 of Diamonds 'No management commitment';
- 7 of Diamonds 'Throwing solutions over the wall and HOPING that people will use them';
- 8 of Diamonds 'We're going to INSTALL ITIL…it can't be that hard';
- 10 of Diamonds 'Never mind about following procedures….just do what we usually do';
- Jack of Diamonds 'Saying yes but meaning no';
- 3 of Spades 'Hierarchic culture. The boss is always right even when the boss is wrong';
- Queen of Spades 'Not my responsibility';
- King of Spades 'Empowering people.

Them and Us culture --
opposing and competing
forces

2 of Spades

'Them and Us culture - opposing and competing forces'

This type of organization is typified by IT people complaining about customers and users, 'They are always....', 'They don't understand...'. **They** being this unseen, unkown set of beings whose sole purpose in life seems to be to annoy IT people.
Often if you ask if these IT victims ever see or talk to users, they stare at you as if you are mad. 'Talk to them?...., We don't get to talk to them'. The communication is often done somewhere else in the organization and the results of the communication are rarely passed down, or are so watered down or changed that it is meaningless and irrelevant.

This attitude creates a lack of trust, a lack of willingness to engage or listen to the other side. This is often accompanied by the 2 of Clubs: 'ITIL uses the terms 'customers' and 'users', what terms do you use?'......The answer being 'dorks', 'morons', 'idiots', 'a pain in the ...'. Terms not included in the ITIL glossary but often used.

The cartoon on the card shows an IT person making a presentation, "Plan, Do, Check, Act ....what does the 'Do' stand for? 'Do' unto the users before they 'Do' unto you!"

Characteristics:

- Do IT people often complain about customers and users?
- How many IT people have regular contact and communication with the user community?
- Does IT market itself to the user community?
- Are customer and user satisfaction surveys undertaken?
- Do IT people really KNOW what the user and customer dissatisfiers are?
- Do users ever get to present to groups of IT staff about the business and what it does? And how IT supports and enables their work?

We have two cases here. One is from Robert Stroud, a well known figure in the ITIL world, the second is from David Pereira, an experienced ITIL practitioner based in Brazil.

> **Robert Stroud**, Vice President, Service Management, CA. Robert is an International Vice President at ISACA and the Chair of the CobiT Steering Committee, and also serves as Treasurer and the Director of Standards and Compliance with the itSMF International Executive Board. Robert was a member of the ITIL V3 advisory group.
>
> "My, how the world has changed in the last two decades. Twenty years ago I could catch a plane with a paper ticket, a manual bag tag and a smiling check-in agent. Today the whole process is technology based, and if the information technology (IT) systems don't work,

then you don't travel. What if IT and the business don't communicate, or if we ('we' being the customers or the business) implement a new charge and don't tell IT? What if IT schedules a system upgrade in the middle of the business day? Successful enterprises today realize the value of IT and recognize it is an integral part of the business services. However, business and IT do not always understand each other, and despite the recognized need for integration, neither partner makes enough of an effort to understand the other.

There is an 'us against them' attitude, one of 'I'm doing my part, why aren't you doing yours?'. And both parties are guilty of this, as they are worried that if they hand over any of their responsibilities, the other department might take it over. The reality is that if each department is too busy worrying about its own role, neither is concerned with the holistic endpoint - the customer.

Changing the attitudes of business and IT is not an easy feat, but through diligent work it can be accomplished. Communication is a key aspect, and the first step. A dialogue between business and IT must be started; the objective is to find common ground to begin working together, collaboratively. From this, a new business initiative or project, which can be used to transform not only the discourse between the two sides, but also the organization, can emerge.

To communicate effectively with each other, the plateau that communication is based on must be changed. For example, for many years IT has attempted to talk business terminology, but typically, the IT organization finds it difficult to transcend 'bits and bytes' to business-based processes or outcomes. Rather than focusing on business and IT, the discussion should focus on the industry customer. Management reinforcement of this collaborative communication is necessary to ensure that both parties work together.

The chief information officer (CIO) plays an integral role. If not already aware of, and familiar with, the relevant organizational objectives, it is necessary to revisit them. (Essentially, this is going back to the basics to understand the business, not IT, goals and objectives, and the strategies being enforced by the business as a directive for how to move the organization forward.) The CIO must be familiar with the current business terminology rather than just the customary IT language that he or she uses on a routine basis.

Another way to enforce the collaborative communication is to set up cross-functional teams that will allow dynamics of the discussion and what is delivered to be changed and improved.

Managers need to set the right objectives and the right metrics. Ultimately, how they are measured is what will drive behavior. Imagine trying to get a sales person to sell without commission. There would be no incentive to perform to the best of one's ability. Performance needs to be measured and, therefore, be measurable, to ensure optimal results. So, if governance metrics are set that identify the performance of the sales person and a required number to sell, the incentive to perform is in place, even without commission. The same is true in any other business - performance must be measured.

This is where IT governance comes into play. The highest-level objective of IT governance ensures that IT meets or exceeds business requirements based on business metrics matched to IT processes and activities. IT governance allows the organization to set goals, objectives and measurements to ensure that the metrics used are business-based. IT can then execute on those metrics and deliver to them, focusing on what is critical to the business, and drive behavior to support the end goal.

The specific solution depends on the business demographic, the organization and the organization's culture. An effective shortcut followed by many organizations already familiar with IT governance can be found in the Control Objectives for Information and Related Technology (CobiT) framework. CobiT includes a series of tables that link business goals to IT processes. Seventeen generic business goals are listed within a subset for organizations based on a balanced scorecard (BSC). Management should validate which of the scorecard items are leveraged and used for the business, from which IT processes can be understood and executed to support the goals, and ultimately lead to metrics and deliverables.

Take, for example, the idea of a stoplight at a busy highway. If someone wants to cross the highway, there are two options: cross the street at any point, or walk up to the light where there is a crosswalk that provides a level of security, like a good governance process. When the light is red for cross traffic, the cars stop and it is OK for a pedestrian to cross the street. The same is true of accepted goals and metrics. There is a set of principles, goals and metrics, and expectations; it is clear what red means and what green means, as a result of the BSC.

For organizations not already familiar with IT governance, the *Board Briefing on IT Governance, 2nd Edition*, published by ITGI, provides a good starting point - a practical overview and introduction to activities an organization can use for a high-level IT governance plan and strategies to be implemented.

Achieving IT and business alignment is a relatively simple concept - IT and business must work together - yet one that results in consistent failure. Through collaborative communication, management reinforcement, cross-functional teams, and effective IT governance to ensure that the correct metrics and measurements are in place, business and IT can effectively work together."

David Pereira, a senior consultant with ITXL in Brazil. David has a wide range of experience helping organizations improve using ITSM best practices.

"In my ITIL classes, as well in my speeches, I used to say that satisfaction can be measured using a mathematical formula: $S = P/E$, or Satisfaction = Perception / Expectation. The issue about satisfaction as far as mutual relationships are concerned is that usually these two variables have a different interpretation from the perspective of the involved parts (clients, IT and 3rd parties).

The great issue about the 'Them & Us Culture' is that it is all about listening. In our projects we can observe a kind of repeating pattern that can be summarized as: "IT is so arrogant, they don't listen to us", and on the other side: "The business guys are so arrogant, they are not able to explain what they want and expect that we guess everything".

This kind of conversation is very interesting because, in theory, everybody wants the same thing: to contribute to business success. However, in the practice, nobody is concerned about 'the business', they are concerned about how to make their own life easier."

Case:

"After an initial assessment of ITIL maturity in a chemical company in a South American country, the CIO became very worried about the level of maturity that was awarded to the service level management process: next to zero. He was also uncomfortable about the insights that we collected during the interviews with the end users and the clients (who pay the IT costs) because there was a general consensus about the lack of IT professionalism. It showed that the IT guys did not behave as professionals.

The CIO was tired of these kinds of complaints, because regardless of the effort that the IT team devoted, the users always said that IT didn't deliver what was promised, the quality of the services was poor and IT didn't add any value to the business.
On the other hand, the IT team complained about the kind of users that they had to deal with: 'confused, incoherent, arrogant, bad tempered, stupid' and another hundred terms that disqualify the users from being equal partners who deserve respect and to be taken seriously.

This situation created such a level of distrust that any kind of initiative to establish a service level agreement was inconceivable."

What was done?
"We had the idea to perform a series of ITSM simulations using Apollo 13. In each simulation we put both users and IT people together, but we decided to assign in advance the roles. We allocated the user roles to IT staff and vice-versa. Another decision was to select a client of IT as Flight Director (the role responsible for organizing the team work).

In some sessions we could quickly see how deep the bad feelings were between users and IT, but as the simulation progressed we began to observe that the perception about the need to have agreements, the limitations of resources, the time that was necessary to perform some activities and the dependency of vendors, was gradually changing. Both sides started to share the same experiences, both sides felt the pain and the need to work together.

At the end of the sessions we distributed the evaluation forms for the simulation and we collected some quotes that summarized how people 'felt' about the result of the simulation:

"Now I know what it is like to be in the IT shoes"
"Now I can understand that is not possible to assign the same priority to everything"
"We need to improve our comprehension about what is a relationship based on agreements"
"We need to be client oriented" (this phrase was written by an IT guy)

We could clearly see that attitudes had changed. In the simulation both sides had experimented with a different way of behaving, and both sides saw the positive effects of this new way of behaving. This is what helped to change attitudes.

A number of weeks after the simulation we started a pilot project for ITSM process improvement with the participation of end users, and the result was very good. Everybody was able to contribute with their own point of view, but the team was also able to design a process respecting the point of view of the other party. Today, in the chemical company, the relationship between IT and users is much better."

This is another case of using a simulation. There are a number of simulations on the market, not just Apollo 13. It is not important in this case that Apollo 13 was used. It shows that a simulation confronts people with their own attitudes and behavior. In the simulated environment people can apply new behavior; they see, feel and experience the impact which can help to change attitude and, in changing attitude, it can mean they behave differently when they go back into their live working environment.

Other cards that underpin this are:

- The Joker 'Unable to specify the VALUE required by the business';
- 4 of Spades 'Internally focused';
- Jack of Clubs 'Let's outsource the business';
- Queen of Clubs 'No understanding of business priority and impact';
- 10 of Spades 'The superiority complex 'we know best!';
- 5 of Clubs 'Neither partner makes an effort to understand the other';
- Queen of Diamonds 'The solution the Customer sees isn't the one that IT sees';
- King of Diamonds 'IT strategy's contribution to business strategy (or lack of)';
- 2 of Diamonds 'We don't measure our value contribution to strategy'.

3 of Spades

'Hierarchic culture. The boss is always right....
even when the boss is wrong'

This type of organization is typified by a leadership style of S1. (In terms of the situational leadership styles of Ken Blanchard.) S1 is 'directing'. I tell you what to do and you do it! There is little conscious effort to apply any other leadership styles such as 'supporting', 'coaching' or 'delegating'. In this type of organization people are told to DO ITIL, we WILL BE DOING ITIL. Little effort or energy is spent on winning the hearts and minds of people. In this type of organization 'awareness' sessions are seen as unnecessary, and the IT manager often gives the 'five minute kick-off speech' about ITIL and is then rarely seen again.

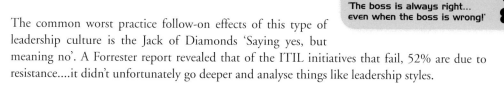

The common worst practice follow-on effects of this type of leadership culture is the Jack of Diamonds 'Saying yes, but meaning no'. A Forrester report revealed that of the ITIL initiatives that fail, 52% are due to resistance....it didn't unfortunately go deeper and analyse things like leadership styles.

The cartoon on the card shows an organizational consultant talking to the CEO. The consultant is reading from a memo prepared by the CEO: "I see you have changed the selection criteria for new managers.....must be 'yes' men....willing to grovel to the boss!"

Characteristics:

- Are staff input and ideas for improvements often ignored?
- Do managers force their ideas through?
- Is time given to awareness and communication before changes are implemented, to ensure buy-in?
- Do staff complain about managers forcing plans through?
- Do IT staff behave like victims...'I don't agree but I HAVE to do it', '..this is going to fail, or be delayed...but we've been TOLD to do it'.
- Do managers delegate well?
- Do managers coach and empower people to be more independent and able to make their own decisions?

Other cards that may be relevant in this type of environment are:

- 10 of Clubs 'No respect for, or trust in IT management';
- King of Spades 'Empowering people (or rather lack of)';
- 5 of Clubs 'Neither partner makes an effort to understand the other';
- 10 of Spades 'The superiority complex – we know best';

- 5 of Spades 'Punishment culture';
- Ace of Spades 'The blame culture';
- 5 of Diamonds 'No management commitment'.

4 of Spades

'Internally focused'

This type of IT organization can be typified by internally focused IT goals, measures and metrics, with little link with business goals and needs. It is this type of organization that the ITIL V3 Service Strategy book is aiming at. It may be that the IT organization is internally focused because the business doesn't trust IT or actively engage with IT. It may be that IT simply doesn't understand how to engage with the business. It may also be the fact that there is no option for the business to go elsewhere, so why should IT bother and make an effort. Most of the ITIL projects we see are typified by this. Ask people if they KNOW what the customer dissatisfiers are, ask people if they KNOW what value they must deliver to the business, and the answer is usually 'we think'. IT assumes and doesn't KNOW.

This is also one of the high scoring cards chosen during ABC workshops using the ABC cards.

The cartoon on the card shows a goal keeper standing in his goal. Only he is facing the wrong way. The ball bounces on his head and goes into his goal…..scoring in fact an own goal.

Characteristics:

- Is there no clear link between IT goals and business goals?
- Is IT regularly invited to business strategy and planning sessions?
- Are there business account managers and service level managers?
- Do IT managers spend a lot of time 'in the business'?
- Do improvement project business cases refer to business impact?
- Do IT KPI's and reports show the link to business value? Continuity?

Other cards that are related to this may be:

- King of Diamonds 'IT strategy's contribution to business strategy';
- 8 of Clubs 'IT thinks it doesn't need to understand the business to make a business case';
- Queen of Clubs 'No understanding of business priority and impact';
- 2 of Spades 'Them and Us culture – opposing and competing forces';
- 3 of Diamonds 'Too little business involvement in requirements specification & testing'.

This internal focus can also be as a result of other cards, for example:

- 5 of Clubs 'Neither partner makes an effort to understand the other';
- 4 of Clubs 'IT not seen as an added value partner to the business';

- 7 of Hearts 'Demand & Give. I demand and you give in';
- King of Hearts 'The CEO: Which part of NO didn't you understand'.

This type of behavior can result in a vicious circle. The business doesn't trust us or involve us, so we will become internally focused. This, in turn, results in the fact that the business doesn't trust us or involve us……the ultimate result of this can be outsourcing, or the IT manager being cordially invited to seek a new job.

5 of Spades

'Punishment culture'

This type of organization is characterized by 'failure is not an option'. Not in the sense that IT can no longer fail to align itself with business needs, but that any type of mistake is not tolerated. Learning by mistakes is not seen as valuable. This type of punishment culture can stimulate a reactive IT organization, nobody does anything extra for fear of reprisals, nobody wants the challenging innovative projects for fear of failing. People only do what they are paid to do. In this type of organization people may not give open feedback or criticism because others may be punished. It is like a 'tell tale' at school, nobody wants to be seen as teacher's pet.

The cartoon shows somebody in the 'stocks'. His head and arms are sticking out of the holes. He has broken eggs dripping off him. Next to him stands the CEO. The CEO says to an unseen audience: "….anybody else not following procedures will get the same…."

Characteristics:

- Are people punished for mistakes?
- Is learning from mistakes valued?
- Are mistakes and failures evaluated so that preventative measures can be taken to ensure future success?
- Are people fearful of taking on new or uncertain projects?
- Do people say "I'm not sticking my neck out"?

Clive Strawford, an independent consultant who has worked extensively for IBM in the Far East has submitted the following case.

"While we understand that people seldom go out in the morning saying to themselves "I'm really going to **** things up today", mistakes do happen, and some pretty catastrophic ones at that. At one organization I worked at, a mistake even made the national news! Not too surprising when thousands of people had their credit card transactions reversed not once, but six times in all! A nice little windfall for the guy in the Middle East who had just purchased a car on his credit card!

So how do we reduce the likelihood of mistakes? After all, 'to err is human (but to really mess things up you need a computer)' is the saying and availability is so often the key for successful operations especially in the financial industry.

When I first started working, punishment was the answer but, in these more enlightened days, we have mostly dispensed with punishment, except for the most serious disciplinary matters. We understand that rewarding people actually makes them more caring about their job, makes them seek out new initiatives, empowers them! Now most of us are targeted on success and the more senior will have bonuses, or are incentivised based on their success. When we do err, we are no longer penalised. Instead, we understand that the mistake must have been caused by an error in the process or a lack of training, and we have processes to deal with either eventuality. In short, we attack the root cause, or we are taught the error of our ways rather than being penalised.

This is not the case all over the world though. In one particular Far Eastern country where I worked recently, reward schemes are unheard of and mistakes are still treated through punishment, mostly financial ones. Staff are given a basic salary and at monthly pay time, pay is reduced if any errors were made.

Penalties are so entrenched in these organizations, that the only management information gathered and KPI's in existence are there solely to support the penalty system.

For example, at one of the world's top 10 banks, second line support teams are financially penalised for having 'too many' tickets raised against their team. At another, the service desk is penalised for taking 'too many' calls!

Not only are these measures rather intriguing, the methods used by teams to ensure they did not get penalised are equally so. For example, the service desk reduced the call numbers by reducing their working hours and the number of staff available on the phone lines! The second line support teams prioritised all incidents that had not been logged, since the less time an incident was open, the less likelihood that it would get logged against them or their team.

As you can imagine these solutions did wonders for customer satisfaction and really fostered an open, honest and trusting environment!

The rationale behind penalising people is fairly straightforward, albeit a little naïve. The belief is that staff will not make mistakes if they are frightened of being penalised and so will take more care in their work. While it is a deterrent, as anyone who has been on a management course knows or who has been trained in ITIL, penalising people in the workplace tends to make them overly cautious, less likely to take responsibility, more secretive and less open to innovation. This was certainly the case in the organizations above where innovation was stifled and taking responsibility frowned on.

But can we change this concept? In one mobile phone organization in this Far Eastern country I tried to explain the justification of a reward regime rather than a punishment one. This particular organization had come bottom in an internal survey on capability measured by their headquarters.

Although I put forward all the well-worn arguments, it was still very difficult for managers to understand the logic. Surprisingly, even the workers believed punishment was the only way to reduce errors and, although they were not very happy when they were penalised, accepted the punishment as a necessary evil.

One of the problems they could not get over at first was the fact that a reward system would not necessarily be more costly than a penalty one. They could not believe that done correctly, it should be cost neutral or even save money.

To show them what could be done I took their current KPI document and transformed all the penalties for errors into rewards for successes and showed by taking the previous month's penalty charges that the reward system would not have cost the department any more than they had already paid.

This did a little to dispense the worries; enough for the CIO to agree to parallel run the reward system against their own system for three months to see if the costs would pan out. As it turned out the success regime would have cost a little less and they were mightily impressed. I would like to say that this simple exercise changed their way of looking at the problem but culture is not so easily altered and after the exercise they carried on in their usual way. However, the thought processes that were instigated by going down this path did have an overall effect. After the three month exercise, the organization had moved up from bottom in their internal survey to fifth, which was not only an enormous coup for the CIO, it resulted in knock-on consultancy orders for the organization I was representing. A very pleasing result all round!"

Other cards that may be relevant in this type of organization are:

- 10 of Clubs 'No respect for, or trust in management';
- 3 of Spades 'Hierarchic culture. The boss is always right even when the boss is wrong';
- Jack of Spades 'Avoidance culture';
- 8 of Hearts 'The buck stops anywhere but here'.

6 of Spades

'The Hero culture'

In this type of organization the IT experts are seen as heroes, they are worshipped by their peers who want to be like them, and they are handled with gloves by the managers who don't want to upset or annoy them. These people then develop a superiority complex and start behaving as they wish. Often there are few consequences attached to their negative behavior. Documenting things is beneath them and not worthy of their considerable technical expertise, testing things almost implies that they don't know what they are doing, so they are loath to test. Transferring their highly valued knowledge to other lowly, intellectually-challenged IT employees is unheard of. People that do not understand them are hardly worth talking to or taking seriously, especially managers and users. These people also generally believe that IT would be a better world if we could only outsource the business......We know because we were technoids. These types of people also display the type of behavior shown on the 6 of Hearts 'That problem isn't in my book, therefore it doesn't exist'. Believe us this REALLY happens. See the section on the 6 of Hearts.

The cartoon on the card shows a technoid unbuttoning his shirt to reveal underneath a Superman shirt.

Characteristics:

- Are the same rules applied to all IT staff?
- Do managers turn a blind eye to the undesirable behavior of technical specialists?
- Is there evidence of 'kid-glove' handling of people?
- Do certain IT staff believe they can get away with pretty much what they like because managers 'dare not' punish them?

Other related cards are:

- 3 of Clubs 'Knowledge is power';
- 6 of Clubs 'ITIL never work here';
- 10 of Clubs 'No respect for, or trust in management';
- 5 of Diamonds 'No management commitment';
- Jack of Diamonds 'Saying yes but meaning no';
- Queen of Spades 'Not my responsibility';
- King of Spades 'Empowering people';
- 5 of Hearts 'Without me the world will stop spinning';
- 6 of Hearts 'That problem isn't in my book, therefore it doesn't exist'.

7 of Spades

'9 to 5 culture'

This type of organization is typified by IT people who only do what they absolutely need to do. People begin exactly on time, work is wound down early so that people can get away on time. Lunch breaks are long, people are not quick to volunteer to do any overtime. It can be because these are the rules of the organization and they are strictly controlled and enforced through regulations or unions. It may also be because there is no real personal ownership or responsibility. No responsibility for the quality of service, possibly no pride in what people are doing. It can be because there is little value or recognition for doing more, so people don't, since managers don't value it or reward or praise people for doing more. It may be the result of a lack of respect for management. Or it may be as a result of the way the business treats IT.

Changing a real 9 to 5 culture in which the organizational rules dictate working hours is different to creating an environment in which people are 'willing' to do more. This willingness comes from challenging, rewarding work, a sense of value or worth.

Giving feedback and rewarding somebody that has done more can make a difference, having users give praise and thanks for work done can make a difference. If you do something that you are proud of, something that challenged you, something that you felt was an achievement and everybody ignores it doesn't stimulate in you an automatic desire to do it again. The same applies in IT organizations.

The cartoon shows the space shuttle a minute or so after the launch. The shuttle calls mission control: "Houston we have a problem!". The response from mission control is: "Thank you for calling the Help Desk....unfortunately it has passed 17:00 and we are closed. We will be open at tomorrow at 09:00.....have a nice day!"

Characteristics:

• Do people go home promptly on time?
• Do people avoid starting tasks around 4 p.m.?
• Are users frustrated by not having support at all times when they are working?
• Do evening or nightly IT failures mean regular downtime during the day?

Other cards that may be relevant in this type of organization are:

• 5 of Spades 'Punishment culture';
• 3 of Spades 'Hierarchic culture. The boss is always right even when the boss is wrong';

- Jack of Spades "'Avoidance culture';
- Queen of Spades 'Not my responsibility;
- 7 of Hearts 'Demand and Give. I demand and you give in!';
- 2 of Clubs 'No respect for, or understanding of users'.

8 of Spades

'Plan, Do, Stop....no real continual improvement culture'

This is another of the more popular cartoons which typifies the fact that many ITIL improvement initiatives are seen and managed as projects. Results are handed over to the organization and the project disbanded. Often because there is no real ownership or accountability for the processes, or no authority for process managers, people can revert back to the old ways of doing things. Often people simply don't realize that ITIL has always been about continual improvement and the continual alignment of processes to business needs. We believe that *The CSI* book should have been the first book released with ITIL V3 so that the ITSM community could start focusing on what it should have been doing over the last 10 years with ITIL.

The cartoon on the card shows somebody pushing a large boulder up a hill. The boulder has the words 'Plan, Do, Stop' written on it. The boulder cannot go any further because its path is blocked by a pile of ITIL books.

Characteristics:

- Are processes regularly evaluated for performance and relevance?
- Are the service improvement plans regularly evaluated?
- Who is actually responsible for improving existing processes?
- Do process managers have authority for changing existing processes and procedures?
- How often are customer and user surveys carried out on the processes or services?
- Is there evidence that processes and services are assessed as a part of major change programs and new IT solutions to ensure that processes are realigned?
- Is the selection criteria of new people aligned to ensure new people have the right attitude and behavior and will fit the culture?

Harold Petersen, Director and Principal Consultant, Lucid IT Pte Ltd, Singapore.

"Several years ago, I had an assignment in Australia to design and implement a centralised service desk, including all people, procedural and tool aspects of the related processes. We had to transition several existing support centres into one central service desk. The assignment was tremendously successful, not in the least because the customer met all the prerequisites for successful organizational change. Senior IT management had a strong sense of urgency to 'fix' the comparatively expensive and scattered support structure in order to improve customer satisfaction and service levels. They followed through on their sense of urgency and vision by actively supporting the implementation project until completion:

- The tailoring of blue print 'best practice' processes was taken seriously and applied in a very practical way by involving existing support managers in design workshops.
- A completely refurbished floor was set up and equipped with white boards, 'war rooms', colourful design etc.
- PABX, IVR and ITSM tools were purchased and configured to underpin and automate the processes.
- Most importantly, a team with the right mix of skills and experience was recruited into a well defined organizational structure, including service desk manager, team leaders, service desk analysts, request fulfilment teams, tool administration and reporting people, major incident managers and a problem management team. The people were trained in ITIL, customer service skills and in their new procedures, and – importantly – we facilitated some extensive and recurring communication sessions and knowledge exchange between the service desk teams and second level support teams, such as various application management teams, outsourcers, and internal network and architecture teams. This improved the co-operation between first and second line, underpinned correct call routing, and also increased the rate of fix on first call rates, due to improved first line knowledge of the business, applications and infrastructure.

The implementation was an astounding success for all concerned. Service levels were up (well, they were truly measurable for the first time), customer satisfaction went through the roof and, importantly, service desk employee satisfaction was great too (and attrition therefore low).

What then is the 'worst practice' in this anecdote one might ask?

The 'worst practice' was something that evolved quite some time after these great successes.

As happens with successful IT managers, the service desk manager and her boss moved on to greener pastures. The next service desk manager had not been part of the ITIL implementation journey and started to pay less attention to the 'check' and 'act' aspects of the plan-do-check-act cycle. He reported less frequently than what was defined in the procedures and didn't include quite the same KPI's that used to be reviewed in the past. His new boss – also not having been involved in the original implementation – didn't pay too much attention to the reports, let alone use them to check on service desk compliance, performance, costs and value delivery (the service desk is doing fine, so 'she'll be right').

Due to the fact that the new service desk manager was generally a capable support and people manager, and the team was still largely in place, the effects of the above were minimal and the service desk manager was still achieving fine customer satisfaction. After a successful period the new service desk manager also moved on and was replaced by an externally recruited manager. Around that time, the majority of the original service desk team had moved on as well. The service levels started to really suffer.

Service desk manager number three tried to patch incident resolution delays by assigning problem managers and major incident managers to regular incident management. They ended up not carrying out their real role any longer, which affected their job satisfaction as well as proactive resolutions and knowledge management. The service desk manager's boss was starting to ask for ad hoc reports in reaction to business complaints about the deteriorating service desk performance. There were moments of panic. Everybody was always busy. Almost every week, new ad hoc reports with different metrics were requested. The morale at the service desk went from bad to worse. The once well oiled system had become inconsistent.

The reason for all of this was ultimately the lack of:

- Consistent process document management ('planning'), since the original handbook had never been updated and was not referred to any longer.
- Consistency (after personnel and management changes) in 'checking' KPI reports and 'acting' upon findings, which ultimately undermined the effectiveness and efficiency of the 'doing' and hence service levels and customer satisfaction.

The beauty of the Deming circle is that it really works, if truly managed with heart and soul, rather than just complying 'on paper'. The new managers developed a renewed sense of urgency to improve the service desk. This new sense of urgency was triggered firstly by the above mentioned deterioration of service desk services, but also because internal auditors uncovered the fact that process documents were missing, standard reports were no longer created, and the audit trails of 'doing' what used to be 'planned' in the old procedures had become inconsistent.

At this point, someone remembered the old ITIL-based service desk handbook. The source document could not be found in the service desk network files. Some loose pages were still floating around, with priority and escalation tables, but they no longer existed within the 'holistic' context of a complete process. Some of the original service desk staff were able to retrieve a backed up version and they established a plan to re-instate the old situation of plan-do-check-act, applied to best practice ITIL blueprint processes that were tailored to their environment. My organization was also contacted again to carry out a 'current state' assessment to provide further analysis of the details behind the audit results, assist with further tailoring of the handbook to the new situation and then communicate around the re-establishment of the procedures in the handbook.

The basis of the procedures was still represented by the tool configuration. There were still some people who had been there during the first ITIL implementation. There was once more a sense of urgency. As a result, it did not take long to redefine and baseline the procedures in a new version of the service desk handbook ('plan'). It also became clear that the profiles of service desk manager and team manager roles needed to be applied more rigorously and some corrections were made in the job/role assignments. A clear split was once more applied between request fulfilment, normal incident, major incident and problem management. People were re-trained and managed towards process compliance ('do') and the link that had been missing for some time was firmly put back in place: 'check' monthly KPI's and 'act' to trigger continuous improvement.

The situation was swiftly restored due to a sound best practice basis and timely action."

Other related cards are:

- 5 of Diamonds 'No management commitment';
- 7 of Diamonds 'Throwing solutions over the wall and HOPING that people will use them';
- Queen of Spades 'Not my responsibility'.

9 of Spades

'Promotion on ability' (not)

"...excellent suggestion Ms. Savill...perhaps one of the men would care to make it."

Promotion on ability

This type of organization is characterized by people being promoted on years of service rather than on capabilities. Performance does not necessarily mean a chance to obtain better positions or new tasks, roles, responsibilities. This can often lead to apathy. Why should I excel if it isn't rewarded.

Another equally damaging example of this is promoting people above their capability. Promoting somebody out of their comfort zone, without empowering them or enabling them to fulfil their new role. People don't like to admit weakness or say they are not capable, especially in organizations where the boss is always right, or a punishment culture exists.

The cartoon shows a meeting. There is one woman sitting at the table. The chairman of the meeting says "…excellent suggestion Ms. Saville…..perhaps one of the men would care to make it!..."

Characteristics:

- Are people generally promoted on length of service?
- Are people hardly ever promoted on ability or performance?
- Do staff feel that people are promoted based upon who they know?
- Can you name young achievers who obtained their position on ability?
- If you ask people why certain managers are in certain positions, what will the answer be?
- If you ask people 'are those managers capable?' what will be the answers?

Ivor MacFarlane, IBM. Ivor is another well known and respected member of the ITSM community. An author of ITIL V1 and ITIL V3 books and member of the itSMF international executive committee, Ivor has added a short case of what he sees as being worst practices in this area.

Short term-ism

"The new IT manager was keen to impress and motivate his staff. He had read the management practice books and felt they should see the bigger picture, be aware of industry trends and had spent all his training budget. This would make it clear he was a modern and caring manager.

So … staff were trained in ITIL, all put through Foundation. The junior managers (who actually made the place run) struggled and studied and worked their way through Managers – many of them even passed. But all of them got the idea, saw the light, realised how an integrated approach to ITSM would make their lives better. They could see the golden future where processes were appropriate and maintained, and all the elements of IT worked together because ongoing work had been done to make the processes match.

A brave new world had been set out in front of the staff – and what is more they had been given the tools to build and deliver it. Metrics would reflect what the business needed and harmony would reign.

The new manager – after the training was over – held a staff meetings (as per page 42 of his 'how to be a caring manager' book).

The case for a serious, wide ranging service improvement program is set out for the boss. He understands the approach, realises the benefits that will accrue to the business, and sees how it will make the IT organization a better place to work.

Then he sees the time frame: feasibility and planning phase; assessment of current situation; development of improved processes; implementation and familiarisation; organizational, staff and customer change initiatives. A big organization changing the way they think and deliver – classic example of turning the tanker – well worth it, especially when the tanker was aiming for the sandbank that was marked on the map as 'outsourcing shoal'.

But the time frame for real benefits is in 18 months, and the manager knows that this organization rotates its management level staff every 24 months, and he has been there seven months already. So – no good to him then. No benefit in doing the right thing for his successor to reap the benefits, he will be judged on the returns while he is in that seat.

So, the project is rejected – instead the focus is only on band-aid repairs that will look good now. OK, some good things get done but the underlying faults from unmatched and incomplete processes remain. The investment in asset and configuration management that would have delivered the foundation for all the other ITSM elements are not put in place.

The result is short term improvements but a serious long term downward trend in staff morale, an increase in staff turnover (and the good ones with the perception and the ideas are those who find it easier to get other jobs).

In 18 months the manager gets his promotion. His replacement looks at the department and realises the staff don't have any real enthusiasm for his ideas for change, and the IT is outsourced.

Of course this isn't the short term boss's fault, nor the suffering staff's fault, yet they and the customers who could have had better service are the ones to suffer. There are two levels we can consider that would help:

1. The organization should examine its turn-around times, its staff assessment and – especially – its silo measures. It is perfectly possible for a department to hit its targets and its budgets at the cost of the business as a whole, not as a means to support it. A

multinational oil company changed its attitude on managerial appointment turnover a few years ago, possibly driven by the increasing costs of training, house moves and excess mileage, and it delivered a quick increase in the average length of and number of 'infrastructure style' projects aimed at addressing underlying defects – and not just in IT either.

2. Pragmatic realisation and manipulation by the junior managers – the perfect service improvement initiative delivers some quick wins – not just for the managers' benefit but also for the customers, users and CFO. Couple this, though, with elements that address the underlying needs for improvement. Configuration might start with understanding the links between services, servers and applications – but at the same time a plan for further detail was made and started. And while the new integrated service management tool will not deliver full benefits for 18 months – the salesmen keen to supply it will wine and dine the boss, whilst getting the call-logging element in place will speed up service desk record and response times."

Other related cards are:

• 3 of Spades 'Hierarchic culture. The boss is always right even when the boss is wrong';
• 10 of Clubs 'No respect for, or trust in management'.

"...I'm just listening to what this user has to say!"

The superiority complex
"We know best!"

10

10 of Spades

'The superiority complex – we know best'

This type of organization is characterized by IT thinking it knows best. IT knows what is best for the business. Many IT organizations we come across deny this. One such organization wanted to invest in ITSM to improve the service to the business. It wasn't necessary to perform a customer satisfaction survey because the business doesn't know what it wants and it will, therefore, be a waste of time.

The investment was to develop 12 SLA's and present these to the business, and get the business to agree to them. A team of consultants were hired in at great expense and spent months documenting extensive, detailed service level documents. When they were ready they were presented to the business for signing. The business unit managers refused to sign the agreements; they hadn't been consulted, furthermore they weren't waiting for SLA's, they were waiting for IT to start involving them and talking to them, asking what they needed. They were waiting for IT to be more proactive. This was a hugely expensive exercise in producing several hundred pages of paper that was thrown in the bin.....but IT knew best what the business wanted.

The cartoon shows the IT manager standing behind a user. He bends down and puts his ear next to the rear end of the user and then says: "....I'm just listening to what this user has to say!..."

Characteristics:

- Are customer satisfaction surveys a regular occurance?
- Is the business involved in ITSM process improvements?
- Does IT proactively inform and notify the business of changes?
- Do IT people complain about the lack of IT awareness and competence of business people?
- Is the business given enough information to make informed choices about IT?
- How often, and for what reasons, are business people involved in IT projects?
- Are there strategic committees of business and IT representatives?
- Are IT business cases aimed at 'business value?'
- Are there always 'senior users' in IT project boards?

Other cards that underpin this are:

- 2 of Clubs 'No respect for, or understanding of customers';
- 4 of Spades 'Internally focused';
- Jack of Clubs 'Let's outsource the business';
- 2 of Spades 'Them and us culture – opposing and competing forces'.

Jack of Spades

'Avoidance culture'

This type of IT organization is characterized by 'burying your head in the sand and HOPING it will go away'. This can also be closely related to the punishment culture. If there is a culture of blame and punishment, people are more likely to avoid putting themselves in a position to be shot down. Another reason for this can be the relationship between business and IT. If IT has little credit within the business, and the business little faith or trust in IT, they will be critical and complain and everything that IT does or proposes will get criticized….it is therefore better not to bother. It can also be as a result of the complexity and challenging nature of business requests, 'we can't do that, we are not capable, let's not set unrealistic expectations, best just to avoid getting in that position'.

Another example we have seen of this is where the IT organization is unwilling to invest in IT training and yet people are expected to develop new solutions on time. People want to avoid being 'dumped upon'. Other situations similar to this arise when there is resistance, for example the roll-out of ITIL. If there is open resistance and criticism, then project and service managers often want to avoid the conflict and the arguments so they ignore it and hope it will go away by itself. It usually does 'openly' go away, but comes back as hidden, invisible resistance. This is a very common chacteristic and human trait. We want the easy life, let's avoid things.

Another example of this is the 'Victim' feeling in IT. We are being dumped on by the business. We tried once to resolve it but they sent us away. Therefore we won't try again. This is avoiding your accountability as an IT organization. An IT organization is accountable for the responsible management and control of IT and IT projects given to them. If you are dumped upon and feel a victim of the business it is your responsibility to change things. Simply moaning about it and feeling sorry isn't going to change anything.

The cartoon on the card shows a man with his head buried in a bucket of sand. He says to his secretary "….tell me when the business stops complaining."

Characteristics:

- Do people avoid giving feedback to each other?
- Do people avoid conflict?
- Are sayings like 'don't rock the boat' and 'don't stick your head above the trenches' used in the organization?
- Do people not willingly volunteer for difficult or risky projects?
- Is there a 'punishment culture' or a 'blame culture' within the organization?
- Do managers back-up IT staff at all times and protect them from the business?

Case:

Kirstie Magowan, of Verso Solutions Ltd in New Zealand, provides a case relating to this.

"You need to know where you are....

One thing I stress to my customers is the importance of taking some baseline measurements before starting to introduce ITIL based processes into their organizations. Two customers I worked with had quite different viewpoints on the importance of this information.

Customer one had a pretty poor relationship with the business; they received a constant barrage of complaints about their poor service and rudeness to customers. Very few days went by when someone didn't show up to complain about some part of the IT service, or lack of service.

The IT manager in this case refused to do a pre-ITIL customer satisfaction survey because he didn't want to encourage any further complaints by making business users think about the quality of the service they were receiving. He really didn't want to know the full extent of the dissatisfaction with IT services that was present in the business.

We carried on and introduced incident management, but the culture of the IT department was the biggest obstacle to improving the service. The service desk manager was the driving force behind the implementation of ITIL-based processes, but she had very little support from the rest of the department. The fact that she was able to get any funding to move ahead with this project surprised me, but I think it was probably a silencing tactic – they were just sick of her insistence on the value of ITIL.

Unfortunately this was a project that was probably doomed to failure from day one. Most of the department had no understanding of ITIL and there was no funding for any of them to have training and, sadly, the evangelism of the service desk manager probably turned them off even further.

I believe that the incident management process made some significant improvements to their customer satisfaction and anecdotal evidence supports this, but with no baseline study done, we will never know; and without evidence of success there will be no further funding for this project.

The ITIL implementation at this site has stalled at incident management and I doubt it will proceed any further. The service desk manager has since moved on and is happily employed in an environment that embraces ITIL and where she is able to make a difference.

Customer two had a totally different view on the value of pre-implementation measurements. Although they knew that their customers were not happy with IT in general, they wanted to know exactly how unhappy they were. Prior to going live with their new toolset, we sent out a customer satisfaction survey. As expected there were quite a lot of negatives and the overall score left a lot of room for improvement.

This customer took this as a challenge and something to work towards. At the end of three months we redid the survey and the results were dramatically improved. Because of all of the baseline measurements we had taken prior to implementing new processes, we were able to see that things were much better. Incidents were being resolved on time, customers were being contacted and, most importantly, customers were happy.

There was still a way to go until service could really be considered to be 'great' but with the metrics we were able to present to the business we were able to justify bringing in three new service desk staff to help drive the improvement ahead. Without those baseline measurements this would not have been possible.

The moral to this story is that no matter how bad things are, you are always better to know the true state of play – if you don't know where you are starting, how you know where you want to be or what direction you need to take to get there."

This case graphically indicates the importance of a dialogue with the customers, to show we understand and respect them, to show that we want to understand the impact on their business and their priorities for resolving specific issues. Ultimately what was created was a satisfied customer. Rare in IT. Perhaps we should follow Basil Fawlty's advice from Fawty Towers: " A **satisfied customer**. We should have him stuffed. ...."

Other related cards are:

- 5 of Diamonds 'No management commitment';
- 7 of Diamonds 'Throwing solutions over the wall and HOPING that people will use them';
- Jack of Diamonds 'Saying yes but meaning no';
- Queen of Spades 'Not my responsibility';
- Ace of Spades 'Blame culture';
- 8 of Hearts 'The buck stops anywhere but here.

"...my responsibility is receiving USER complaints.. Not DOING something about them!..."

Not my responsibility

Queen of Spades

'Not my responsibility'

This type of organization is typified by people using job descriptions and roles as an excuse for not doing something. Or using the lack of clear job descriptions in the same way. Strong hierarchic organizations and an authoritative management style can be a reason for people refusing to do things. It may be a form of resistance to these types of management styles that causes people to refuse to do things and declare 'not my responsibility'. This is also a characteristic of organizations where tasks, roles and responsibilities are unclear and people genuinely do not know they are responsible for certain tasks or results.

Another example is people not feeling responsible for KPI's or goals. When there is no clear link between the goals and individual performance, people can genuinely believe it is not their responsibility or they will use it as an excuse.

The cartoon shows a Help Desk employee sitting behind a desk, his feet up on the table. A user is standing in front of him with a letter in his hand. The Help Desk employee says "...my responsibility is RECEIVING user complaints....not DOING something with them!"

Results taken from the key learning points of more than 1000 students who have played the Apollo 13 simulation show that this is the top learning point. It is the most important success or fail factor.

Characteristics:

- Do people know where tasks and role descriptions are?
- Do people know the tasks roles and responsibilities of all process roles and all departments within IT?
- Do users complain that promised actions don't occur?
- Do users complain nobody ever informs them of things?
- If people are confronted with something, or asked why something wasn't done, do they point the finger somewhere else?
- Does everybody feel 'responsible' for results?
- Do people confront each other when they see that responsibilities are not being taken seriously?
- Do managers confront employees for not following agreed procedures?
- Do people make suggestions and take ownership for improving their own procedures?

Other related cards are:

- 5 of Diamonds 'No management commitment';
- Jack of Diamonds 'Saying yes but meaning no';
- 8 of Hearts 'The buck stops anywhere but here'.

King of Spades

'Empowering people' (not)

John Kotter, in his eight steps to transforming organizations, names 'empowerment' as one of his key success factors. This card is closely related to the card 'Lack of management commitment'. In this type of organization people are not empowered to change. They may not be given enough training, time, resources or information. This can be remedied by making it visible. What is actually more dangerous is when management pays 'lip service' to empowerment. What does that mean? Managers organize meetings to inform employees and to give the employees the chance to offer input. They do this because a change consultant or a communications expert says this is what they should do. However, the improvement suggestions or input is only taken on-board if it fits in with what management has already decided.

The cartoon on the card shows the IT manager talking to an employee who has just made a service improvement suggestion after being asked to by the manager. The IT manager says "…nice suggestion….but not the one I had in mind!….Try again!"

Characteristics:

- Do managers ask people what they need to be able to complete their tasks?
- Are resources and time made available to people to work on ITSM improvements?
- Do managers protect employees from conflicting requests and priorities?
- Do process managers have the authority to carry out process management?
- Are people adequately trained and coached to perform new tasks?
- Are people empowered by the 5 P's?
  - clarity of roles, authority, training;
  - clear processes and procedures;
  - supporting technology to enable process tasks;
  - supporting agreements with partners;
  - and, most importantly, clear insight into the results to be realized.

Case:

A team of IT second level support, covering PC's, servers and networks, all got together with their managers in a hotel for a brain storming session. A lunch was arranged and some creativity sessions. The aim was to identify and agree improvements. At the end of the day the teams were positive, charged and keen to carry out what they had decided upon. The CIO then came in, walked to the front of the room and declared: "So you have had your nice day out, team building…now that you are all together and in a positive mood I can share with you what we as a management team decided last week....". He then presented a set of decisions that totally undermined what the team had spent the whole day doing....you could visibly see the shoulders sinking, people slumping in their chairs, folding of arms. People were going red in the face from anger and frustration and there were audible sighs of frustration. The CIO seemed totally oblivious as he droned on. "So I have spoken long enough, Monday I'll get together with the team leaders to work out the action planning. Now you have all earned a drink, I believe the bar is open. Enjoy yourselves, unfortunately I have to go now."

Did this team feel empowered? Do you think this team is now fully supportive of management? Do you think the manager has successfully reduced resistance?

Richard Voorter, Senior Consultant, Ideas to Interconnect BV (i-to-i).

Case:

"A large construction concern in the Netherlands had been busy for a number of years with ITIL. The IT organization was outsourced and ITIL was implemented as an out-of-the-box solution. The employees and managers from the IT department were familiar with the high level concepts of ITIL and declared that this was how they worked. The IT organization was inefficient and, as a result, the outsourcing was not cost effective. The inefficiency was a result of poorly implemented processes and dissatisfied teams of employees.

An additional and equally important side effect was dissatisfied customers. In less than two years, four service managers had been made redundant because they were unable to make an impact on the situation.

Eventually the alignment between the customer and the IT organization was successfully realized. How? A new service manager was employed who entered into an ongoing dialogue with the customer. This gave the service manager a clear picture of the situation from the customer perspective, and gave the customer an insight into the status and the planned actions. In this way he created more time for making phased improvements.

At the same time he started a dialogue with his team. The team was reorganized, people were given functions more suited to their skills and capabilities. The right people were placed in the right positions.

The service manager decided to work step by step to gradually bring the processes and procedures to the required level. The customer was informed of this approach and kept up-to-date with planning and progress. The first steps were to improve incident and change management.

His approach was, on the one hand, to give strong steering and guidance to the team at the process level, whilst at the same time giving the team the freedom and opportunity to use their own creativity to develop the working procedures and how they wanted to work together.

When the process and the procedures were seen to be working, they were documented and formalized. One of the team members was then made responsible for the process. In this way, within six months the processes and procedures were given form.

By ensuring that the right people were put in the right function, by enabling and facilitating people to develop their own working procedures, and by making them ultimately responsible for the way they worked together, the service manager realized significant improvements in efficiency, effectiveness and quality.

Repositioning staff and stimulating them to improve their own work resulted in increased staff morale and enthusiasm. The working atmosphere was improved and this also had a positive impact on the users. Equally important was the understanding and acceptance that the ways of working would need to evolve over time. The team members were also made responsible for the continual improvement of their procedures. The quality was no longer dependent upon the service manager. The service manager was now able to operate as a coach.

What were the most important aspects of this approach?
Tackling the problem directly and not just talking about the problem. Entering into dialogue with the customer and agreeing a realistic planning horizon and realistic improvements. Ensuring the right people were put into the right functions. Steering at the process level, but letting staff develop their own procedures and ways of working. And improving in small steps that match the growing maturity and capability of the team.

What was the impact of this approach?
The employees and the customer are enthusiastic and satisfied. ITIL is now being used as an instrument to realize 'goals' and not as the 'goal' itself. The value proposition of the outsourcing arrangement is being realized. The business has a regular dialogue with IT. IT is now seen by all parties as win-win. The service delivery capability is now realized through the team and not through the service manager."

Other related cards are:

- 5 of Diamonds 'No management commitment';
- 7 of Diamonds 'Throwing solutions over the wall and HOPING that people will use them';
- Jack of Diamonds 'Saying yes but meaning no';
- Queen of Spades 'Not my responsibility';
- 8 of Hearts 'The buck stops anywhere but here.

Ace of Spades

'Blame culture'

Our ICT world seems to be dominated at the moment by the finger of blame. Business blaming IT, and vice versa. Inside IT companies this can be a culture that prevents creativity, stifles innovation and inhibits people trying to change. A blame culture, or punishment culture needs to be balanced with a reward culture. But the finger of blame also extends into the ITIL world itself. There seems to be an enormous amount of press around ITIL, with blame being apportioned for it not being what people expected it to be.

The cartoon shows a group of managers all pointing the finger of blame at each other.

In this section we want to add a small piece by **Richard Pharro**. Richard is the CEO of APMG, who are responsible for the new certification scheme for ITIL V3.

We asked Richard his views on the importance of ABC and where we seem to be going wrong. We also asked him to select a card he wanted to write about. He chose the Ace of Spades. Below you will find the results of our interview with Richard.

What are your views on the importance of ABC?

"My personal view is that ABC is essential. Success with ITIL or any other similar framework is all about people. People need to have the right attitude, skills and knowledge channelled towards the right behavior, otherwise you will achieve nothing. In this book you call it the ABC, I call it professionalism. ITIL will give you the knowledge, but knowledge alone is not a guarantee of success."

Why are ITIL initiatives currently failing to live up to expectations?

"I don't profess to be an ITIL expert and I don't have experience of deploying this framework, but in conversations with industry experts and leading champions I hear that the people aspect of deployment is vitally important. Success in any business is more about the people than the systems and the frameworks. The ITIL V3 philosophy cuts across all levels of business and IT, and it requires collaboration and engagement with the business. This means a different role and behavior for IT, which many IT organizations are already comfortable with. But it remains a challenge as we move into the future."

What is the biggest barrier to ITIL V3 at the moment?

"The biggest challenge is to do with people accepting change - accepting the new concepts, and being prepared to change. People need to take the trouble to understand V3 or learn the differences between V2 and V3 and what it really means for them. Many people will say, "Oh the difference is strategy - we already do strategy, we don't need this". Maybe this attitude comes from arrogance or complacency - 'we know all this', 'you can't teach us anything new', - and maybe the attitude is partly fear. It is new, it is different, and it means closer alignment with the business, so some people may feel it is too far ahead of its time and their organization's current maturity. Maybe the attitude is, 'We'll wait and see what everybody else does with ITIL V3'. But not taking the time or trouble to understand ITIL V3, for whatever reason, means that organizations could be missing an opportunity. The opportunity is to take from ITIL V3 what they need to ensure that ITIL realizes value for their business, and to ensure that as IT becomes increasingly important, we can demonstrate that we have IT under control and we are reducing the risks to the business."

Which card did Richard feel is the most relevant ABC card?

He chose the Ace of Spades. Pointing the finger of blame. 'The buck stops anywhere but here!'. "At times it feels that APMG are held responsible for everything that is perceived as being wrong with ITIL. Whatever we do and whichever direction we take is going to be criticized by some people."

Why is this?

"Partly it has to do with the above issue - people not taking the time or the trouble to understand the changes in ITIL V3. It is also due to the fact that none of us like to change and, if we change, we like to feel we are leading the change, or in control. Many people feel they were not involved in ITIL V3, it is something being imposed upon them and, as such, they are resisting. This is also what happens in many organizations when ITIL is adopted. It is felt that it is being imposed upon them, they have no input, and they have to take what they get. There will always be resistance. What is important now is how to deal with the resistance."

What is the vision of APMG with regard to ABC and the way forward?

"There has been a lot of effort to launch the new certification scheme. We know that some dates have slipped but we are working with our examination panel, the Examination Institutes (and through them the training companies), OGC and itSMF. Together with these key stakeholders we shall decide collectively how to develop the scheme. This also means ensuring that the ABC issues are addressed. To use the terminology of your ABC, we are not so arrogant that we think we can create this vision alone, we can see a scheme beyond just V3 content, and we are humble enough to know that we need to work together with others to realize and achieve this. ITIL V3 is a good start, but the world is bigger than ITIL. The journey has just begun."

Another case for the Ace of Spades comes from **Mark Smalley**. Mark has been involved in the application management side of IT for a number of years and is active in promoting the ASL (Application Service Library) and BISML (Business Information Systems Management Library) frameworks.

"A culture where people often blame others for their own deficiencies is by no means limited to the IT world. The issue is about taking - even claiming - responsibility for a task. I often hear people coming up with lame excuses why they haven't been able to produce the goods on time. "I left a voicemail but he didn't call me back". "It's the wrong form". "I didn't have enough time". The excuses are always about somebody else, not the person in question. The 'blamers' depict themselves as victims of the behavior of others and seem blind to the fact that they could have done more themselves:

- "I left a voicemail but he didn't call me back" - call him back yourself!
- "It's the wrong form" - find out what the right one is!
- "I didn't have enough time" - warn the project manager before it's too late!

This victim behavior can be fatal for projects. Deadlines get missed because there's not enough proactive behavior. Costs increase due to rework. Poor communication causes reduced quality."

Case:

"A couple of years ago I was working for an Application Management Services provider on a large release for a customer. The work involved was broken down into various parts that were assigned to, in total, more than twenty people. As usual, the work packages were interrelated: the progress of one part depended on the progress of another. So far, so good. But as the work progressed, certain team members started to lag behind with their work and complained about not having enough time, not having the right information, the requirements not being clear enough etc. They were blaming others for their lack of progress, while they could have done more about it themselves. They focused on the impossibilities instead of the possibilities. The deadline was approaching and we were looking at a delay and a penalty or submitting a substandard release."

What was done to break down or overcome this ABC?
"Due to the backlog we regularly worked on into the evening and one evening, just before leaving and after having a couple of people blame others for their lack of progress, I drew this sign on a white board.

No Victims Allowed

The next morning, as people arrived, they noticed the sign and asked what it meant. This is what I was hoping for. I now had a way of introducing the subject of unproductively blaming others. I also printed some business card sized cards with this new 'traffic sign' and occasionally gave them to people to remind them or others of the behavior that was troubling us. Gradually, the blamers shifted from being *unconsciously* incompetent to being *consciously* incompetent. Some of them progressed further and worked on their behavior and became consciously *competent*. Others didn't, but that's life: you win some, you lose some. I was pleased with the step we'd made and it was good enough to get the release submitted on time."

Other related cards are:

- 5 of Diamonds 'No management commitment';
- Queen of Spades 'Not my responsibility';
- 8 of Hearts 'The buck stops anywhere but here'.

2 of Hearts

'The user'

'Creature at the END of the evolutionary chain...'

This is the poor long suffering user who has been the victim of unsuccessful bureaucratic ITIL implementations and the victim of the technoids who deliver poor quality service.

However the user isn't always the poor, long suffering victim of IT.....Oh, all right, he is...or she is. But the user is also the person guilty of insisting that 'everything' has the highest priority. Often the users don't know or care what the impact of their 'demands' are on other business-related IT projects or changes. Just so long as MY IT is working.

When you look at the worst practice cards ask yourself "Is the user the victim of this card.....or is the user the instigator of this worst practice?"

Unfortunately many IT people still do not know what the real user needs or issues are, many have never seen a real user. Perhaps IT managers should ensure that all IT people actually get to visit a user, or invite a user to come and give a presentation to IT people about the 'use' of IT in support of the users business. Maybe this will help us finally improve our Customer or User focus.

3 of Hearts

'The Help Desk technoid'

"Hello HELPLESS Desk....what do you want now?"

This is the IT Help Desk employee. In organizations that say they are 'user' or 'customer' focused, but don't deliver on those 'words'. These are the Help Desk employees that find it annoying when users phone up....or users that can't solve the simplest things themselves...or users that don't read the manuals...or users who try fixing things themselves and generally make things worse. Fortunately after years of beating the Help Desk technoids about the head with HDI conferences and thick heavy ITIL service support books, this breed is dying out. Look at all the adverts for IT call centres and Help Desks. The photos are always of happy, smiling attractive young men and women who are clean and professional and look like they came out of a set of 'Dallas' – the TV show. None of them look like the technoids we meet!

We agree things have changed and Help Desks are becoming increasingly professional. The Help Desk is often the victim of other worst practice cards such as 'knowledge is power', in that there is frequently too little knowledge transfer to the Help Desk.

4 of Hearts

'The IT manager'

*'The best way to improve services is to outsource.....
the business'*

This is the IT manager who has grown up through the ranks of being a technoid...somebody forced into the daylight and into the realms of the users and customers. Generally somebody who is more comfortable speaking technobabble with the technogeeks rather than talking to the business and users.

Often in this type of organization there is little trust from the business and IT is treated like an inferior subset of beings. Which reinforces the technology focused inferiority complex of this type of manager. This is also the type of manager that doesn't even think or realize he or she needs to change and will be sitting dumbfounded when suddenly outsourced. Why me? What did I do wrong?

Obviously not all IT managers are like this. Many are dedicated, highly professional managers. What we would like to know however is this: "Who then are all the IT managers who are the reason that we originally gave our worst practice presentations, which 10 years later are still getting people nodding their heads and agreeing that the worst practices apply to their organizations?"

As an IT manager you should use the ABC cards and identify, together with your teams, which ABC worst practices are still relevant. Then, as a manager, you should show your ABC capabilities, your commitment to resolving them.

Also as an IT manager you should give the ABC cards to your teams and employees and ask them to choose the worst practice cards that apply to management in YOUR organization.....which includes you. Use them to get some 360 degree feedback. Show them you have the attitude and display the behavior to change and you are promoting an open, feedback culture focused on improving......I dare you!

5 ♥

The Consultant

Without me the world
will stop spinning.

♠
5

5 of Hearts

'The consultant'

'Without me the world will stop spinning'

These are the consultants with the barely disguised superiority complex. The consultant with an arm full of certificates that explain how capable they must be. These consultants feel so superior they don't think it necessary or wise to involve the business in scoping technology solutions. The business doesn't understand IT and shouldn't be allowed a say in what IT gets purchased or deployed.

These are also the technology consultants and architects who try to explain to the business why the business should invest in a particular technology solution. One of the main business complaints is still that 'IT thinks too much in terms of systems and not enough in terms of business'.

It is these consultants that gave rise to the business manager telling us 'IT people speak in technobabble'.

6 of Hearts

'The techno geek'

'That problem isn't in my book, therefore it doesn't exist'

This type of attitude and behavior really exists, certainly in organizations typified by the 6 of Spades 'The hero culture'. I once called the Help Desk to report a very strange PowerPoint problem, and they referred me through to a techno geek. The conversation went pretty much like this:

Me: "Really if I click on file, and select a directory every filename is displayed as 'unkown file'"

Techo geek: Loud and long exhaling of breath. "Listen, I am a certified Microsoft engineer, I have been doing this for five years, believe me that can't happen!"

Me: "Well I am sitting here looking at my screen and that is what it says."

Techno geek: "Is there anybody else in the office?" (meaning is there somebody sensible I can talk to), "Can I talk to them?". I put my bemused colleague on the line who confirmed indeed what I was saying.

Techno geek: "Listen that can't happen, I'm not even going to look into it. Go into file directory, double click on the file and it will automatically open PowerPoint for you and load your file.... happy!!!" (followed by the sound of the phone hanging up).

7 of Hearts

7♥
stakeholders

Business Unit Manager

Demand & Give. I demand
and you give in!

'The business unit manager'

'Demand and Give. I demand and you give in!

This type of organization is characterized by business managers who continually make demands for new IT projects and changes. They do not accept a 'no' from IT. IT struggles with limited resources to meet the growing demand. Often IT is unable to produce facts and figures to show that it is unrealistic to achieve all of the demands. Ultimately not all demands can be met and IT gets the blame.

Koen van Vliet, director of Avighna consulting. Koen is a business consultant and not an IT consultant, which is why we asked him to share his views and experiences on demand management.

Case:
"I've worked with a large insurance company in The Netherlands. I was a business project manager and thus positioned between the business manager and the IT department. The project's goal was to guarantee a smooth continuation of all insurance services in the coming year. This project took about eleven months.
In the first month the business manager invited me to a presentation of the commercial plans for the next year. A very nice, well organized PowerPoint slide show! In the presentation he also showed his first rough planning. Deliver business plans on the first of July. Great, but two months too late! I decided to tell him this and the conversation went as follows: "Hi Paul, I am Koen and I will be your business project manager for the coming year. I have enjoyed your presentation and I am really happy that you have shared your planning with us. I have only one comment, you are two months late.....". I won't repeat his reply, because this is a decent book, but you understand that he was not amused. He decided to escalate things to the director of the firm. When I offered to go along with him, he declined my offer.

This was the first of many conversations we were to have. Weekly we sat together to discuss the status, issues and problems. I don't need to tell you that the discussions were tough in the beginning. He was convinced that he was the one to decide what would happen and what wouldn't. Just like the guy in the playing card: "I demand and you give in!". I decided to try to change his attitude towards me and IT, but how?

After thinking things over for a while I knew what to do. Everytime he was 'demanding' things I showed him the consequences of his choice and some alternatives (and related consequences). Then I asked him to choose. Essential to this strategy is that I didn't tell him that the things he was demanding were not possible. "Everything is possible, but these are the consequences". After a couple of weeks he asked me why I came up with the consequences and alternatives and why I didn't 'just do as I was told'.

This was my chance. I explained to him that he was very good at his own job, but couldn't possibly estimate the IT consequences of his request (note: I don't use demand….). That is my job! And, thankfully for him, I am also good at my job. I think from the perspective of my customer, I want to help him to make the best choice according to price/quality ratio. (Some people would call this 'the essence of project management'.)
I guess my story was quite convincing, because he thanked me and told me he appreciated this attitude.

And so we went on for a couple of months. Me doing my job, he doing his. And then out of the blue, I was completely astonished! He came up with another commercial wish like this: "Koen, we've discussed another new wish in our management team and I would like to hear your opinion on this before entering it as a project change". As you can imagine I was totally surprised!

He continued to inform me of upcoming project changes before discussing them in the management team, so that he could tell them the consequences directly during the meetings. He took over my job!

Later on I asked him why he had changed his attitude this way. He said: "I saw what you did in our discussions, it took a while, but I realized that I appreciated this. You didn't discuss our plans, or tell us we were wrong, you just pointed out the consequences and came up with alternatives. That is a positive way of saying 'no'. I decided to try this in my own management team and it worked! So that's why I changed my point of view and attitude."

Is this a cultural change? No, I don't think so, but it worked out positively on a small scale. And guess what? The same business manager has asked me to be next year's business project manager again!

Perhaps within one year it will be cultural change ;-)"

8
♥

stakeholders

The CIO

The buck stops
anywhere but here!

♠
8

8 of Hearts

'The CIO'

'The buck stops anywhere but here'

Fortunately as IT is becoming increasingly important, and business managers are hiring in more and more people with a business background to fulfil this role, the times are changing. It used to be that CIO meant 'Career is Over' and, indeed, the CIO was an expert in ducking and diving and avoiding having to take the blame for a massively embarrassing, costly IT project failure. CIOs are now business savvy, have an excellent relationship with the business, are well respected by their IT staff and are visionary leaders capable of shaping IT's future within their business...... really! It must be true a CIO told us....

9 of Hearts

'The supplier'

'OK so the functionality isn't great but look at the flashy user interface'

Car salesmen have nothing compared with these slick IT sales professionals. Supplers who are willing to listen for hours to your problem description even though they know after two seconds what they are going to offer. These people are generally paid on commission, the more expensive product they sell you, the higher the commission. Therefore the chances of them saying "no don't buy this product, it is too expensive and doesn't meet the needs of what you have just described" are about the same as the chances that England will ever win another football world cup.

These are the suppliers who sell Training, or Consulting, or tools. A holistic approach combining People, Process, Product and Partner is a catchphrase in their company marketing brochure. Ask them to explain their vision on PPPP to you, ask them how they ensure a holistic approach to solving your ABC issues.....If they squirm and wriggle in their seats then they are the type of suppliers this card is aimed at.

10 of Hearts

'The quality manager'

'....waiting for the IT organization to improve'

We want to add a small piece of text from Paul's ABC worst practice article taken from the *Global Best Practices* book.

When I began my career in computing 25 years ago as a system manager, otherwise known as 'technoid'.I was informed in the computer publications of the time that IT'ers would need a new focus if they were to survive:

- I would need to communicate in terms the business could understand, and deliver service to customers and users as IT was becoming more and more important .....10 years later I was a manager of a team of system and network managers, a herd of 'technoids', the industry was preaching ITIL to us, and how we techies would need a new focus if we were to survive.
- We would need to communicate in terms the business could understand, and deliver service to customers and users as IT was becoming more important. And now in 2008 the results of an itSMF survey in the Netherlands revealed the number 1 strategic priority of IT organizations is to 'improve the quality of products and services to the business'!

So why has so little changed?
Darwin proposed a theory of 'survival of the fittest'. A species would evolve from generation to generation, adapting to the demands of its environment in order to survive. Based upon his premise you would logically conclude that from generation to generation the technoids would evolve and adapt to changing business demands... apparently not. It would appear the theory doesn't apply to technoids. Or perhaps the technoids are like the great white shark, perfectly adapted to their environment, they haven't changed in millions of years. Perhaps the technoid is a perfectly evolved and adapted species? Grunting in technobabble and annoying the business is what it was designed to do.

Jack of Hearts

'The ITIL consultant'

'A procedure flow and some procedures are all you need'

Consultants are getting younger and younger....or we are getting older and older. As such they have less and less actual experience and yet they feel capable of telling IT organizations what they should be doing and how to change.

These consultants feel so superior they don't think it necessary or wise to involve the IT staff in ITIL design....they won't understand it, they'll just moan and resist. We'll write the procedures for them and hand them over at the end of the project.....then we can run away and deny it was our fault.

These types of CONsultants have earned the name CONsultant, with a heavy emphasis on the word CON.

The ITIL Consultant

A process flow and some procedures are all you need

In order to break down this worst practice we suggest any customer thinking of hiring ANY consultant ask for a CV that explains the practical experience in dealing with ABC issues. Then when you get them sitting in front of you in an interview. ask them "Give me a practical example of an ABC issues you have resolved?"

The Project Manager

Of course we will finish on time and within budget

Queen of Hearts

'The project manager'

'Of course we will finish on time and within budget'

Still 70% of IT projects are over time, over budget or fail to deliver quality requirements. This has always been a core competence of IT project managers.

This type of project manager has paranoia. The business hates him (or her), the IT organization hates him(or her), the ITIL process managers hate him (or her) as this type of project manager feels entitled to operate outside the boundaries of any control of service level, change, release or configuration management process.

King of Hearts

'The CEO'

'Which part of NO didn't you understand?'

These are the CEO's that haven't yet realized the strategic importance of IT to their own company, or the CEO that hasn't yet implemented a good IT governance mechanism, or the CEO that has no faith or trust in the IT managers with their IT investment proposals that lack any form of business case....or in fact don't even contain the word business anywhere in them.

This is typified by an organization that hasn't implemented good IT governance practices. Governance practices that ensure both business and IT 'desirable behavior' are embedded in governance mechanisms.

A ♥

stakeholders

The HRD Manager

... .Our IT staff are now strategic assets?...

A ♠

Ace of Hearts

'The HRD manager'

...*'Our IT staff are now strategic assets?'*

These are the HRD managers who haven't yet read an ITIL V3 book. If they had, they would realize that IT technoids and technogeeks are now 'strategic assets', responsible for managing mission critical IT. Business continuity rests in their capable, skilled hands........'where can I get a new job?' thinks the HRD manager.

There is a shortage of skilled IT experts, and IT staff do not have the right business capabilities or understanding. The HRD manager has an important role in ensuring this skills and capability gap is filled. Has anybody told the HRD manager? Does anybody know who the HRD manager is?

The Joker: Unable to specify the VALUE required by the business

Alejandro Debenedet, Ex director of an IT services company in Argentina, Alejandro helped to start the itSMF in that region, and is now working for EXIN international.

"For many years I have worked in what we could call the NON-ITIL part of the world, Latin America. I have trained hundreds of people from Foundation to Service Manager courses and had many different types of students. I have also conducted many assessments and ITIL implementations. In every case, the feeling and notion prevailed of: "Why are we doing this?, What is the VALUE of this? Will this be part of the solution or will it make things worse?!"

Countries in Latin America are always viewed as short sighted, informal, with no real commitment. Years of bad systems administration and the different set of cultural values from other parts of the world, have created the wrong image, an image that many 'locals' make their own. However, more and more we see a need and search for better services and predictable outcomes (and costs). It is in this environment that ITSM best practices (ITIL as the star, but other best practices or standards, such as ISO 20000 are also growing) are now seen as an important part of the solution, and are here to stay.

Businesses are now demanding that IT organizations deliver value. The mission, vision, goals must be known to everyone in the organization and the value to be realized will, as it were, be the flag, guiding each and everyone in a common direction. Companies now believe in formal training, international certification and recognition, the value of consultants in supporting change, partnerships, etc. Businesses are beginning to understand the value in sponsoring such activities. There appears to be a shared vision, IT fulfilling their mission and realizing value for the business; the business empowering IT. Unfortunately this ideal situation does not always have such a happy ending. This transition and alignment of cultural values and the realization of real value using service management is not easy or hassle free.

Many times the investment in ITSM (time and money) is made before anyone realizes (or communicates) the value that was to be realized by the investment. Sometimes managers understand the VALUE required by the business, but they do not know how to communicate it, or they even FORGET to do so."

Case:

"We were engaged to conduct a training and assessment project for one of the top 10 multinational companies and a leader in their own industry, both in this Spanish speaking country and in many other parts of the world.

They had launched the introduction of ITIL worldwide and had people trained, services defined, processes established, tools deployed.

We were commissioned to train hundreds of people in the fundamental aspects of ITIL and we decided to do this after gaining an understanding of the motivation behind the project and following an intake interview with the senior management.

We did a pre-assessment and were introduced to the high-level aspects of the project. The business value was also clearly described and we were easily hooked by the appeal of this interesting and challenging project.

But we overlooked one aspect: 'We', my colleagues and myself, were the ones requesting the information, analyzing it and establishing a training program based upon it. The information was there, it was of good quality, but it had not been communicated to ALL levels within the organization.

We noticed this in our first training group. People were sitting there like zombies. Some reacted, some interacted, but for most of the time, there was no real 'energy' or 'enthusiasm'. There was no collective awareness of the importance of the training and certification.

We evaluated our training, talked about the results with the management and tried to figure out the problem. With the second group, the same uneasiness prevailed. If we kept going this way, the objectives would not be met and the business value will never be realized, or at least not with ITSM."

Case: What was done to break down or overcome this ABC?

"At this time we decided to stop the planned training and openly try to discover more information. What was the barrier? What was the perception of the people involved in the training? Could it be that the business had one vision that was shared by IT managers but not understood by the rest of the organization? The exchange of information started in a guarded way, and after realizing that we really were interested and were listening, the flood-gates opened and the real situation started to flow like Niagara Falls.

Most of the people that had been trained had never sat down with their manager to talk about the project. Some even feared that, if they failed the exam for certification, they would lose their jobs. Others were expecting promotions as a result but did not know if this would happen, therefore they were not motivated. All of them experienced a lack of interest on the part of the management, no real support for the course, since none of the managers were actively participating. ...and the list grew and grew. We asked for their approval to communicate these findings anonymously to their managers so that we could try to find a solution.

After reviewing the feedback, the management layer recognized and understood their own faults: they never communicated the expected VALUE of the training and its meaning to the overall project, not just locally, but worldwide. They also discovered that if they were not actively involved, the VALUE would stay as a definition or a wish, it would simply be words and management plans, and would never be a reality in the mind of the rest of the people. They had to play it as a team, and not just as managers saying what needed to be done. The value is perceived better if everyone is a part of it. Managers needed to 'walk-the-talk', lead by example, show why it was important.

A change was then made to the agenda of each training course. There would be an opening talk by at least two managers (one from IT, one from the business side) where the information that we discovered during our intake would be shared with the attendees. Also there would be a series of individual and group meetings where the current and future responsibilities would be discussed. An elected attendee in each training course would make notes during the course, capturing ideas and suggestions that could be used as input to the actual project. This list would be then be discussed in open sessions so that the managers could say what would be done with the ideas and suggestions, and the employees could see that there was management commitment to their ideas, and management commitment for changing things.

These changes had the expected effect so we had a happy ending. People enjoyed the training thereafter and the results were as expected.

The key then is **knowing** what the value is for all the interested parties. The vision must answer the question 'what is in it for me?' for all of the stakeholders, especially those expected to change their behavior. Not only is the business aspect crucial, but also the individual's. They all need to have the same information and share the same objectives. The value to be realized must be specified, shared, recognized and agreed.

In an ITSM project each component has a unique contribution to make (the individuals, the project, the training, the certification, the improvement measures, etc.) and the sum of them will therefore achieve the ultimate goal of providing the VALUE required by the business.

This also goes to show that deploying ITIL training is more than simply training to achieve certification. For example, EXIN as an examination institute, does not only develop and distribute exams; it cares for the training quality, the company behind it, the trainers, the content of the course, and how all the pieces fit together to make the IT professional complete in knowledge and recognition.

Some people underestimate this part and only focus in a training-to-certification program. Still, the training should be matched to the context of the organization in which the trainees will be expected to use their new found knowledge.

If that is achieved, certification will be naturally obtained and the overall feeling of all the parties involved (the business, IT and the individuals) will be one of completeness, a job well done, and money and time wisely invested."

The Joker: A fool with a tool is still a fool.......unless

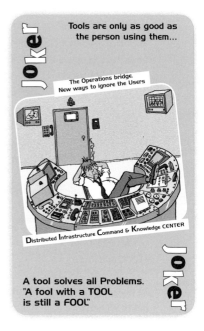

Tools are only as good as the person using them...

The Operations bridge.
New ways to ignore the Users

Distributed Infrastructure Command & Knowledge CENTER

A tool solves all Problems.
"A fool with a TOOL
is still a FOOL"

Many IT organizations are technology focused. This is perhaps understandable as many of the emloyees are 'techies' or 'technoids' as we called them in our book *IT Service Management from Hell*. As such, many have difficulties in understanding and appreciating the value of 'processes' and 'procedures'. In this type of organization it can be hard to sell the concepts of processes. Very often this type of organization thinks they can throw a tool at the problem and suddenly they will have ITIL.

We have three cases here. One is from Benny Kamin founder of the itSMF chapter in Israel. Another is from Aad Brinkman, a senior ITIL consultant from the Netherlands who conducted an investigation into 'awareness' for ITIL implementations as part of his thesis. The third is from a 'tool supplier'- Don Page from Marval. We know that Don is much more than that, he is a champion of ITIL and ISO20000, but this is our 'paradigm'

– anybody who has anything to do with selling us a tool is a tool supplier. Indeed one exercise we performed using the ABC worst practice cards revealed that the tool suppliers were seen as only being interested in selling a tool. Don clearly shows that not all tool providers think that way.

> **Benny Kamin** is one of the leading ITIL pioneers in Israel, He is the president and the founder of the Israeli itSMF chapter and the CEO of I-til Consulting. Benny quickly realized that the ITIL uptake in the Israeli market was still very much 'technology' focused. His challenge was how to ensure a technology focused customer didn't end up being 'a fool with a tool'.
>
> ## Case:
>
> **So, ITIL is a great solution: processes, procedures...**
> "Yahh. ITIL is a great solution, if you manage to convince your IT management board to adopt ITIL. But the Israeli IT manager is technology oriented. After each ITIL presentation about processes and procedures there will always be a manager who asks: "So, what does it take to INSTALL ITIL, and how much does it cost...?"
>
> **How to convince technology oriented customers to deploy ITIL?**
> The customers (and my wife) are always right, and you need to find a way to convince them to see your way, if you are convinced they are on the wrong path.
> If they come up with list of problems, and they ask for a solution, but they are not open to hear about processes and procedures, then you have to market ITIL in a different way.
>
> A customer of mine – a huge Israeli bank - faced many IT maintenance issues, but no-one was open to invest a few million in an ITIL implementation. "We need solutions now, not within

three to five years", is a common quote. A short ITIL assessment revealed there was a vast gap: IT put all its efforts into a professional-technological approach, neglecting the need to provide IT services to customers. No matter how many presentations about ITIL they saw, no-one was brave enough to invest in processes.

We took a different tactic: to get to ITIL via technology. If you cannot show the benefit of ITIL processes, you may show the value of CMDB to the IT. Unlike processes, which are a virtual entity – you can present a CMDB to the management. It has screens, you can connect it to the management systems, and you can provide an Impact Tree view.

But, how can you manage CMDB without work processes?
In this case we decided to 'do' first and to 'think' later. To show the IT organization all the benefits of CMDB first, then to show them the risks and consequences of it being out-of-date, and what was needed to ensure that it remained a valuable tool; in other words the ITIL processes later.

To obtain a 'quick win' we decided to fill the CMDB with 'flat trees' only. After gathering the list of all banking-applications (and there are 600 of them!) we attached servers for each application. We could instantly provide a SIM (Service Impact Management) view of the application trees. By providing fast value to business, we succeeded in convincing the bank to invest in the next step: to implement real ITIL processes around the CMDB.

The phase of ITIL processes
After you have a CMDB running, it is easier to convince your management to invest in change management processes: "We must keep our CMDB updated". There is a shift in 'attitude' that suddenly processes and procedures are needed to ensure the technology continues to deliver value.

Now came the moment to change the behavior: The CMDB implementation was acompanied with 'knighting' new responsibility for each IT engineer: each one of them became a 'service owner' for one or more business services, and each 'service owner' is responsible to keep 'their' business service updated. After all, each one of them is willing to see 'their' service impact tree updated. It's 'their' tool now.
From now on, each change in the production environment has to have the 'service owner's' signature, otherwise there is no permission to release!

Having achieved a first success we could then focus on 'other ITIL customers' within IT.The DRP manager is looking for a tool to check the difference between the disaster recovery plan environment to the production environment. He is a great customer for ITIL continuity management process.

Having a service Impact tree can collect data about availability of a business service. That's a great opportunity to deploy ITIL availability management process.
Once we had managed to create 'buy-in' that this ITIL stuff can actually work and can add value, we gained more momentum.

How the people get along with ITIL?

That's a delicate issue. In order to shift from a technical approach to a service management approach, we decided to educate the 'service owner'.

By nature people resist any kind of change, especially when you change their work processes. Therefore we invested a tremendous amount of effort in awareness. We provided presentations and training, we set documentation about ITIL within the internal knowledge system, we even advertized the project via the itSMF conference and local IT newspaper in order to gain the maximum attention from all of the IT personnel. The result was great: the technical people were just glad to be a part of this new approach.

The journey from a technical to a business oriented approach is long one, but beneficial.

Today, being a 'service oriented' department makes its employees proud, and the new culture develops. Managers are seeking the benefits of ITIL processes, we don't have to force it any longer. They are demanding procedures and processes.

This example shows a holistic approach: from Product to Process and People. My company was the partner that helped drive the change through. Raising the technology or product level of maturity to the next layer and embedding the ITIL approach in the people themselves. Slowly changing Attitude and Behavior."

Aad Brinkman, senior consultant, Apreton. Aad has also conducted a survey into 'ITIL awareness'. He provides a case from the Netherlands.

"A large educational organization was founded following the merger of several schools. The new ICT department, managed by a new ICT management team, became a hotchpotch of the former ICT departments and system managers.

The management wanted to offer a better quality service and the much larger organization demanded a different approach. At first the cultural aspects of one school in general, and the separate schools specifically, were completely ignored. To support the change process they chose ITIL as their method and immediately bought a tool. This tool was adapted by the system managers without any support and without any knowledge of a process-oriented approach. The tool underwent some major adjustments. It had a lot of custom-made components and was aimed solely at supporting the work without any regard for the management side of things which the tool should also be supporting. Things were not working as they should and a consultant was hired to help solve this problem.

The consultant recommended stopping the outsourcing of the Help Desk as this would not solve the problem at hand. He then organized workshops to clearly define the processes. The consultant recommended involving the ICT customers. Also, ICT contacts were invited and they assisted the consultant in scoping the change process. By doing all this, it became very clear that the knowledge of ITIL and processes within the organization was very limited. The consultant explained to the management the consequences of a process-oriented approach in relation to their own tasks, authorities and responsibilities, and their relationship with the process managers. That gave them a bit of a scare.

The organization decided to hire a change manager.

Halfway through 2007 the consultant was approached again. Things were still not running smoothly. Incidents and changes were not being dealt with on time and the customers were very unhappy. As it was 'not done' in this organization to voice opinions out loud, customers discussed their unhappiness with the system managers during 'corridor chats'. The system managers blamed the new ITIL way of working which 'limited' them in their tasks and responsibilities. As a result, the consultant proposed to spend four weeks at the department in general and with the change manager in particular.

These four weeks made it very clear that:

• The change manager did not have the commitment from the system managers - they were doing their own thing;
• The way the change manager worked instigated a lot of resistance;
• They used the tool to communicate between departments;
• Nobody's behavior was addressed and if it was, there were no consequences.

The consultant learned that the change manager planned to leave the company and proposed to take on this role temporarily. At the same time he would coach the staff of the ICT department as he would now be 'on the inside'. This made it possible to address people's attitude and behavior in the capacity of change manager and not as a consultant. At the same time the consultant would have a closer look at the tool. The management agreed and freed up some budget because they wanted to solve the problems.

In his role as change manager, the consultant was considered part of the company and people felt free to talk to him. Because of his everyday presence he was able to see a lot more of the staff's natural behavior. After some time as a change manager the consultant was able to present the management with a clear understanding of the problems.

The consultant recomended that they should play the Apollo 13 simulation game to enable everybody to see and experience their own behavior. The consultant convinced the management to become involved as this would add a powerful dimension to the game. The three simulations that were played out were quite shocking at times. The results however were very clear and, most importantly, were discovered and written down by the participants themselves. The ICT manager wrote an article for the department's magazine that was sent to all the members of staff. The first step towards open communication between departments had been made. At the same time the consultant, now in the capacity of ICT service manager, provided reports from the ICT department to the customers. Soon these reports were used as input for meetings between ICT and its customers about their reporting needs.

The organization was desperate for a new tool because of all the changes made in the way of working, the new process management and the reporting demands. At the same time, the Facilities department discovered the benefits of the changes made in ICT. Plans were made to join the front office of ICT and Facilities and a project was started to introduce the ICT way of working to the Facilities department. The purchase of a new tool was postponed. The management were very aware that good processes and having the right person in the role of a process manager is much more important than having the right tool. To accommodate support of the improved processes, it was decided to update the tool with the latest version and to redevelop the tool to match up to the new requirements.

The Apollo 13 game achieved both improved communication and the sharing of knowledge amongst departments. The change process has taken four years so far and appears to be very successful. The management appreciated that change would not happen overnight and supported the whole process with time and commitment. The support departments are now able to offer a true service because of their changed attitude and behavior.

This project supports the conclusions of the survey *Awareness at Service Management Implementations* which made it very clear that during these projects time and attention to ABC and changing of ABC are critical success factors. The use of aids to help people experience ABC (through simulations and games) also takes a prominent role in this process."

Don Page, CEO of Marval and one of the leading champions of ITIL and ISO20000 in the world.

"Selecting the right ITSM tool is a business decision, not a technical one. For some reason, the moment organizations have to produce a requirements document for the purchase of an ITSM tool, they go into techno babble, often having unrealistic technical requirements that rarely address or support the business problem that the solution is actually required to address. This is generally seen when the technical specification far outweighs the really important requirements to support the business. Because 'software' is involved, the specification/choices are all-to-often steered by technical staff rather than the service professionals and the needs of business users.

The bottom line is 'support is support' and the process required to support a computer is no more difficult or complicated than supporting a coffee machine or business service.

To be honest, the only thing that delivers world class service is excellent staff, underpinned by flexible process and reliable software; therefore the key requirements should focus on supporting business services, productivity, communication and customer satisfaction.

In a recent government project, the chosen software tool required software training that exceeded the general ITSM solution education by a factor of 10. In other words, for every hour spent talking about the principles and processes of ITSM and how to manage using these tools, ten hours have to be spent discussing how to make the software work. Sadly, this is backward. For every ten hours discussing the principles of ITSM, one hour should be spent discussing how to implement those concepts in the software tool and map to the required business processes.

It's not ITIL that fails; it's the people implementing it. In many cases the wrong tools have been selected, but the organization continues investing because it would be too politically embarrassing to back out. With some companies spending over one million dollars and ending up with nothing more than a glorified call-logging system.

Selecting the right tool is like brain surgery: 'It isn't the cutting that takes the time. It's all the preparation, analysis, and figuring out where to cut that's time consuming.' Remember 'a fool with a tool is still a fool."

The Joker: Frameworks & processes and procedures

Our attitude is the processes and the procedures will solve it. The framework itself is more important that what you do with it, or what it CAN do and solve. Take any given framework in use in your organization and ask yourself: "What problem was this framework desired to fix and have we fixed it?"

We also have an attitude with these frameworks such as ITIL that you 'implement them' or, worse still, 'install them'. 'We need to install ITIL!'.

Implement and install instead of 'adopt' or 'apply'. We like 'adopt' because we think of adopting children. Something that needs careful consideration and something that takes a long time before the process is finished….just like adopting ITIL.

Oustourcing saves costs… whilst maintaining quality

Either we just don't understand it. We think hey, installing the latest generation of hardware and software is hard, this ITIL is just procedures, right? How hard can THAT be? Which means we are stupid. Or we are so convinced of our own capabilities and believe that it will be easy. Which means we are arrogant. Arrogant or stupid, or are we just stupidly arrogant in the way we approach these frameworks?

Are we innocent and naïve? We didn't know, nobody told us. We are a young industry finding its way still in the big bad world. No, we have had more than 15 years to grasp the concepts of ITIL and what it should help us achieve…..we just don't do IT well.

Concrete examples:

ITIL tag as it was called by a manager in Denmark. Another name is the ITIL hot potato. Get rid of it as soon as possible. An incident ping-ponging around the organization. If it lands on your desk, you pass it on as soon as you can. Then YOU don't have to worry about it. The incident manager runs around as if blind-folded trying to find who has it.

Solution: changing the authority of the incident manager to be able to claim resources and put them in a room to solve it before they can do anything else. This requires agreement with line managers as to the priority and the allocation of resources.

Here are some of the worst practices we see

Managers not 'walking the talk', expecting everybody else to change but they don't need to. They undermine the processes. Strong executive leadership is needed to confront these managers. If this is missing, then it will not change and these people will not listen to advice from 'below'. The most popular cartoon that I have, requested by many operational people, is the one about commitment. Yet another example of poor leadership. We are committed to ITIL, just so long as we don't have to do anything. An example of this is the manager that gives a five minute introduction at the beginning of a project and then disappears. Never to be seen again. A spin off to this type of behavior is lack of respect and copying this type of behavior.

Before long this becomes the accepted way of behaving.

Case:

"At an ITIL introduction session before running a series of Apollo simulations I invited the CIO to the presentation about ITIL implementations and the ABC. I showed the cartoon about commitment and there was a lot of laughing and nodding in the audience. The CIO was shocked that this feeling existed, he had never heard about it before, but seeing the spontaneous reaction woke him up. He agreed to do the introduction to each Apollo simulation and agreed to be there at the end of the sessions to explain what would happen with all the feedback and learning points. People really felt empowered and energized to change when they thought there was commitment. Some quick wins were funded and sponsored by the CIO and attention was given in memos and a newsletter by the CIO. Momentum was created."

Case:

"The same thing happened at another customer. This time the CIO thought: "Yes but that isn't me...they are laughing at the cartoon". He did not attend the Apollo sessions, only the last one, for the last five minutes. He gave no backing or commitment and didn't show any interest to pick up the improvement suggestions from the organization, from the people themselves who were willing to change and wanted to be involved.

His lack of commitment and lack of follow up on suggestions caused the energy to drop, momentum stopped, the staff refused to sign on for the program or take it seriously. They were working against the adoption of change because of this management behavior."

A recent **Forrestor report** revealed that the biggest reason (52%) that these types of initiatives fail is **'resistance to change'**.

One of the biggest challenges is to get people to recognise the urgency for change and to see, feel and accept the benefits that process working will realize.

This was an example of resistance to change. Not because they didn't recognize the benefits of processes. The Apollo simulation won them over. The simulation left them feeling briefly empowered and willing to change. Leadership and management commitment created the resistance. A direct result of this is the worst practice card the 10 of Clubs 'No respect for, or trust in IT management.'

Joker: Breaking down the silos

"... I was told we have to break down the SILOs... so I just took your WALL out..." ... The SILO mentality

...The SILO mentality

Pablo Coutere de Troismont, a consultant from Xelere, an Argentinian based company.

"The choice of this card is because one of the biggest problems that we encountered in several ITIL implementations in different organizations, is that the areas of development, production and technology work in isolation (SILO mentality), fulfilling their objectives, but not having a holistic vision aligned with IT services that support business processes.

Unfortunately, it is very difficult for an organization to carry out an ITIL implementation and solve this problem. It is one of the most significant obstacles in projects like this. Working in isolation can be ingrained in people for many years. For this reason, most of these initiatives are undertaken by external consultants specializing in ITIL implementation. Consultants who work on the cultural change through workshops and key activities.

It should be borne in mind that an ITIL deployment comprises three aspects: processes, people and technology. People are a key issue on which we must work to achieve a successful implementation of ITIL."

Case:

"An IT services provider, composed of different specialist areas, could not achieve a commitment from all areas for the internal ITIL deployment initiative. This was due to the complexity of trying to change the current ways of working within support and operations. The behavior that had been embedded and accepted over time.

This organization was growing and had started to provide new services and to support more customers with an increased workload in each area. This made it difficult to achieve a cultural change internally because people, in addition to the growth in their daily duties, had to carry out the project of introducing ITIL.

These projects are very different from the typical technology projects, since ITIL implementation has to do with a cultural change in the organization, getting people to work in an end-to-end delivery chain, involving all departments, avoiding the silo mentality.

This organization, decided to hire a consultant with experience in implementating ITIL, in order to carry out the project. The greatest contribution made, in terms of breaking down the 'silos' between areas, was to pursue process design workshops with people from different areas, so as to achieve greater participation and consensus.

However, to give the participants the feeling that it is worthwhile, the most important success factor is the commitment from the team of directors. They must give the right messages to the people who will be affected by, or involved in, the project. They must stress the importance of everybody's participation in order to succeed. This message from the top level will help to convince people to come the workshops, at least the first workshop.

The workshops were made up of people from different departments. We made a careful selection of people to be involved. People with power or respect from their own teams or departments, and people who were to play an important role in the processes, such as process managers and process owners. The workshops focused not just on the ITIL process activities and designs, but also the implementation issues, such as getting buy-in, and working across silos. During the workshops people were delegated tasks to perform. People said this was a new way of working for them, working in a team with people from different departments, discussing it in this way helped them to agree a common shared goal.

Following the workshops, we continued to convey the importance of the activities that were agreed and the importance of embedding the initiatives as part of a continuous improvement approach that involves people from different departments and areas, thereby avoiding the silo mentality.

One of the most interesting findings of the workshops was the acknowledgment that people from different areas, who needed to work on a common goal, have seldom sat together at the same table! Participants said they suddenly understood their role in the end-to-end delivery chain, and suddenly understood how dependent others were on what they delivered and what they did, or did not, do.
Participants said that the dialogue helped them to understand the goals of each of the departments, and helped to discuss and agree common goals and ways of working that all agreed with and all were happy to use, in a collaborative way."

Chapter 6
Building blocks to develop your own instrument

In Chapter 4 we focused on ABC, what it is and some interventions you can try for dealing with it. In Chapter 5 we focused on real life worst practice cases and some practical interventions that worked. In this chapter we want to recommend other building blocks or instruments you can use in support of your interventions.

Based on our experience, both as consultants and simulation and workshop facilitators, we now want to share a few building blocks which can be extremely useful and powerful instruments for you to use when you work on your own ABC initiatives. ITIL V3 names some of these building blocks themselves. Most consulting firms will also have their own choice of consulting instruments and tools. These are ones we have used successfully to facilitate organizational change and address ABC issues.

Please read about these building blocks to get a good impression about how they can help bring you success, then develop your own skills by using them, developing them and sharing them with your colleagues. But remember these are only instruments. The most important instrument for getting ABC to work is YOU.

People, Process, Partner, Product and Performance

Service Design talks about the 4 P's. We have added the 5th P. And have called it originally….the 5 P's. We should start with the last one, **Performance**. This is, in fact, the key 'P'. IT departments must perform. They must deliver value. The Service Strategy book in ITIL V3 stresses this. IT must demonstrate that it can support and enable the business, so that the business can make money, so that the business can use IT products and services whenever they need them and so IT can develop and deploy new products and services to facilitate business change and growth. IT must demonstrate that it has IT under control and is managing risks to ensure availability, security and continuity of business operations. That is, after all, why you work in your company. Or are we wrong?

You should have insight into what it is that the business demands from IT in terms of performance. You should have insight into how you currently perform. You should have some kind of reporting framework or dashboard that contains a set of key performance indicators showing that you deliver what you promised to your business. This dashboard should also show exactly which indicators are not on target and must be improved. This is the basis of continual service improvement and, indeed, ITIL has a whole book about this. Everybody in IT should know what it is they need to do to deliver value to the business? Many do not. That is why our 'value' exercise was designed using the ABC cards. ISO20000 also stresses that top management must ensure all employees are aware of how their activities contribute towards results. It is a fundamental need if we are to behave effectively…..knowing how we need to behave and how we need to perform.

The capability to deliver the performance depends however upon the quality and capability of the other 4 P's. How well they are developed and integrated. Let us look at them in a little more detail.

People

The term 'People' covers you, your employees, your customers, your manager, your IT director. It is everyone who is involved in delivering services. We start with 'you' to show that you are part of the solution and possibly part of the problem? We often hear it said 'people' need to change, it is always other 'people' that are to blame. Indeed it is people that display the ABC aspects we have described in this book. It is these ABC aspects that will determine the success or failure of your ITSM initiatives. People will determine how well you perform. It is people and the ABC aspects that, if they are not developed, will prevent you from performing, and thereby create a risk to your IT and business operations.

People need to show desirable behavior. This desirable behavior must be agreed and then developed, for example, during interactive workshops with all the employees who are involved in IT service delivery. They must all agree on what this desirable behavior is and they must all demonstrate it. With everybody we mean everybody, including IT management and customers. Aspects of people include:

- Are they following the agreed procedures?
- Are they helping their colleagues?
- Are they customer focused?
- Are they improving their work?

Naturally training is an essential element, indeed certification. However certification must be linked to the ability to actually transfer the knowledge gained into practice.

ITIL V3 describes ITSM capabilities as a strategic asset, comprising of People, Process and Technology. As such people are a strategic asset that must possess ITSM capabilities. Through effective training and leadership styles, through an understanding of shared goals and through fostering a culture of personal accountability, ownership and responsibility people can be transformed into strategic assets. By consciously recognizing and managing the ABC issues, you can ensure that people do not become the risk factor.

This was the single largest success and fail factor identified by students participating in the Apollo 13 business simulation. See the results below:

% named as key learning point	P	Key characteristics
4.6	Partner	• Manage the end-to-end supply chain • Steer the suppliers • Clear agreements and targets for suppliers
6.0	Product	• Tooling to: - automate the workflow - provide configuration insight - support knowledge sharing - enable reporting and decision making
17.1	Performance	• Dashboard & KPI's to steer and to demonstrate success • Effective priority and escalation mechanisms at all levels between business & IT • 'Explicit' agreements known to all • Translate KPI's into process design and agreements and accountability
27.6	Process	• Defined, deployed, demonstrated processes • Process management • Apply continual service approaches to processes
44.7	People	• Clearly defined and embedded tasks, roles, responsibilities and accountabilities • 'Act' customer focused not just 'say' customer focussed, walk-the-talk • Team working and removing silos and barriers between departments • Conscious, managed communication lines at all levels, internally and externally • 'Address the soft issues' • Personal ownership and accountability

Process

Process is the complete set of procedures, work instructions, role descriptions and so on. The process is the way we work. Processes must be effective, efficient and must deliver the agreed output in terms of products, services and quality. In ITIL V3 terms, processes are what deliver value. Processes will describe what people need to do. Process descriptions are also instruments that can be used for quality audits, process improvements initiatives, and education and training. We do not need to elaborate on this. The ITIL books do this in detail.

This was the second highest success and fail factor named by students participating in the Apollo 13 business simulation. The need for defined, agreed process descriptions, flows and instructions, developed by all. The need for real 'process managers' with authority, and a need for continually reviewing, improving and aligning process capabilities to changing business demands.

Partner

Partners are roles like suppliers, other departments or advisers. Partners are part of the service delivery chain. And they also need to be controlled by processes and performance indicators. Partners can bring solutions, products or knowledge you do not have, or you decide not to develop yourself (due perhaps to costs). Good use of partners can bring better and/or more efficient performance. Once again ITIL V3 describes the importance of managing partners.

But do not forget to integrate your partners in YOUR processes. Do not forget to develop together with them the desired behavior (people aspect). It is also important to understand the word partner, or supplier. What makes a partner more than a supplier? The ABC issues are fundamental to a partnership. Attitude, understanding, belief, open communications, trust and commitment. A successful partnership is more than a set of contractual agreements and aligned processes and procedures.

Before you select a partner, whether it is a training partner, a consulting partner, or a tool partner, you should implement 'demand management'. What do we mean by that? Demand that the partner specifies how they will help address and resolve ABC issues. Ask for their vision on ABC, ask for demonstrable, proven capabilities in addressing ABC. This way you will be able to ensure that partners really do possess the capabilities (or partner agreements themselves) to help you transform ITSM into a strategic asset.

Product

Product stands for tools, systems and other technology needed to support your service delivery processes. Products will help you manage your workflow and processes, manage complex technology, produce reports and share knowledge.

Your challenge is to develop the best possible fit between People, Product, Process and Partner to deliver the agreed Performance. Failing to adequately integrate and align each of the 4 P's can cause you to fail to deliver on performance.

To do so here are some tips:

- If you analyze the current status of your team or department, you must discuss all of these aspects. (Are our people well skilled, do we communicate well, do we behave responsibly, do we know what the business demands? Are our processes and procedures working? Are they delivering the right products, services, quality? Are our tools supporting our processes, are they up-to-date? Can they produce the right level of reporting? Do they support knowledge sharing, Are our partners delivering value? Are they there when we need them? Do our underpinning agreements support what we promised our business?)
- You must link aspects to each other to get more information about the real situation. For example: 'If you find out that the Processes are not well followed, you should investigate if this is caused by People, Products or Partners. So explore all these aspects'.
- Let employees explore these aspects themselves.
- If you are seeking improvement initiatives, ask the employees which elements of People, Process, Partner and Product need to improve in order to increase the performance of your team or department.

- If you implement new processes do not forget to check if all 4 P's are in place. For example, if you implement incident management you should check the following aspects:
  - Process: did we describe the processes clearly and correctly? Are the tasks, roles, responsibilities and authorities well defined for each process step?
  - People: did we train people well? Did we involve them during design?
  - Product: did we integrate the process in our tools? And does the tool support each person in carrying out there process activities?
  - Partner: did we integrate partners in this process?

Focus on people

According to Kaufman, "An organization is only as good as its people."

From the first part of this book we all learned that people are the most important focus area when you want to improve performance in your team or department. However this is not the easiest part of your job, which is why we wrote this book. However there are a few elements that can bring you success.

We will now look at a few of the most important elements:

Work in teams

Every improvement initiative which brings value to the team, process or service needs to be embedded in the organization. This will cost time and energy. Unfortunately most of the time is spent creating buy-in, motivating people, working against resistance and defending ideas. This is why you should work in teams. The main actions are:

- Create shared value of the required situation;
- Create shared vision on the approach;
- Empower the team to be able to improve (time, resources, management commitment);
- Develop shared solutions (process, procedures and rules);
- Control the performance as a team;
- Analyze the performance and implement change.

Let the team establish their own rules

Do not define rules for others. Work on a shared vision which leads to internal rules set up by people. If people truly believe that you should solve incidents within four hours, they will develop their own rules.

Define desired/desirable behavior

This is part of the IT governance framework (oops, another framework). But this is a crucial part of working with people. It is important that everybody who is involved in the area of the IT delivery process is present when the desired behavior is discussed. Everybody from manager to employee must tell the other their opinion and must listen to the other's vision. Both need to put forward their ideas, this brings the team closer to a real shared and committed vision on desired behavior. This is why we developed the ABC card set, so that people, in teams or groups, can discuss non-desirable behavior as identified on the worst practice cards.

Exhibit leadership

When we have agreed the desired/desirable behavior, we need to act according to this. This means that we need to reward example behavior and punish undesirable behavior. And management needs to act themselves according to the agreement; if they show the wrong example, people will follow. These are the common 'throw away' lines and management catchphrases like 'walk-the-talk', 'lead-by-example', We hear them more often than we see them.

Successful leaders first impose change on themselves and then cultivate it in others.

Measure performance

Do not forget to measure! People's behavior is not that easy to measure, you should look at examples that show desired behavior. During evaluation sessions you must explore with the team the current behavior. We can use the so called 'incident method'. Each person in the team will describe real examples of desired behavior, which can be positive or negative. (You can use the ABC card deck). If the outcome is that we do not see some desired behavior, then you can start an improvement inititative.

Kolb – the learning cycle

In order to get the ABC aspects into the new behavior of the people in the ICT department, it is important to develop the learning skills of the team. We need to be aware that each individual will learn in his or her own way. The learning cycle consists of four stages:

- Stage 1: Feeling – learn from experience.
- Stage 2: Reflection – learn from observing and reflection.
- Stage 3: Thinking – learn from preparing, designing.
- Stage 4: Doing – learn from experimenting.

During your improvement initiatives you can guide your team through these stages. I will give you an example:

During a meeting, a team of capacity management staff decided to use active monitoring to monitor two critical components in the infrastructure. They decided to check every morning, every noon and every afternoon the disk utilization of the server and the utilization of the router. The results would be registered in a spreadsheet. The team started on Monday.

Stage 1: Feeling
The team experiences the new way of working. One of the team members is very negative. It costs a lot of time and on Wednesday he stopped registering the figures. The other team members liked the graphs and when they reported the results to the service manager, he also found them useful.

Stage 2: Reflection
On Wednesday there is a meeting. During this meeting the team discusses the new way of working. The person who stopped is asked to explain why? He said, "It's stupid work, costs a lot of time and I can't see the point. Just go and buy a tool if you want to look at graphs and things!" At this stage you should not go into the detail about the solution. Take time to explore the new way of working. Ask questions like: "Why is it stupid work? Why are we doing it? Why is it necessary? What does it mean if we don't do it? What are the consequences and risks of doing it and NOT doing it? How can we improve it?" During this stage we can find out what went wrong and how we can improve it. Try to get as far as possible to the root cause of the behavior and then identify possible solutions.

Stage 3: Thinking
Now let's try to develop a new solution. In this stage the team should define new requirements, new solutions. For example: we could develop a small piece of software to check the utilization automatically, or we could only check manually at the end of the day.

Stage 4: Doing
The team should decide to work with the new way of working. They should start experimenting with the new approach. Ok, maybe this goes wrong again, but then we restart the cycle from Stage 1 again.

If you work with teams you will experience that each person will learn differently. Kolb calls this the learning styles.

You have the following types of learners:

a. People who want to do. "Ok, I'm in, let's do it."
b. People who want to prepare themselves. "First I want to think about it before I do it."
c. People who want to understand first. "I first need to understand, I first need to have…, we first need to describe the procedure…"
d. People who want to know if the new way of working makes sense. "What is the added value to the team, the customer, the service…?"

If you know which learning styles there are, then you can decide where to start in the learning cycle. Remember you can start at every stage you want.

How will people learn the most?
Learning type **a** will learn if you give this person the obligation to start immediately with the new way of working, unprepared and without structure. The structure will come over time as they go through the stages.

Learning type **b** will learn if you give them time to think about it. When there are no time limits. They will prepare themselves, will explore risks and create confidence.

Learning type **c** will learn if you put the person in clear defined structures and give them clear objectives. If you give them time to study and try to understand in detail what they must do and what the models, methods and structures are. They must be able to ask detailed questions.

Learning type **d** will learn if the solutions are practical, if they can link the new way of working to added value for their work.

You can imagine that if you have all four of them in your team, it's not easy to improve processes. Each person will look at the improvement/problem from his/her own perspective. It's very important to use these learning styles in the team because this develops the competence 'learning to learn' of the team.

Some tips:

- Do a kolb-test to explore the learning styles in the team and share them.
- Respect each style and let each person explain his/her experience.
- Give people time to ask questions, some of them need this.
- At the start of a program agree with the team in which stage you should start. If you have a lot of do'ers in the team, start in Stage 1, if you have a lot of people who need time to understand, or are insecure, start in Stage 2.
- Document the new way of working. This gives structure to the type **c** learners and creates a clear starting point for the type **a** and **b** learners.

Commitment and buy-in

We all know that one of the key success factors of successful improvement initiatives is commitment and buy-in. Commitment is an often used word in ITIL implementations and everybody agrees its importance, everybody says it is needed and many say it is missing. What is commitment? What does it look like? Commitment should mean:

- All stakeholders involved in the initiative recognize and **agree the need** for changing. Kotter refers to this as the sense of urgency, which may be different for different stakeholders (where are we now).
- All stakeholders are aware and **agree to the goals** and aims of what the initiative is trying to achieve (where do we need to be).
- All stakeholders involved in the initiative share and agree what desirable behavior is, what undesirable behavior is, and **agree to behave** according to this.
- All stakeholders involved in the initiative **do what they promised**. Spend time, effort, energy and money on realizing desirable behavior.
- All stakeholders involved in the initiative will adopt a common stance. Which means they all support the initiatives, and they stand behind the choices or discuss these professionally with others in order to improve the initiative(**walk-the-talk**).
- All stakeholders **demonstrate a desire** to make the initiative a success.
- All stakeholders **address people** who are not displaying or demonstrating desirable behavior. Not just managers, but all staff.

So, what is commitment? We decided to extract a number of dictionary terms to clarify what it is we mean and what it is we should look for and expect. Use this as a sort of assessment:

'… to **promise** or **give** your **loyalty**, **time or money** to a particular principle, person or plan of action..'

'…to express an opinion or to make a decision that you **tell people** about…'

'…**willing to give** your **time and energy** to something that you **believe in**….'

'…or a promise or firm **decision to do** something…'

'…something that you **must do** or deal with that takes your time…'

So if you don't see this 'desirable behavior' that signifies commitment, carry out the final bullet point above.

How do you show that commitment is lacking or that you need it?

This is why we have developed the ABC card set and this is why we use instruments like the Apollo 13 business simulation. These are great ways of opening up dialogue and discussion. People can give open feedback. Using a simulation is a great way of creating buy-in to the fact that ITSM best practices such as ITIL really do work. At the end of such a session you can get people to commit to doing something about things.

We have developed a small humerous framework to help you. It is one that we created for an ABC worst practice article, to show we are just as guilty of leaping onto the band wagon and displaying worst practices. We have included here a short extract of part of the article together with a framework you can use to determine the level of commitment and buy-in in your organization to an existing initiative.

> "….However, as there seems to be an explosion of frameworks at the moment, and even a new book to explain all the frameworks you can choose from (CobIT, ISO, ITIL, MOF, Prince, EFQM), and as I am part of this culture too, my attitude is 'me too, I want one as well', my behavior is 'I know I shouldn't… we don't need another framework, but I'm going to create one anyway'. So I have created my own framework and am calling it the MOTHER of all frameworks.
>
> MOTHER = Maturity Overview To Help Enable Results
>
> The Americans invented the MOTHER of all bombs to be the most powerful explosive of all time, the Russians countered with the FATHER of all bombs, four times more destructive. I have developed the MOTHER of all frameworks, probably just as destructive as all the other frameworks in use at the moment. The analogy is really quite good. A bomb comes with a warning: 'handle with care, if not used with proper supervision this could cause serious unexpected damage', I think all these frameworks should also carry this warning!

Maturity level	Characteristics	Attitude	Buy-in
Indifference	• Awareness • Unconvinced • Unwilling • Undermining • Visible resistance	"I'll follow procedures only if I HAVE to and am TOLD to"	NO
Interest	• Recognition • Buy-in to possible benefits • Willing to listen • Reactive involvement	"I'll follow procedures because other people seem to be....but if anybody else stops I will too"	YES, BUT...
Engagement	• Understanding • Belief • Active participation • Visible contribution	"I'll follow procedures because they seem to be making a difference" "I'd better follow procedures because everybody else is"	YES, AND
Commitment	• Enthusiasm • Passion • Proactive promotion • Defending the way of working • Criticism of those that don't comply	"This is the way we work.... why should I not follow procedures?"	YES, BECAUSE

As you can see any idiot can create a framework and convince people they know what they are talking about…..you can use this framework to test how far you are with any other framework adopted…..see what type of characteristics people display to judge whether behavior and attitude are changing and whether there really is buy-in and commitment. Have a look at it and judge where your ITIL initiative is at the moment."

Too many of the ITSM improvement initiatives fail because of a lack commitment. See our most famous cartoon:

The question is how to develop this commitment and buy-in?

Involve all stakeholders in creating a shared vision of the problem

Create the shared vision of the problem 'we' have in this organization. Involve the IT manager, the team leaders, employees and even customers. Work on a shared vision by sharing views, ideas, problems, risks, consequences etc. Do not accept any unclear or vague feedback from the stakeholders. For example: do not accept words like "yes we need to do something…" or "ok, I'll take it with me and think about this…". NO!! Ask: "What do you mean with something?" or "Do you have ideas?" or "What is it you want to think about?". Make it clear, let people SAY the words you want to hear like "Yes, I will go to the board to present this…" instead of "We should tell the company …." Make it personal like "What do YOU think about this? When you say 'we' who is this 'we', which individuals are you talking about?"

Define a shared vision on the solution

Let the problem owner explain when he or she is happy! How does the problem owner see the solution. The solution must be defined in terms of:

• Desired behavior;
• Results like lower costs, increased customer satisfaction or greater availability.

Also define how we can measure it and which reports the problem owner wants to receive in order to feel happy.

Define desirable behavior for each stakeholder

Make clear what we expect from each other. Do not accept a manager saying: "Ok, good idea please come by in the management meeting and present your idea!" NO!!! You tell the manager your idea and let HIM share this with his management team. Then it becomes his idea, he must take ownership and needs to report back to the management team about the progress. Of course he can ask you to do it, but only if he tells the team that this is a great idea.

Defining desirable behavior means SAYING which behavior YOU will show!! "I (the IT Manager of this department) will support you if there is any problem, please come into my office and I will take the time to listen and try to find an answer….."

Hearing it from the mouth of a person means "what I say I must do."

Put the problem where it belongs

This may sound rather negative, sorry about that, but it's very important to act like this. Name it, label it.

Just an example:

A project is not going that well. Some steps are taking too much time and you feel that your manager (who previously showed a lot of commitment) is not supporting this project in his management team meetings. You talk to the manager ('my door is always open…') and after a good discussion he says: "Ok can you draft a memo which I can send to the management team…..".

You know that this doesn't solve the problem, still your boss will not 'defend' this project in the management team meeting. So you return the ball and say: "No, it must be you who talks to the management team, you must show that you really support this project. If you don't accept this responsibility then we might as well stop this project."

Oops, would you dare to talk to your boss like this?? Does your organizational culture allow this? 'Desirable behavior' in governing IT demands this. Governance is about managing business risks associated with IT. If you feel that the business faces risks of project delays, wasted money, failure to achieve goals and objectives, it is YOUR personal responsibility and accountability to say something. Therefore, we would hope that you would say something. Explain it in this way. Explain the desirable behavior needed by all if business risks are to be mitigated and business value is to be realized. Remember, it is not you and your personality against your manager's personality. It should not be your hierarchical position against you manager's hierarchical position, it should be about governing IT. If your manager takes the challenge, he or she shows commitment and buy-in and it could mean the difference between success or failure. If your manager doesn't take the challenge, then you know how important this project is to them.

Another example. We all promised to support the first line support team with clear information and solutions, because we all agreed that the more clear and accurate the communication between second line and first line support is, the better the performance we can deliver.

An employee of second line support sends an email to the Help Desk which says: 'Please tell customer to reset printer w34r5 and reset the interface unit on the second or third floor, it is only the interface on the PC that doesn't work…'.

This Help Desk employee doesn't understand this email, it is totally unclear. But the employee understands a little bit about printers and knows the answer. He resets the interface, calls the customer and resets the printer. The customer is happy.

How many of you close the call and that's it? Ok, if this is your approach the second line person will never change his way of communicating. The problem is that if he doesn't get feedback he will never change his behavior. One approach is to send the email back and tell this person that you cannot solve the incident because you do not understand his email. You ask him to make it clearer. You repeat this until the answer is clear. Even if this second line support employees is mad at you, this is the consequence of what we agreed.

Of course we hope that you would first resolve the incident (happy customer), then close the incident (happy process manager, happy service level manager) and then go back to your second line colleague.

Show the problem owners and sponsors your progression

If you start an improvement initiative, define when the project or program has finished. When are all stakeholder satisfied? Also define performance indicators that show the progress of the program and report the results to the stakeholders. Show them that performance is increasing, show them when targets are met or close to completion. This will increase the buy-in from people. Now this may sound like stating the obvious and insulting your intelligence. However, remember we have already quoted the results of a Parity report '*Only 27% of IT managers have directly measured the return on investment from ITIL implementations, and under half measured the value that IT service management delivered to their business....*' So, apparently it is not so obvious and common sense.

Why would a manager show no interest if the performance indicators show an increase in customer satisfaction? Why should a manager stop spending money on your improvement initiative while you are minimizing the costs of external suppliers? What would you do if you have to pay Euro 100 each week to get Euro 1000 at the end of the month?

Showing your progression with reliable reports and figures also proves you are in control. That you are able to manage this program. That you are steering the program towards the agreed output. This displays trust. You can imagine that if you show this to your manager, then this also influences his buy-in and commitment.

Change agents

Changing people, teams or organizations means hard work. It is not only the change itself which needs to be attractive, effective and bring more value, but it is also the process of changing which makes the change effective. To change organizations you need to work with people to develop new procedures, work instructions, new ways of working and new behavior. The people who are part of this change process must have trust that these changes will create a better work situation and that they are likely to follow the program leaders. What we need is a change agent who is able to lead the team to a better performance.

What do we expect from a change agent?

- This person must show examples of desirable behavior;
- This person must be able to motivate people;
- This person must lead the team to change;
- This person is able to facilitate the change process so people will create their own work situation;
- This person can listen, talk and explain;
- This person is respected and trusted;
- This person will 'embed' change in the day-to-day processes and into the behavior of people;
- This person will monitor and steer the new processes and will correct un-desirable behavior from people.

Who are change agents?

- First of all the manager of the department. If he or she doesn't show the expected behavior, you might as well just forget about realizing the required effects of change;
- Team leaders;
- Process managers;
- Employees;
- …

Yes, you are absolutely right if you say: "So, all people in the team could be a change agent". We really mean that each person in the team should be a change agent, from employee to manager. And this is your main task, to get everybody to become a change agent. Change agents 'make change happen'.

But, some people are a little bit more of a change agent than others. And, as a leader of change, you should select the change agents around you who can help to ensure that the ITSM improvement initiative is successful.

DIGMA©

DIGMA© is a powerful instrument that can be used to create a clear shared picture of a desired situation within a team or department. It will guide you step by step from the desired situation towards the design of the approach.

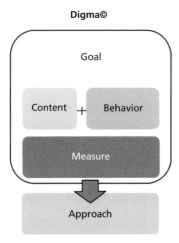

Digma©

Let us go through the steps in the model.

D (Doel) stands for Goal. In this box we describe in clear terms how we all see the desirable situation. This description is written in a way that shows the situation when the program is finished.

For example:

• "The service desk handles all priority 3 incidents within four hours, all according to the agreed performance. We inform our customer in a timely manner about the status of each priority 3 incident."

I (Inhoud) stands for Content. In this box we describe all the content aspects which need to be in place to create the desired situation.

For example:

- "We need the SLA, we need to know the performance indicators and the values."
- "We need to have a clear definition of the categories so we can classify each incident in the correct priority class."
- "We need to have access to standard solutions."
- "Our tools needs to make it possible to create reports related to this performance indicator."

G (Gedrag) stands for Behavior. In this box we need to describe the behavior that will result in the desired situation being achieved.

For example:

- Second line support needs to share solutions with first line support.
- Second line support needs to inform us about the status of incidents so we can plan our time and, if needed, can promptly inform our customer.
- The Help Desk needs to register each incident accurately and ask relevant questions in order to classify each incident correctly.
- The Help Desk needs to have a routing table in order to route each incident directly to the right person.
- The life cycle of incidents are monitored by incident management.
- Incidents that cannot be solved within four hours are escalated to the incident manager.

M (Meten) stands for Measure. In this box we need to describe the indicators that prove our improvement initiative is on track, or that we have reached the desired situation.

For example:

- We have a weekly graph that shows the average time to solve priority 3 incidents. It shows that we are heading towards the four hours target.
- We see meetings between first and second line support aimed at improving the process.
- We see a decline in the number of mis-routing activities, with the aim to have 90% correct.
- We see that 100% of all incidents that are not solved within four hours are accurately communicated to the Help Desk. We keep track of them using graphs, and using the role of the incident manager.
- We see that 100% of all incidents are registered.

- We see that 80% of all incidents are classified correctly at the first contact with the user and 100% after re-classification.

A (Aanpak) stands for Approach. In this box we need to describe the approach. In this box we need to document HOW we are going to develop the desired situation using all the content, behavior and measurement aspects. The challenge is to combine these elements into an effective approach.

For example:

- First and second line support will develop a routing table. The effect is that we create ownership and can also give them the responsibility to keep this table accurate. It's their product. We develop content, using the behavior aspects we want to develop.
- First and second line support will develop a list of questions to be asked during the intake of an incident. We still spend time on unclear incident descriptions, and both teams can address this by improving this list. This solution is not seen as rules drawn up by the service manager or process manager, but as their own tool to help them with their work.
- The incident manager and the Help Desk team will design and implement a report that shows the average time taken to solve priority 3 incidents. This short project will mean that we can develop a small procedure that specifies which attributes need to be completed by the Help Desk. The Help Desk can then take care of this themselves, can explore what the impact is, and can train themselves in how to do this most effectively and efficiently.
- We need to have regular meetings with first and second line support to discuss the follow indicators: number of incidents with wrong routing; number of incidents with wrong classification; number of incidents with un-usable descriptions...

You can see that the approach will combine all elements, will create ownership in the teams and will incorporate continual improvement activities which help to ensure that the targets are met. The approach is not describing the HOW but the WHAT. How it's done is discussed by the team. They will develop their own improvement processes that guarantee a continuous focus on getting things implemented, and will adjust these until we have reached the desired situation.

How to use the DIGMA© model?

The DIGMA© model is used at the start of each change/improvement/implementation initiative. With a team of people all involved in this project, the first step of the project is a DIGMA©-session to fill in the boxes. Based on this information, the project manager can develop an approach to get the things done.

During the session you can use flipcharts to list all the ideas of the team. Discuss them, explore them and come to a conclusion. Document all of the results and check over time if these are still appropriate.

During the program you will have to re-use all materials to check if we are still on track or if there are new insights that can be used to improve the approach.

Tips and tricks to use DIGMA©

1. Take one or two days to explore all aspects of DIGMA© with a team of people involved in the improvement initiative. This team consists of employees, team managers, process managers and maybe even the IT manager.

2. Be sure that what we write on the flipcharts is clear to everyone. No unclear sentences like 'management', 'people', 'some people' etc. Just clear like: 'incident manager', 'Mr Wilson', 'the first line support employee'. If you are not clear, then even thougheverybody might agree at the time, when it comes to action, nobody will assume responsibility…

3. Write down the results on paper and let the team read them and think about them. At the next session check if this is still the situation that we all agreed to.

4. Check the consistency of the model. If we write down that we want to monitor an indicator, check if we have written the indicators graph in the 'content' list and if we have described the behavior aspects in the 'behavior' box. Also check if all aspects are related to the goal box. If not, we face the risk that although some initiatives are carried out, they don't actually contribute to the goal. If we find that certain actions are important, we should move them to the next improvement initiative and start DIGMA© from the start.

5. If you have too many discussions on what to put in the boxes, look at your goal box again. Maybe the description in this box is too broad. Maybe if you narrow this it helps to focus and clarify things. So don't use sentences like 'people are working faster and more accurately'. The word 'and' can make the discussion too broad.

6. Use an external facilitator for this session, or somebody from outside the group. This person can easily ask 'silly' questions to make things clear. In organizations we are not always aware of our terminology and our blind spots. If somebody says, "people from upstairs" they all know who are they mean, but if you ask "who are they?" the participants need to think. Or if you see some habits like nodding, smiling or puffing, you can ask them about it. "Why do you nod NO?" One of the answers which is rather common is "Did I?" In this case explore the reason. People from inside the team do not see this, but behind this behavior there could be specific reasons or fears.

Performance Improvement

What we are doing in the world of ITSM is rather common in the BPM-world (Business Process Management). In BPM we see the same elements such as processes, design, measure, steer, improve, report etc. One important aspect of BPM that brings value to your ITSM team is the 'performance improvement' elements. In this 'building block' there are three elements of particular interest:

1. Relate business goals to ITSM performance indicators.
2. Process improvement, getting rid of unnecessary process steps.
3. Dashboards.

Let's look a little bit closer at these.

One phrase that is heard very often is 'business alignment'. It is a nice phrase but what is it and what can we do with it? Let's look at an example. In our BPM business simulation called 'The

Greatest Move' the team must play various roles in a company called 'World Wide Movers'. We show the team the following slide:

Performance Improvement

The Greatest Move™

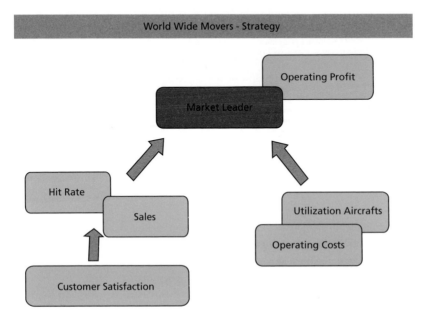

This slide shows that World Wide Movers wants to become market leader and increase operating profit. In order to achieve these goals, the team need to ask themselves the question: "How can we achieve this, which indicators do we need to define, implement, monitor and steer?". The answer is:

- To become market leader we need to secure most of the deals in the market. So we need the indicator 'hit-rate'.
- To become market leader we need to have a high level of sales. So we need the indicator 'sales'.
- But, in order to have a lot of sales and a high hit-rate we need satisfied customers. If they are not satisfied, they will give their orders to our competition.
- To increase operating profit we need to fly with full aircraft. That is why we need to have this 'aircraft utilization' indicator.
- To increase operating profit we need to lower the operating costs. That's why we need this indicator.

All indicators are assigned to a role (department) in the team.

Hit-rate (80%)	owner: Sales manager
Sales (1.000.000)	owner: Sales manager
Customer satisfaction (80%)	owner: Service center (sub indicator – response time)
Aircraft utilization (+60%)	owner: Planning
Operating costs	owner: Operations manager
Market leader	owner: Director
Operating profit	owner: Director

Each indicator () has a target set by the Director.

During the game these indicators are used to meet the overall objectives. They are the guidance for analysis, steering, improving and reporting.

Back to ITSM. How many of you have ever made this type of analysis? If not then now is the time. Indeed the ITIL V3 Service Strategy book also pays attention to these aspects of 'business value'.

• Take an empty piece of paper;
• Go to a business director and ask him 'what is your goal';
• Then agree and list within your ITSM department which indicators you need to have to support this goal;
• Then check which ones you have;
• Skip the ones that are not linked to this goal;
• Add the ones that really support this goal;
• Set targets;
• Develop a dashboard;
• Develop and implement processes to register, monitor, report and improve the performance;
• Tell your business that from now on you will focus performance on achieving their goals.

Interpreneurship

This building block is important for those of you who are looking for employees to become responsible, proactive, business focused, entrepreneurial etc. We want to see people who work in this type of company act and behave as if they are running their own company. They take actions as if they were the boss, they present investments decisions and proposals specifying value and risks. They present them in a way that enables the sponsor to make decisions and approve the 'business case'. Let us focus on some examples to explain interpreneurship.

Many employees are very negative about decisions made by management.

An example:

A team is responsible for improving the performance of the Help Desk. One of the solutions they found was to update the tool that was used to the next version. They invite the vendor who provides a proposal for the upgrade. The team arranges a meeting with senior management in order to present the proposal. During the presentation the manager asks a range of sensible questions such as: " What does it cost? What returns does it give us? How much of a cost saving can I make if I invest in this tool? Did you think of risks? Are there any guarantees that the vendor will not charge more money for the customization and implementation?". At the end of the session the team is asked to go away and improve the proposal.

Outside the meeting room they are very disappointed. "He doesn't want to invest!", "He doesn't understand", "Ok, if this is what he wants…."

One simple question which needs to be answered in this case is: "What would you do after this presentation if this was your money?"

If you must invest E1000 when would you do this? I hope when you are almost sure that the ROI (Return on Investment) is acceptable, say two or three months or years. This is an example of what we call interpreneurship.

Another example is about making decisions or taking actions:

You are responsible for a very risky and complex change that is being carried out over a week-end. You need to upgrade the centralized logistic server and, in order to do this, the whole application and data will be restored on a shadow machine so we can run the evening/weekend jobs. Because the shadow machine is expensive you hire one from the vendor. This machine is using disks (Raid 5). Then halfway through the change a few of the disks of the shadow machine raise errors. You contact the vendor and the advice is to sign a service contract to ensure that the specialist support will react within two hours; this costs E4000 for a period of three days (week-end + Friday). You try to call your manager several times without success. You then decide to sign the contract. The change goes through without any more errors. The disks do not fail. On Monday your manager calls you in, and on his desk you see the invoice.

Reaction 1 from your manager: "You know you are not allowed to sign any contracts, you spent Euro 4000 during this weekend and that is not allowed.. This is a warning, now go back to work…"

Reaction 2 from your manager: "Please tell me why did felt you needed to sign this contract during the weekend?" You explain the risk, you explain that if this was your company you would do the same because of the insurance. If one other disk had failed we could be sure that we would not have availability next Monday and this would have cost the business even more. I tried to contact you but time was running out."

"Ok, I like your initiative, and I'm happy you did it, but Euro 4000 is a lot of money! Next project try to avoid this type of reactive investment."

Which one do you think is an example of a company where they support intrepeneurship?

It is like empowerment. Try to delegate responsibilities and authorities as low as possible within the organization. Make employees responsible for a job, task or project. Let them run this as if this is their own company, foster a feeling of personal accountability, an understanding of business value and risk.

ABC card set – case and example exercises

We have described in this book the ABC of ICT cards and how they can be used. The following section details what they are and contains a case example of how they were used during an itSMF conference workshop. **This case also describes two exercises you can apply in your own organization**.

We have also produced a workbook containing several more exercises including worksheets that you can use in your organization. If you are interested in the workbook please contact us at office@gamingworks.nl.

ABC of ICT round table session

Document overview

This document contains the results of the **ABC of ICT round table session** held during the 'Best Practices in IT Management conference in 2008. ABC stands for the 'Attitude', 'Behavior' and 'Culture' of ICT. It is ABC that stands between you and the realization of business value using ITSM best practices.

In this article we hope to give you insight and advice into how you can finally resolve these ABC issues. Issues that are the reason why many ITIL initiatives fail to realize the hoped for, and needed, results. IT is now too important to business operations, we can no longer afford to fail to bring IT under control. The ABC issues MUST be tackled and resolved.

- **Section 1** contains a brief introduction as to what ABC is, what ABC worst practices are, and why they are relevant and worth serious consideration.
- **Section 2** introduces the ABC of ICT card set, an instrument that can be used to help organizations assess their own ABC worst practices and the risks that these pose. *This card set was used during the round table session to identify key ABC worst practices as identified by the participants.*
- **Section 3** contains the results of the exercise and tasks performed using the ABC card set during the session.
- **Section 4** contains a set of conclusions and recommendations to IT organizations that they should use these ABC cards as an assessment and dialogue instrument within their own teams, departments and organization.
- **Section 5** contains quotes and comments from delegates about the ABC cards.

Section 1: ABC of ICT

ABC of ICT stands for the Attitude, Behavior and Culture within ICT organizations. In the past 10 years or so, IT organizations have increasingly adopted 'best practice' frameworks such as ITIL to bring IT under control. However, many organizations have failed to realize the expected benefits of these frameworks. Why is this? Because of ABC issues. It is our belief that it is the ABC 'worst practices' that will determine the success or failure of your ITSM improvement initiatives, not the frameworks and the models. *It is ABC that will prevent you from realizing the value offered by these frameworks. It is ABC that presents a business risk.*

IT is becoming increasingly important to business operations, and to all types of businesses, with the result that we can no longer afford to fail to successfully apply these types of frameworks. It is time we recognized and resolved the ABC worst practices once and for all.

It is this need to bring IT under control that has partly led to the rise of IT governance. According to a Weill & Ross investigation into best practices for IT governance, it may be described as:

Specifying the decision rights and accountability framework to encourage the desirable behavior in IT

We in IT have focused for too long now on the first part, the *'frameworks'*, and not enough on the second part - the *'desirable behavior'*. This is why many IT improvement initiatives fail. A Forrester report revealed that 52% fail because of 'resistance to change' (Attitude). A further 29% fail because of a lack of business interest or involvement (Attitude). Findings from our own 'Apollo 13 – An ITSM case experience' business simulation (see the article '**Using simulations to increase the success of your ITSM initiative**' published in the IT Service Management Global Best Practice book – volume 1, 2008, Van Haren Publishing) also reveal that the key learning point, identified by more than 1000 students is that '**people related issues**'are the most significant success or fail factor in improving IT performance. Issues such as the need for:

- clearly defined, agreed and accepted tasks, roles and responsibilities;
- personal accountability;
- creating buy-in and commitment;
- leading change and 'walking-the-talk';
- 'acting' customer focused instead of 'saying we are' customer focused;
- breaking down organizational 'silos';
- managing the soft issues relating to organizational change.

Unfortunately neither existing frameworks and 'best practice' guidance, nor training or certification programs, conference sessions or articles adequately tell you how to address these issues. Fortunately in the Netherlands things are changing. The itSMF has recognized the need to give attention to ABC, and has included ABC as a separate conference stream.

ABC is like an iceberg, much of it hidden below the surface, and difficult to see, but nevertheless dangerous and capable of inflicting enormous damage.

Section 2: The ABC of ICT card set

Because there is currently too little help from the ITSM supplier community to assist IT organizations in resolving these ABC issues, we in GamingWorks, working together with Van Haren Publishing, have developed a set of ABC of ICT cards.

The ABC card set contains 52 worst practice cartoons. These are worst practices that industry experts recognize and agree, and these are worst practices that we regularly present at itSMF conferences. Whenever we present them people nod (enthusiastically) in agreement and recognition. (We are a little concerned at the smiling, enthusiastic acknowledgement – it sometimes looks almost like pride "Yes! Yes! That is what we do!")

This card set has been designed as an awareness and workshop instrument to help teams, departments and organizations:

- identify, recognize and agree whether these worst practices apply to their organization;
- look at worst practices from the perspectives of different stakeholders;
- identify how stakeholders are impacted by a worst practice and identify which stakeholders display which type of worst practices;
- enable teams, possibly comprised of various stakeholders, to get together to discuss the worst practices;
- discuss and agree the consequences and risks of these worst practices;
- recognize and create 'buy-in' to the 'need' to find a solution to resolve them;
- discuss and agree possible solutions to resolve the worst practices;
- provide input to 'continual service improvement' initiatives.

The card set is aimed at creating dialogue and discussion so that these ABC issues can be brought out into the open. Once they are brought out into the open and recognized, action can be taken to address them. *So long as they remain hidden and so long as we avoid talking about them or discussing them, they will remain a danger that may turn into resistance.* Resistance that will prevent your organization from achieving success and, as a result, pose a risk to the business.

The card suits represent **Attitude** (Clubs), **Behavior** (Diamonds), **Culture** (Spades) and **Stakeholders** (Hearts). There are five Jokers representing People, Process, Product, Partner and Performance.

So how can you use the cards? What can you do with them?

The cards can be used at the start of a change program, for example the cartoons can be posted on a website and people invited to vote on the relevance of the cartoon within their organization. This will raise awareness to the issues and will help reveal a 'need to change'. This will also help gain insight into people's attitude towards the change.

Three of the cards were posted on the itSMF Netherlands website, as a sort of mini-survey to try to identify whether people recognized these worst practices. The findings were:

Statement 1: 'We are not customer focused enough in IT'.
Result: **89%** agreed.

Statement 2: 'We are poor at sharing and reusing knowledge in IT'.
Result: **86%** agreed.

Statement 3: 'Current ITIL training and certification does not adequately address ABC issues'.
Result: **94%** agreed.

These results clearly show that we in IT have some problems still to resolve and current training and certification doesn't help resolve them.

The cards can also be used as an assessment instrument, by inviting teams to identify and agree worst practices relevant to their own team or organization. A number of exercises can be performed using the cards, for a wide variety of stakeholders.

And finally the card set can also be used as a normal set of playing cards.

Section 3: The ABC exercise and results
The ABC of ICT round table session was a 45 minute event. In the session seven 'round tables' were created, with each table containing up to six participants. Participants were given a set of ABC of ICT cards and a series of tasks to perform:

Exercise: Customer and user focused
During the round table session we focused on one specific exercise. This exercise was the customer or user focused exercise. 'We are not customer focused enough in IT'.
The reason for this choice was:

• The results of the mini-survey placed on the website (see above).
• The results of the findings of the itSMF's own 2007 survey which revealed that the number one strategic priority of many IT organizations in the Netherlands is the need 'to improve the quality of products and services'. This was the same number one as 10 years ago when we first presented our worst practice cartoons. Why has so little changed after 10 years with all these 'best practice' frameworks?

The objective of the exercise at the round table session was to try to confirm the results of the mini survey, and to identify why we are not customer focused enough. What examples of worst practice Attitude, Behavior and Culture do we display that are symptomatic of this lack of customer focus, and what are these worst practices we need to get rid of before the 'best practices' start delivering real results.

The first task given to the team was:

Task 1:
- Place the USER stakeholder card, 2 of Hearts, in the middle of the table (user = creature at the end of the evolutionary chain).
- Place the 2 of Clubs on the table ('customers', 'users' or '***dorks***').
- Read out the following to the team: "*We have had ITIL for more than 20 years. ITIL was all about the users and the customers and providing services that deliver quality to the users and customers. In a recent mini-survey on the itSMF site in the Netherlands this cartoon was published (2 of Clubs) with a statement. 'We are not customer focused enough in IT'. You would expect after 20 years of ITIL that this was a ridiculous survey to place there, as this is obviously no longer true. However 89% of respondents AGREED with the statement!*"

Task 2: Ask each individual to agree or disagree with this statement:

'We are not customer focused enough in IT.'

Record the answers on this form. Those who agree must give one example of behavior they have seen that supports this; those who disagree can also give one example.

The key findings in the exercise were, for us, somewhat surprising. We had suspected that the high result on the itSMF website survey was influenced by the type of people who had responded. We suspected that most of those who responded were people who had read the Paul Wilkinson and Brian Johnson book '***IT Service Management from Hell***' and simply wanted to endorse the twisted and warped view of IT in this book! Many of the cartoons in the book were used to create the ABC of ICT card set.

Results of statement during the round table session:
'We are not Customer focused enough in IT'
86% agreed with the statement

What surprised us was that this was a wider selection of IT professionals, most of whom had probably never been influenced or corrupted by 'IT Service Management from Hell'.

Examples of behavior to support the statement 'we are not customer focused enough in IT

- The customer behind the customer needs to be taken into account;
- We need round table sessions with our customers;
- Grey areas in service delivery (entitled/not entitled to support – the customer is the victim!);
- We have problems realizing 'time to market' of new services and solutions;
- IT is too busy with its own processes;
- We are too internally focused;
- We can keep the end user happy, but not the business manager;
- IT doesn't understand the business;
- There is still no clear, single point of contact for customers;

- Language and communication towards customers are still an issue;
- We don't take the customer seriously;
- We focus too much on technology, ...because that is *SO* interesting (2);
- If we were customer focused ENOUGH we wouldn't need all the models (frameworks);
- Users are poorly represented in IT projects;
- We display a tunnel vision by only involving a subset of the user community;
- IT is convinced *it* knows how the business should act;
- IT thinks it knows best what the business needs (2);
- If you call the help desk you won't get a direct solution;
- Costs of IT are confusing;
- Otherwise we advisors wouldn't have any work anymore!;
- Most IT staff have no idea;
- We have a 'blinkered' view;
- The customer is a pain in the ...system;
- Is the customer always right?...you might never achieve the customer requirements – we need to think ahead;
- We still need to be more proactive.

Examples of behavior to support the claim we ARE customer focused enough
- External provider is paid and judged by the hour; market mechanisms apply;
- 80% OK, 20% problem;
- As externals we try to develop new services;
- Otherwise we would miss revenue....the customer is our business.

(It was noticeable that the comments of examples of good behavior seem to have been made by external suppliers, whilst the results of the next exercise do not match this view!)

The above exercise was aimed at generating discussion within the group, what IS customer focused behavior? What does it look like? What type of behavior is NOT customer focused? This allows a team to share views of desirable and non-desirable behavior.

The following task was intended to place the participants into the perspective of the 'customer' or 'user' and to try to identify what the 'user' would see as the worst practices that support the 86% findings. (This is as attempt to break out of the finding in Task 1 above that we in IT are too internally focused.)

Task 3:
- Lay the cards out on the table.
- Read out the following to the team: "*Now imagine we are asking the user (2 of Hearts) 'If we give the user the ABC cards which three cards would he or she choose that most typically represent the worst practices in ABC in your organization?*"
- Let each person choose three and record these on the form supplied.

The overall findings of this were as follows. The figure between ( ) represents the number of times this worst practice was chosen.

Attitude:
- IT not seen as an added-value partner (4).
- Neither partner makes an effort to understand the other (4).
- My TOOL will solve ALL your ITSM problems (4).

Behavior:
- We don't measure our value contribution to strategy (5).
- Throwing ITIL solutions over the wall and hoping people will follow them (5).
- Process managers without authority (4).

Culture:
- 9 to 5 culture (4).
- Not my responsibility (4).
- Blame culture (4).

These were the cards chosen by the individuals and the number of times that a card was chosen.

card	suit	Description	No of time chosen
2	♣	No respect for, or understanding of users	✓✓
3	♣	Knowledge is power	✓✓
4	♣	IT not seen as an added value partner to the business	✓✓✓✓
5	♣	Neither partner makes an effort to understand the other	✓✓✓✓
6	♣	ITIL never work here	✓✓
7	♣	My TOOL will solve ALL your ITSM problems	✓✓✓✓
8	♣	IT thinks it doesn't need to understand the business to make a business case	✓✓✓
9	♣	Walking the talk	
10	♣	No respect for, or trust in management	
J	♣	Let's outsource the business – we'd be better off	✓✓
Q	♣	No understanding of business impact & priority	✓✓
K	♣	ITIL is the objective,... not what it should achieve	✓✓
A	♣	ITIL certification means I know what I am doing	
2	♦	We don't measure our value contribution to strategy	✓✓✓✓✓
3	♦	Too little business involvement in requirements specification and testing	✓✓

4	♦	Not capturing the right knowledge for reuse	✓
5	♦	No management commitment	✓
6	♦	Everything has the highest priority....according to the users	✓
7	♦	Throwing solutions (ITIL) over the wall and HOPING people will use them	✓✓✓✓
8	♦	We're going to INSTALL ITIL....it can't be that hard	✓✓
9	♦	Maybe we should have tested that change first	✓
10	♦	Never mind about following procedures....just do what we usually do	✓
J	♦	Saying yes but meaning no	✓
Q	♦	The solution the customer sees isn't the one that IT sees	✓✓
K	♦	IT strategy's contribution to business strategy	
A	♦	Process managers without authority	✓✓✓✓
2	♠	Them and Us culture - opposing and competing forces	✓✓✓
3	♠	Hierarchic culture 'The boss is always right....even when the boss is wrong!'	
4	♠	Internally focused	✓✓
5	♠	Punishment culture	✓✓
6	♠	Hero culture	✓
7	♠	9 to 5 culture	✓✓✓✓
8	♠	Plan, Do, Stop....no real continual improvement culture	✓✓
9	♠	Promotion on ability	
10	♠	The superiority complex 'We know best!'	✓✓
J	♠	Avoidance culture	
Q	♠	Not my responsibility	✓✓✓✓
K	♠	Empowering people	
A	♠	Blame culture	✓✓✓✓
2	♥	The user...creature at the end of the evolutionary chain	✓
3	♥	The Help Desk technoid...Hello HELPLESS desk....what do you want NOW?	✓✓
4	♥	The IT manager...The best way to improve services is to outsource.....the business!	✓✓✓
5	♥	The consultant...without me the world will stop spinning	
6	♥	The technogeek...That problem isn't in my book, therefore it doesn't exist	✓
7	♥	Business manager...Demand & Give. I demand and you give in	✓✓

8	♥	The CIO...The buck stops anywhere but here!	
9	♥	The supplier...OK so the functionality isn't great but look at the flashy user interface!	✓
10	♥	The quality manager...waiting for the IT organization to improve	✓✓✓
J	♥	The ITIL consultant...A process flow and some procedures are all you need	
Q	♥	The project manager...Of course we will finish on time and within budget	✓
K	♥	The CEO...Which part of NO didn't you understand	
A	♥	HRD manager...our IT staff are now strategic assets?	
	Joker	...The silo mentality (Process)	✓
	Joker	Outsourcing saves costs....whilst maintaining quality (Partner)	✓✓✓
	Joker	A tool solves all problems (Product)	
	Joker	Unable to specify the VALUE required by the business (Performance)	✓✓
	Joker	IT as a business enabler and differentiator (People)	✓

Now the team has a list of worst practices that they themselves have identified. However they don't necessarily feel any need or commitment for them, or for doing anything about them. The next task was designed to try to create the need for change.

Task 4:
- Consolidate the findings and identify the teams' overall top three ABC worst practice cards.
- Discuss and record examples of symptoms and behavior that support these cards.
- Record the consequences and the risks of these top three cards.

This raised an interesting discussion as to how to choose a top three because individuals had already chosen their own three. How could we determine the most important? One way could be to identify how many times a worst practice card was chosen, however the most effective way would be to focus on the 'consequences' of the Attitude, Behavior or Culture cards chosen, and to focus on the 'risk' to the business. This will help the team discuss and identify consequences in terms of 'downtime', 'delay', 'costs', 'availability and continuity of business operations' and 'failure to achieve business goals'. By discussing consequences, participants will themselves discover the three most in need of resolving which will help create 'the need or urgency to change'. Unfortunately during the round table session there was insufficient time to discuss the risks in detail as there was so much discussion trying to identify and agree the consequences.

These were the cards named as the top three cards by each of the teams, together with examples of behavior and the consequences.

Team 1

Card:	Symptoms: *Describe example of behavior seen that closely related to card*	Consequences: *In terms of customer satisfaction, costs, downtime, delay.*	Acceptable risk?
5 ♣ Neither partner makes an effort to understand the other	• Continual discussion about what and who wants what • Independent budgets and investments • No alignment between business and IT plans • No business meetings for IT	• Business goals not realized • Conflicting goals • Overlapping investments • Disconnect between strategy and operations • Delayed solutions • Dissatisfied customers	
8 ♠ Plan, Do, Stop! ....no real continual improvement culture	• Understatement of effort and scope of project • Understatement of impact of project • No strategic cycle, only operational focus	• Higher costs • Ad hoc and reactive • Demotivation • Fire fighting (again!) • No real progress • Risk of going out of business	Not acceptable
J ♦ Saying yes but meaning no	• Resistance to do things • Not following procedures or sticking to agreements	• Delays • Requirements not carried out	

Team 2

Card:	Symptoms: *Describe example of behavior seen that closely related to card*	Consequences: *In terms of customer satisfaction, costs, downtime, delay.*	Acceptable risk?
7 ♠ 9 to 5 culture	• 'Lunch break'.. exchange server is down	• Business functionality down • "According to the SLA that's OK!"	No
10 ♥ Quality manager ..waiting for the IT organization to improve	• Process written in 2006! Two years nothing done with it, no updates or improvements!	• Paper tiger! • Inefficient operations • Ineffective processes	No
4 ♥ IT manager... the best way to improve services is to outsource... the business!	• "They're always moaning about something! It is never good!"	• No user or customer focus • Ignore the customer needs • IT not responsive to business needs • Business will eventually look for another provider	No

Team 3

Card:	Symptoms: Describe example of behavior seen that closely related to card	Consequences: In terms of customer satisfaction, costs, downtime, delay.	Acceptable risk?
Q ♥ The project manager... Of course we will finish on time and within budget	• Not on time • Not within budget • IT services not ready in time • Less quality delivered because of pressure on time overrun • Scope boundaries change	• Missing business requirements • Increased cost • Dissatisfied business	
J ♣ 80% of downtime due to users.... Let's outsource the business – we'd be better off	• Lack of user training • Wrong and changing requirements	• Projects deliver no real benefits • Increased cost of support	
The Joker "There is no keyboard?!..... We've been outsourced,...it is a cost reduction initiative"	• Not my responsibility • Not in my back yard • We know what is good for you	• Users feel they are not taken seriously • Circumvention by obtaining own solutions	

Team 4

Card:	Symptoms: Describe example of behavior seen that closely related to card	Consequences: What are consequences? In terms of customer satisfaction, costs, downtime, delay.	Acceptable risk?
3 ♦ Too little business involvement in requirements specification and testing	• Poor, and continually changing requirements • Incorrect prioritization	• Delays • Investments in wrong solutions • Investments do not support the business	
Q ♠ Not my responsibility	• Grey areas of who does what....who is allowed what • No real accountability	• Business suffers • Delayed time to market • Things don't get done	
4 ♠ Internally focused	• IT too busy with technology and not the business use of technology • IT too busy with its own processes	• Technology not aligned to business needs • Processes don't deliver business value • Lack of alignment between IT initiatives and business goals	

Team 5

Card:	Symptoms: *Describe example of behavior seen that closely related to card*	Consequences: *In terms of customer satisfaction, costs, downtime, delay.*	Acceptable risk?
4 ♠ Internally focused	• Dissatisfied customers	• Outsourcing	
7 ♥ Business manager... Demand & Give. I demand and you give in	• Continually changing priorities • Rework	• Higher costs • Takes longer	
2 ♦ We don't measure our value contribution to strategy	• No insight for decision making	• Poor decision making • Wrong investments	

Team 6

Card:	Symptoms: *Describe example of behavior seen that closely related to card*	Consequences: *In terms of customer satisfaction, costs, downtime, delay.*	Acceptable risk?
8 ♦ We're going to INSTALL ITIL.... it can't be that hard	• Takes longer than planned • Increased bureaucracy • Continually changing priorities • Rework	• Dissatisfied customers	
3 ♦ Too little business involvement in requirements specification and testing	• Wrong choices and decisions • Increased mistakes	• Costs • Rework • Delays • No value	
4 ♣ IT not seen as an added value partner to the business	• IT not invited to participate	• Dissatisfied customers	

Team 7

Card:	Symptoms: Describe example of behavior seen that closely related to card	Consequences: In terms of customer satisfaction, costs, downtime, delay.	Acceptable risk?
10 ♠ The superiority complex 'We know best!'	• Superiority feeling within IT • We know best so shut-up	• Doing the wrong things • Dissatisfied customer	no
2 ♦ We don't measure our value contribution to strategy	• No ability to determine added value of IT for the company	• Business doesn't have the right information to be able to make decisions	no
K ♣ ITIL is the objective,... not what it should achieve	• Arrogance	• Too focused on processes and technique and not on the customers and users, or value • Inability to steer on value realization	

An additional exercise you can try is the following:

The ABC of ICT

Exercise: 'Value?'

Are you GAMBLING with YOUR IT?.....
Use the ABC card set to find out!

Background to this exercise:

We used the cards in a workshop at the itSMF Best Practice conference. More than 60 delegates were asked to name the top three worst practice cards that THEIR users would choose in relation to THEIR IT organization.

The TOP scoring worst practice card was:
• **We don't measure our value contribution to strategy**

The results of a poll conducted on the Van Haren website, using the ABC cards revealed the following:

- **Poll**: '*The senior business management in my organization **understand and act** on our IT metrics reports*'

72% disagreed and **28%** agreed.

Our challenge is simple. The situation is even more worrying. Why? Before you can start to deliver value you need to know WHAT THAT VALUE is.

We have played the Apollo 13 business simulation with 1000's of IT employees. **More than 90% of IT employees don't KNOW what value they should be delivering to the business?** Do YOUR IT employees KNOW what value they should be delivering?

The 'Value' exercise

Exercise instructions:

- Place the Value Joker on the table
- Read the following to the team:

Imaging now the CEO is sitting opposite you. He says "*So you are spending all this IT budget on improving ITSM to add **VALUE** to MY business. Do you **KNOW** what VALUE I **need** you to deliver?*"

Task 1: (5 minutes) **Conduct the following exercise individually**:

- Write down for yourself a key value indicator that will demonstrate that you are delivering VALUE.
- If we visit your organization could you SHOW us where this is documented?
- Do YOUR IT reports demonstrate achievement of this VALUE?

Task 2: (5 minutes) **Discuss the results**:

- Does everybody know the VALUE they need to deliver?
- If not, how can you demonstrate achievement if most people don't KNOW what value they should be delivering. **What do the auditors say?**

ISO20000: *Monitoring, Measuring & Reviewing*

- **The organization SHALL apply suitable methods for monitoring and, where applicable, measurement of the service management processes. These methods SHALL demonstrate the ability to achieve planned results.**

  CobiT: ME1 Monitor and Evaluate IT Performance
  Management of the process of *Monitor and evaluate IT performance* that satisfies the business requirement for IT of *transparency and understanding of IT cost, benefits, strategy, policies and service levels in accordance with governance.*

  ISO20000: **Requirements for a management system.**

- **Top management SHALL ensure that its employees are aware of the relevance and importance of their activities and how they contribute to results.**

Now is the time to ENSURE that the whole IT organization KNOWS what the VALUE needs to be, and that ITSM processes can actually measure, AND demonstrate that VALUE.

- Does top management ensure that the goals are known to all?
- Does top management ensure that employees are aware of the relevance and importance of their activities and how they CONTRIBUTE TO RESULTS?
- If the answers to the above two points are 'NO', what is your responsibility? What should YOU do?

Task 3: **Present the findings** (3 minutes per team):

- Do we ALL KNOW what VALUE we should be delivering?
- What should WE all be doing to ensure that we KNOW?

Section 4: Conclusions and recommendations to IT organizations
Conclusions:

- We are still not customer or user focused enough in IT, and we confirm this ourselves.
- People clearly identified with the worst practices in the card set and could relate them to their own organization which shows that the cards do reflect current worst practices.
- All participants were engaged in active dialogue and discussion, to such an extent that we ran out of time because they wanted to continue to explore and discuss issues, clearly demonstrating that the cards achieve their intended aim of creating dialogue and discussion.
- People were able to identify and describe actual undesirable behavior and the consequences within a short, 45 minute session. Showing that valuable assessment results can be achieved within a short time frame (such as a regular team meeting).
- Participants were willing and eager to take the cards away and perform exercises within their own organization because of the dialogue this created. We are receiving emails asking for the example exercises.

- The card with the most choices is 'We don't measure our value contribution to strategy' which confirms our own findings. This is why the 'value' exercise was specifically included in the article 'ABC of ICT V3' in the 'IT Service Management Global Best Practices – Volume 1 book, 2008, Van Haren Publishing. We have added this exercise to the recommendations below.

Recommendations:

- Use these cards within your own organization', to create dialogue and enable an assessment of your own worst practices.
- Either carry out this exercise or pick some cards that you think are particularly relevant to your organization, publish them on your website and ask people to react. Ask people to discuss them in regular team meetings or organize a one hour meeting to perform the exercise.

Section 5: Quotes
This section contains quotes from delegates about the game, and follow up quotes and requests that show the value of the cards.

Maarten Bordewijk, Getronics-PinkRoccade, senior ITIL trainer, Netherlands

"Any IT service management initiative that doesn't address ABC is bound for failure. Any educational institute wanting to give people the capabilities and knowledge for successfully deploying ITIL should use the ABC cards to support the necessary discussion in training modules leading up to formal certification.

When organizing an improvement workshop it helps to list issues and to prioritize them. Participants often find it difficult to be complete in this. The ABC cards provide a complete list of all things that could go wrong. People can instantly recognize issues and pick the cards that apply to them and provide examples of attitude and behavior. It speeds up the process and helps everyone involved to name the issues that really inhibit successful ITSM."

Alejandro Debenedet, EXIN, Netherlands

"The ABC card exercise was a lot of fun, and put people immediately to work, brainstorming on the worst practices and their consequences, aided by the easily recognizable cartoons. It was interesting to see how people from different backgrounds could quickly interact and agree on how the situations apply to daily life and how they need to be approached.

From my perspective at EXIN, I see that the ABC card set helps people understand the problems and the typical worst practices. It helps people discuss the consequences and possible solutions, and with that it achieves something very important: it gives hands-on experience in solving ITSM-related issues.

This is a great aid for people seeking certification in the different levels and practices of ITSM, whether it is ITIL or ISO 20000, or other good practices. EXIN has always developed the exams based on the belief that the candidates need more than just theory, but also practical knowledge, and this helps people gain practical knowledge."

Appendix 1
Authors and their card cases

This appendix identifies which specific ABC card a particular author provided content for.

Author	Card	Page number
Martin Andenmatten	7 of Clubs	
Mats Berger	9 of Diamonds	
Jack Bischof	King of Diamonds	
Aad Brinkman	Joker: A Fool with a Tool is still a Fool	
Gary Case	2 of Diamonds	
Alejandro Debenedet	The Joker: Unable to specify the VALUE required by the business	
Arjen Droog	8 of Diamonds	
Rob England	Chapter 3: A skeptical view, Introduction to Chapter 5	
David Bathiely Ferdandez	5 of Diamonds	
Bartosz Górczynski	5 of Diamonds	
Jeremy Hart		
Brian Johnson	5 of Clubs	
Benny Kamin	The Joker: A Fool with a Tool is still a Fool	
Alexander Kist	8 of Diamonds	
Erna van Kollenburg	9 of Diamonds	
Aidan Lawes	Ace of Clubs	
Paul Leenards	7 of Diamonds	
Peter Lijnse	7 of Diamonds	

Vernon Lloyd	King of Diamonds
Ivor Macfarlane	9 of Spades
Kirstie Magowan	Jack of Spades
Martin Ng	King of Diamonds
Paul van Nobelen	Ace of Clubs
Don Page	The Joker: A Fool with a Tool is still a Fool
David Pereira	2 of Spades
Harold Petersen	8 of Spades
Richard Pharro	Foreword, Ace of Spades
Colin Rudd	3 of Clubs
Walter Servaes	3 of Diamonds
Mark Smalley	Ace of Spades
Clive Strawford	5 of Spades
Robert Stroud	2 of Spades
HP Suen	8 of Diamonds
Sharon Taylor	Foreword, 2 of Clubs, 5 of Diamonds
Pablo Coutere de Troismont	The Joker: Breaking down the Silos
Ken Turbitt	Queen of Clubs
Stephane Vleeshouwer	2 of Diamonds
Richard Voorter	King of Spades
Ken Wendel	5 of Diamonds
David Wheelden	Ace of Clubs
Katsushi Yaginuma	4 of Clubs

ISO/IEC 20000
The Official Books from itSMF

ISO/IEC 20000: An Introduction
Promoting awareness of the certification for organizations within the IT Service Management environment.
ISBN: 978 908753081 5 (ENGLISH EDITION)
PRICE €49.95 EXCL TAX

Implementing ISO/IEC 20000 Certification: The Roadmap
Practical advice, to assist readers through the requirements of the standard, the scoping, the project approach, the certification procedure and management of the certification.
ISBN: 978 908753082 2
PRICE €39.95 EXCL TAX

ISO/IEC 20000: A Pocket Guide
A quick and accessible guide to the fundamental requirements for corporate certification.
ISBN: 978 907721279 0 (ENGLISH EDITION)
PRICE €14.95 EXCL TAX

Other leading ITSM Books from itSMF

Metrics for IT Service Management
A general guide to the use of metrics as a mechanism to control and steer IT service organizations, with consideration of the design and implementation of metrics in service organizations using industry standard frameworks.
ISBN: 978 907721269 1
PRICE €39.95 EXCL TAX

Six Sigma for IT Management
The first book to provide a coherent view and guidance for using the Six Sigma approach successfully in IT Service Management, whilst aiming to merge both Six Sigma and ITIL® into a single unified approach to continuous improvement. Six Sigma for IT Management: A Pocket Guide is also available.
ISBN: 978 907721230 1 (ENGLISH EDITION)
PRICE €39.95 EXCL TAX

Frameworks for IT Management
An unparalleled guide to the myriad of IT management instruments currently available to IT and business managers. Frameworks for IT Management: A Pocket Guide is also available.
ISBN: 978 907721290 5 (ENGLISH EDITION)
PRICE €39.95 EXCL TAX

IT Governance based on CobiT 4.1: A Management Guide
Detailed information on the overall process model as well as the theory behind it.
ISBN: 978 90 8753116 4 (ENGLISH EDITION)
PRICE €20,75 EXCL TAX